I0569685

THE MAN IN THE GLASS BOX

A TALE OF TRUE ADVENTURE

OR ONE MAN'S JOURNEY ACROSS THE UNITED STATES IN A GLASS APARTMENT ON WHEELS

A Memoir

Harper & Loukas Publishing

THE MAN IN THE GLASS BOX

A TALE OF TRUE ADVENTURE

OR ONE MAN'S JOURNEY ACROSS THE UNITED STATES IN A GLASS APARTMENT ON WHEELS

A Memoir

RANDOLPH HUBARD

Other works by Randolph Hubard:
-Nomad on the Pleasure Grounds
-Finding Christmas in New Jersey
-Exit Through the Service Entrance

Title: The Man in the Glass Box or One Man's Journey Across the United States in a Glass Apartment on Wheels
Author: Randolph Hubard
Copyright © 2025 by Randolph Hubard
Published by Harper & Loukas Publishing

Cover design by Lance Banyon
Photo by Kevin Lyons
Edited by Jachin Harte
ISBN 979-8-218-55368-5

Based on True Events,
with certain elements altered
for pacing and clarity

PROLOGUE

In The Middle of Nowhere at The Medieval Motel

It was cold, and it had just started snowing as I walked to the motel just off a lost and forgotten highway, somewhere between Wisconsin and Kansas City. We had been driving for days and this was just another stop for the night. You could see the truck with its fresh tire marks on the ground and its green tarp covering the long square back, the secret it was carrying contrasting against the falling snow.

Tired and just wanting enough sleep so I could get back on the road in the morning, I rang the circular bell on the thick wooden motel desk.

Moments later, a tall, thin man in a brown shirt and blue jeans appeared. *"How can I help you?"* the man asked with a smile.

"One room, single occupant, one night," I replied with the least amount of words I could muster.

He nodded and then saw my rig just outside.

"What you hauling?" he asked.

I paused for a second; *I could tell him,* I thought, but didn't have the energy to go into it. "Top secret, government stuff," I said.

That piqued his interest.

"What do you mean?" he asked.

I looked at him and said, "It's glass, a box of glass."

"No," he replied.

"Yes, yes, it is," I insisted. Just then, the others entered, and he went back to finding a key for my room.

"We're renovating; would you like one of the new ones?"

This was a medieval-themed motel flipping all of its rooms to something more modern.

"If possible, I would like one of the medieval ones," I said.

"Yeah, I think we can do that. I think we can do that," he smiled.

This was a one-level motel in the center of a parking lot with nothing around it—not a gas station, house, or a street sign in sight. Nothing. The place was brown with hints of smokey yellow. Everything had a flat feel to it.

The room he gave me had a purple shag rug. Above the Queen-sized bed on the white, knockdown-textured wall was an airbrushed mural painted in the 1970s of two battle axes framing a medieval shield against a stone castle. The room had a nice finished look with its dark, wood beam ceiling. If you took a deep breath, you could faintly smell burnt tobacco. And there was a perfect view of the parking lot from the window.

Ring, ring goes the cell phone. I recognized the number. It was mine. My home number back in Brooklyn.

"Hello," I said. My flatmate was on the other end.

"Hi, Randy. How the hell is everything going?"

"It's great. It's unreal. It's beyond anything I could have ever imagined."

"Good, that's good." He then dropped his energy.

"What's up," I asked.

"Ah, Randy, I don't want to be a buzzkill, but... the police were just here. You have a warrant out for your arrest."

———————————

In Brooklyn a few months earlier, just after Christmas, on the way home from a night in the city, one of my friends, Richard, lost his MetroCard. As he was fishing through his pockets to find coin, I said, "No problem, Richard. I'll swipe my card, and we can just enter the turnstile together." The technical term for this crime is called fare evasion or fare-dodging.

We squeezed into the subway turnstile together, and out of the blue, three undercover cops flashed their badges and handcuffed both of us. It happened so fast we started laughing. We were taken by subway to the NYPD Transit District 4 station located in Union Square. Richard sat across from me during the ride with the look of fear and mad dog vexation. I tried to remind him of the good times we just had, but to no avail. We were taken inside the police station and cuffed to a wooden bench. The cops were just going to give us a ticket. But the thing was I couldn't identify myself. I had left my wallet on my dresser back in Brooklyn. Fingerprinted, photographed, and told they had to put my credentials in the high crime super-computer database located in North Carolina to check if there were any outstanding warrants on me. For there was no valid identification on my person, I couldn't prove who I was. So, as we waited for the data to come in, I was transferred to one of their custody suites. Richard was given his ticket and released. I begged him to get my wallet and bring it back to the station. He screamed, "I'm not your porter!"

With this information, the booking officer let Richard take my keys so he could retrieve my wallet in Brooklyn.

Hours later, they opened the cell and said, *"Mr. Hubard, you are free to go. Here is your summons; just show up to court on this date, and you can take care of it."*

It was a bit dark and difficult to read the officer's handwriting, but he handed me the summons. I was to appear in front of a judge the second week of January. I glanced at the officer at the desk and said, "I can't make this date... I'm going to be out of town for the next four months!"

His face turned cold as he replied, *"You better show up for that date."*

With no other options, no comfort in my soul, I headed back home. Coffee was my only vice until the sun came up, then I randomly started calling lawyers. You could only assess their character based on whether they took my call and the tone of their voice. One said, *"Come down to my office, and we can talk in person."* So, I did.

Ted Williams from Shubert, Hudson & Williams LLP was rather young to have a full head of white hair. He took me into his office and was soft-spoken as he said, "What do you got, Mr. Hubard?"

I showed him my summons, and he thumbed through his day planner, saying, *"Alright, here's what I can do. I can represent you on the court day and ask the judge to reschedule it so you can appear in person sometime in May."*

"That's it?" I asked.

"That's it."

"What's your fee?" I asked.

Ted sat back in his leather chair, paused for a minute, and said, *"$2,000."*

"Two thousand, American? Just for showing up? Alright, let's do it." We shook hands, and that was it.

What was I going to do? I thought. Then considering all the ways to get out of this thing. I could just go out of town, start this project, fly to New York the morning of my court date, pay the fine, and fly back in the afternoon, with none the wiser. Or, provide Ted his fee to represent the absence in court and then appear in court sometime in the spring. Or the third option, totally and shamelessly ignore it.

Later that day, I called Ted and said, "Ted, thank you for meeting with me today. I'm going to pass."

———————

Standing in the present, under the airbrushed mural in a motel left over from the disco era, writing down the phone number of the police officer who came to my apartment looking for me because I didn't want to pay Ted $2,000 to pretend to be my lawyer left me in a state of panic.

"That's the number, you got it?" replied my roommate as he was having kittens.

"Alright, I'll call him right now, sorry about that."

"Randy... are you alright?"

"Yes, it's just a minor misunderstanding. I'll take care of it."

Concluding the call with the cell phone seemingly hanging up all by itself, taking a deep breath, I dialed the number of the police officer overseeing my case. The call connected me to the desk of the New York police officer who had paid me a visit. This is how it went.

"Hello, this is (Officer) Jenkins."

"Yes, hi, hello, very good, my name is Randolph Hubard. I have come to understand you were at my apartment yesterday. Apparently, there is a warrant out for my arrest."

"WHERE ARE YOU?!" he screamed.

"I'm out of town," replying in a low tone. Just then, I opened the door to my room, which looked out to the parking area of the motel right at ground level, and saw one of my traveling companions, Peter, as he walked by. We smiled and waved.

"I'm out of town until spring. I'll turn myself in once I get back."

"What?" Peter asked.

"Not you, Peter. I'm talking to a man about a horse," I smiled back.

You could feel the officer's frustration through the phone as I gave Peter the thumbs up sign. There was a long pause, and then on a dime, Officer Jenkins changed his demeanor.

"Alright, here's where you need to go."

He gave me a time and the address to turn myself in once I returned to New York. Then he said in a stern voice that echoes in my head to this day.

"Let me just tell you something. If you are in California and you get pulled over, they will arrest you and expedite you to New York."

"I understand, thank you," I said.

"Alright," he said like a disappointed coach at the end of the most important game of his career. Then he hung up the phone.

I put down the cell phone on a small round table by the door. The parking area was now blanketed in white snow. You could see in great detail every flake's crystal pattern as they fell on top of each other. At that moment, I believed three things: it was calm outside, we were in beautiful country, and the police were on their way to get me. Standing in that doorway, I was absolutely convinced I would be arrested – arrested in an airbrushed 1970's style Medieval motel with the keys to a fully furnished *Glass Apartment on Wheels* in my pocket in the middle of nowhere.

CHAPTER 1

The Call to Adventure, and The Clown Survival Bag

How did I get into this situation? I'm miles from home, with a million-dollar *Glass Box* in the parking lot of a fleabag motel, and the cops in New York are looking for me. This is how it started:

I was living in Brooklyn, down to my last couple of dollars, when I found an audition in a small paper for a job called *The Man in The Cube Campaign.* The gig was to, for four months, travel the country and "live" inside a fully furnished *glass apartment on wheels,* promoting a product of unspecified origin.

This was an open call held at The Coup de Foudre Aux Fraises Hotel (CdFAFH) in the city. No mention of preparation for any reading material or anything else. Just asking for you to show up.

The Man in the Cube Campaign

Looking to hire eight actors to travel the United States and "live" in a Glass Apartment on Wheels.

• Must be willing to travel for four months.
• Promote new product.

Audition held at
The Coup de Foudre Aux Fraises Hotel
November 18, 9:00 am

Living in a *Glass Cube,* crisscrossing the U.S. – sounded like a sweet deal. The job posting was a bit vague on the specifics, but the promise of exploring the country was tempting enough. Honestly, who wouldn't want to embark on an adventure like that? Let's face it, pursuing this or any of the wild and crazy things I've tackled is akin to rolling the dice with a 1 in 99.9% chance of success. I thought about it that night, and as I kept thinking about it; the idea refused to go away. It lingered, nagging at the edges of my mind.

It was now morning; I was just drinking coffee, staring out the window. The next thing I knew, I was headed off to the hotel to see what this was all about. If it's chaotic, incomprehensible, and unorganized, I'll bail.

I arrived early at The Coup de Foudre Aux Fraises Hotel (Cd-FAFH) in Midtown, and, to my surprise, no one was there. The headcount was maybe a dozen or so people, but that was it. It was in the lower portion of a large hotel, so seating was aplenty. I signed in on a small, clear plastic clipboard. Soon after, my name was called, and the door opened to a large conference room; my curiosity led the way.

Inside were a dozen or so business-casual individuals sitting at a table in the center. *"Have a seat,"* someone said. I couldn't tell you who spoke, but I took a chair at the head of the long, wooden conference table. The business-casual individuals looked at me like deer in headlights. We all sat in silence. It was dead silent. It felt like waking up in your childhood bed as a full-grown adult in the stillness of the eternal night with an entire boardroom looking at you, expecting something to happen. At that point, the feeling was that someone needed to make the first move. I felt like I had to say something grand. But finally, someone asked, *"Do you have a headshot?"*

"Yes!" I replied with great excitement and utter confusion.

My credentials glided to the individual immediately to my right. And one by one, every single person at that table looked at my picture, then to my resume, then to me, then to my resume, then to my picture, then to me. It slowly passed to the next person and to the next, repeating in actions. The room remained silent.

On my resume, I had under a segment called Special Skills these four words:

1. SKIING.
2. FACIAL HAIR.
3. BAKING.

My paperwork continued from one sterile hand to the next. Then I heard a singular voice break the deafening silence... *"Special Skills, Facial Hair!?"*

Every head in the room turned toward my direction. All eyes were now on me. I was sporting a full beard at the time, and I said back without hesitation and dry as a bone, "Yes, I didn't have this when I woke up this morning."

Everyone laughed. It felt like someone released a thousand helium balloons into the sky. An emotion was hit, and I knew I could build on that. The room completely changed. I wasn't sure if they were laughing because I said one of my skills was rapid beard growth or that I had it written down on my resume. The feeling was like I passed a secret test, and suddenly I was now one of them. I looked around to see if I was going to get a sash or a plaque that said, *You did it!* or something.

Now, it was down to business. You could feel that they wanted to talk, but they weren't sure if they could trust me or not. And why would they? We just sat down together for the first time. No one knew who the hell I was. But they all had a sparkle in their eye; they knew they had something truly special they were working on, and I was about to get the inside scoop. Half of these guys were from a marketing company, and the other half represented the product that was to be advertised. And I was just a guy living in Brooklyn.

This thing was real because it had a name. It was simply called *The Man in the Cube Program*. They were looking to hire actors to "live" in a fully functional apartment on wheels to tour the country and promote this new product. Not actually live inside, but give the illusion that these individuals were living in a glass-enclosed, germ-free environment. They struggled a bit to explain this to me. They had no visuals or mock-ups. And they were limited with the information they were giving out. I had to put together what I could with what they were allowed to say. They didn't give any specifics, simply that they were going to put some people inside of a *Glass Box*.

It was stirring to think what it could be. Perhaps a new low-calorie, plant-based instant breakfast beverage, a brand-new video game system, the latest high-tech kitchen appliance with an art nouveau metallic design, or maybe a kissing booth on wheels. It could be anything! Someone, probably in a white lab coat, came up with the product. Then, someone suggested promoting it in a *glass apartment on wheels,* and someone said, *"Sure, let's do it."* I didn't know what it was. The guy who sat in this seat before me didn't know what it was, and the guy after me didn't know either.

To see if this guy from Brooklyn was a good fit, they had to feel me out. They had to ask questions:

1. ARE YOU ALRIGHT BEING ON THE ROAD FOR FOUR MONTHS?
2. HOW WOULD YOU FEEL BEING WATCHED ALL DAY?
3. HOW WOULD YOU MAKE THE SPACE INTERESTING TO SEE?
4. ARE YOU ALRIGHT WITH SHAVING YOUR BEARD?
5. ARE YOU AVAILABLE FOR THE ENTIRE CAMPAIGN?

I was more than fine traveling across the country in a *glass apartment.* More than fine filling the space with daily human behavior. I can't remember exactly how I answered that question. I remember talking, seeing my hands gesturing. But I couldn't tell you what I said. One gets incredibly nervous in these types of situations. When two or more emotions are swirling through me at once, I have a tendency to say things, unable to recall later anything that was said. As for the shaving question, I responded, "Of course, I have no problem shaving."

I was fine with everything, even though no one actually knew what they were talking about. You can only hope you gave the correct answers, or the ones they were looking for. You always need to be easygoing and talk about beards for a little bit in interviews. Then the uncomfortable pause happened, and someone said, *"Alright, we'll let you know in a couple of days."*

"Great, thank you for seeing me today."

We all got up, looked each other in the eyes, smiled, and

said goodbye. My curiosity let go of any expectations I gathered that morning, and I headed back to Brooklyn.

The season was changing, and the ancient red and blue carnival pattern linoleum floor in my apartment stopped feeling like it was about to burst into flames. It was located in the sunroom that housed six windows, framed by blue curtains, with six four-in-hand knotted neckties (one necktie holding each set of curtains together in the center of the window), acting as a sort of napkin ring that helped reduce the extreme light blaring in from sunup till sundown. The room had a similar feel to a casino. With a plain white ceiling and an eyesore of a floor, it forces the eye to battle between the extremes. And then surrender somewhere in the middle. I sat down in my wooden rocking chair, gathered my pride, looked out the window, and thought, *Not a bad morning. Let's see where this goes.*

Ring, ring, goes the telephone.

"Hello," I cried cheerfully.

"May I speak to Randolph *Hubbard?*"

My last name has often been confused with the main character in the 1805 nursery rhyme, *The Comic Adventures of Old Mother Hubbard, and her Dog,* by Samuel Arnold. So, this was always a minor speed bump in communicating with new acquaintances.

"This is he!" I cried again.

"Hi, it's Anna Myers. We met last week about The Glass Box touring gig."

I was surprised that they called me. But I had also shaved.

"Yes, why of course. How is everything?" I played it very cool.

"Things are good thank you. We would like to see you again. Are you available Monday, say 9:30?"

If they said 2:45 am in the *Sea of Tranquility* on the moon, I would have said yes.

"I would love to," I replied.

"Great, let me give you the (office) address."

I scurried to find a pen and something to write down the address, grabbing the wrinkled envelope of a bill, and said...

"Um Ha, I see... which floor? Alright. Great. Do you need me to bring anything?"

"No, we just want to see you again. Ok, see you Monday."

"Ok. See you Monday, Thanks, bye!" *Click* goes the receiver on my cheap cordless phone.

"Ok, Monday." I cried to myself.

Making it to phase two was rewarding on its own, but I still didn't know how many people they auditioned. And this whole thing could be canceled at a moment's notice. And the great mystery was who's bankrolling this?

This was like nothing I'd ever gone after before. It's not like you could ask someone for advice on an interview for a position with zero details. *Was this a second audition or an interview? Should I wear a tie or a Hawaiian shirt? Do you part the hair, get a perm or pull it straight back? Are we going to have cucumber sandwiches? Are the crust going to be cut off!* I didn't know how to present myself.

This position didn't require a learned set of skills or acquired knowledge, just a desire to do it. It was like an interview for being a human cannonball. *Was this even a job?* And if one did get it, how does one put it on a resume? There was only one other thing I could compare this to. It was this.

When I was a teenager, living in Richmond, Virginia, I saw a flyer on a bulletin board in a high-traffic area in a large concrete and steel building. The ad was a small agency looking to hire an individual to work, mostly weekends, around the city and the surrounding suburbs. The job was for a *Party Clown.* The company was run by a divorced woman living just outside of the city limits. She was running it from her home. Her company was called Wild Things! The full name of the company was *Wild Things! A Party Clown Company: The Entertainment Experts!*

WILD THINGS

A PARTY CLOWN COMPANY:

NOW Hiring

Kids Birthday Parties

Party Clowns

Costume Characters

Family Night

No Experience Needed

555-7890 555-7890 555-7890 555-7890 555-7890 555-7890 555-7890 555-7890

The paper said it was a job for a *party clown*. The flyer was pink and had precut tabs at the bottom with a phone number to call for an interview. The flyer must have just been tacked up for no one had ripped a tab off yet. So, I just took the whole flyer. Without hesitation, I called the number the next afternoon, and a sweet-sounding middle-aged woman answered.

"Hello, Wild Things."

"Yes, hello, very good, I'm calling about the party clown position," I cried.

"Oh, yes. Did you get the number from the flyer?" she asked.

"Yes, yes I did."

She said *flyer*. I think that was the only one she made.

"That's super! Tell me a little about yourself," she exclaimed.

"I'm a student, and I am looking for something low key to do on the weekends between classes and such."

"Super-duper! Can you come in and see me?" she asked.

"Sure. When?"

"Right now," she stated.

Her place was only a few miles away, and I was able to find it without incident, showing up around an hour later. She greeted me at her front door just beyond the white picket fence, and we entered the home. The very first thing she said to me was that she was divorced, and that these were her two children. There were two male teenagers lying on the couch like sacks of potatoes watching television. They didn't even grunt to say hello.

I hadn't known this woman for more than fifteen minutes, and I already knew she was a single mother raising two teenage zombie halfwits watching the boob tube in the middle of the afternoon on a school day. She told me this as I stood for the first time in her living room. I got her name and phone number off a pink flyer on a bulletin board at a local college the day before. And we were now standing in her home.

She was a short, stout woman in her forties with curly, white hair. She walked with a limp, one of her legs was longer than the other. She smiled and asked me to follow her to the dining room just a few feet away. We could still hear the television set from our meeting area.

We sat down at the dining room table that was covered with bags of twist n' shape balloons, grease face paint trays, plastic polka-dot derby hats, magic coloring books, wigs, pink invoice papers, and stacks of personal checks made out to *Wild Things!* She had to move several clown costumes from the chairs for us to sit down. The house was a bit messy, with a layer of dust on the credenza and pictures hanging on the wall. It looked like it needed a good cleaning. And the entire place smelled like a gymnasium. I couldn't understand how she could work in those conditions.

We started talking. She was looking for someone to perform at children's birthday parties on weekends and do light magic tricks and some balloon bending at a restaurant on Tuesday evenings. The ad said, *No Experience Needed.*

No requirement of any previously learned skills, just a desire to do it. Knowingly and willingly having the desire to dress up as a clown and have people stare at you.

That was exactly what a young, dumb kid wasting a year at a half ass college in Richmond, Virginia was looking for. I went into this interview cold turkey. I was just some yutz off the street. Didn't have a clue how to do this. Even though the ad said, *No Experience Needed,* I had no references or any *Party* experience outside of attending them as a kid. Never performed as a party clown before, never bent a balloon or put on lipstick either. But she didn't know that.

"Have you ever done parties for kids before?" she asked.

"Well, there was... I mean when I was a kid I always, like I thought one day... it would be nice to give something back to the children," I mumbled.

"It's really easy. Each gig is for an hour. You do face painting, balloon bending and a little magic. I have three magic tricks. That's all."

"That's it?" I asked.

"Yes, most parties just want a clown. And others want a clown for the first half hour then a full body character for the second half. And that takes up the hour. The rest is pictures and presenting the cake and if they want you to do any special, like hand out gifts, goodie bags, or something like that," she simply stated.

She then took me into a side room that was painted the same putrid pink as the invoice sheets. I thought the dining room table was a mess. The room was bare, except for a small desk and chair in the right corner, nothing on the walls, just more clown stuff. The closet door was half off its hinges, trying to hold the bags of balloons from spilling out on the black grease-stained manila carpet.

"*These are the (magic) tricks*," she said like a homeroom teacher.

She opened a desk drawer that screamed to be oiled and took out an oversized, copper-painted plastic penny and a purple bag with a wood handle and said,

"*This is the disappearing bag.*"

She presented the large coin in a dramatic way. Then she placed it in the bag and showed me the secret metal wire under the wooden handle that flips the inside of the bag to the side. When you turn the bag inside out, it looks like the penny disappeared, when it was simply pushed into a hidden side pocket by the metal wire. It's two bags inside one.

"*That's the first trick,*" she smiled.

She tossed the magic bag on the chair and presented two different-colored silk scarves attached at the ends to each other. At the end of one of the scarves is a plastic ring that you grab with your four fingers and thumb, then you slide the plastic ring from one end to the other, flipping the scarves inside out to reveal two different colors.

"*That's the second one. Super duper.*"

The two scarves glided to the floor. She then took out a *Blow Book*, also known as a *Magic Coloring Book*. It's one of the oldest magic tricks going back to the 16th century. The themes have changed over the decades, but the principle remains the same. It was a blue and yellow coloring book with a llama in a top hat and an alligator in a bathing suit on the cover. She showed the front of the book to me. The coloring book said, *Happy Fun Crazy Exciting Circus Time Coloring Book!* Ages 4-97.

"*This is a three-part trick. Look at the pages,*" she stated.

She then flipped through the coloring book pages and revealed circus characters with no color.

"*Alright, now watch again.*"

She flipped through it a second time, and the same images are now in *full color*, as if someone magically colored them in.

"Now, this is the kicker. Watch!"

She flipped through a third time, and the pages were completely blank as if someone erased everything.

"What!?" I cried.

She then gave me a closer look. It's a series of three alternating pages, and they are of different widths. Depending on where your fingers flip the page, it will reveal a different series of pages (images). If you flip the pages at the top, it's the colorless circus characters. Flip in the middle of the book, it's the colored circus characters. If you flip the pages at the bottom, it's the blank pages. I had to admit that one got me.

"Alright... balloons."

She grabbed a bag of long colorful twist n' shape balloons and something that looked like a big sprayer from the early eighteenth century.

She then attached a yellow balloon to the end of the big sprayer and pumped air into the balloon until it was 75% full. Then tied it off and squeaked it into knots to reveal a dog. I tried to memorize every twist and turn she did so I could duplicate it.

"Alright, give it a go," she said.

I grabbed a purple balloon, and she handed me the big sprayer, pumping it completely full of air.

"Nope, you need space for the knots. Only pump it 75%," she said. I tried again exactly as she requested.

I grabbed a blue one and pumped it to 75%. Then *Fur-plat, snap. Squeak, squeak, pull, pull... Ker Pop!* and presented her something that had the ears of a rabbit, the neck of a giraffe, the feet of a turtle, and the tail of a poodle.

"Good enough. You'll get better with practice. How are you with face painting?"

"Oh. I'm good at that," I lied.

"Great, I've got four parties for you Saturday, still finishing up the schedule for Sunday. Costumes are in the back. Follow me, I know the way."

She then took me to the backyard, and right next to the trampoline was a long white barn that had racks of neatly hung and labeled costumes. Clowns, Santa Clauses, elves, winged fairies, pirates, religious fanatics, superheroes, wizards, and more. With wide shelves of costume heads, huge in size. Like Easter Bunnies, purple dinosaurs, bears, horses, lions, giraffes, turtles, llamas, and every other animal you can think of, but with a slightly terrifying look. And a pyramid of clown and toe-curling elf shoes in all colors of the rainbow.

"Grab one you like and don't forget the shoes."

Choosing my attire from the selection labeled *Clown*, I opted for a black sequined one-piece with gold highlights on the oversized ruffle collar and sleeves. Pairing it with orange clown shoes, laced in black, and a candy apple red permed wig I found perched atop a plastic storage bin. I sealed the barn door behind me before returning inside.

As we both prepared to embark on my final moments at this one-day, trial by fire, Clown College, the chaotic scene continued to unfold. The mismatched ensemble gathered in the barn was now going to be complete with a bag—*the clown survival bag*. A green duffle bag and the low budget array of party supplies she was now cramming inside. These were the final knickknacks given to me before becoming an official clown.

With great difficulty, she orchestrated party plans while engaging with a client on the phone, juggling the components of *the clown survival bag*, trying to do all this while simultaneously checking to see if her two sons were still alive on the couch.

The pink invoices, detailing every aspect of each party, were handed to me with a casual directive: these pages had the name of the client, the address of the party, the name and age of the child, the number of kids attending the party, the character for the party (clown, pirate, purple dinosaur, karate lizard, etc.), and the special requests for the party, such as cutting the cake, presenting a gift, or dancing with the grandmother, etc.

"Show up in costume and leave in costume."

Her tendency to double-book, a recurring issue, meant

I would be more than fashionably late to the last two parties—a challenge that tested not only my clowning abilities, but also my diplomatic skills with frustrated parents expecting a full-grown adult to entertain their children on this special day. These events were meticulously planned weeks in advance, with deposits made by parents who will only have one 8th birthday party for their child. Yet, one would inevitably arrive an hour and a half late. You could only imagine the anger, frustration, and the poisoning of the soul I got from the parents.

"Do you have access to a car?" she asked, muffling the phone with her hand.

"Not always."

"It's fine; you can use mine."

"Ok," I replied.

"Alright, the first party is at 11:30 am on Saturday. Thank God you're here."

I still had no idea what *The Man in The Cube Campaign* was or what I should wear. The black sequined one-piece with gold highlights was long gone at this point. I made it to phase two, yet the scale of the audition remained a mystery. Arriving early and seen quickly, there were likely hundreds, if not thousands, of other candidates they saw that day. I still didn't know who was financing this. Maybe it is an eccentric old millionaire who orchestrated the whole thing—posting a phony ad as a desperate attempt to find a suitor for his daughter before he dies of a mysterious illness. Could this promotion be an elaborate test of mental stamina? I imagined - an old man in a wheelchair, draped in a plaid blanket, bursts into the room on Monday, exclaiming, *"If you can survive this... you can survive my daughter, and my life's fortune will be yours!"*

The night before the second interview, with no concrete facts, I had no doubt, no doubt in my mind the old man would be there, and that it was going to be a promotion for a new instant breakfast beverage.

CHAPTER 2

The Second Interview,
and Expecting to see The Old Man

Monday morning at 9:30 am, I was at The Sparkling Marketing Stone Group (TSMSG) in Midtown, a brand marketing company in the city. Anna Myers. She was tall, and very blonde. She walked with an elegant charm and a great sense of purpose. She was one of the individuals who sat at the conference table during the audition the week before, and she greeted me warmly in the waiting room. She escorted me into a private office and sitting at the desk was *Special Skills, Facial Hair*. We exchanged nods and handshakes, as if we were old friends. I half-expected to see the old man in the wheelchair.

Special Skills handed me a set of 11"x16" color pictures of it – *The Box*, the *Apartment on Wheels*. These photos, captured by an ordinary flash camera, contained a simple white Ryder Tandem Straight Truck with green highlights. The logos were yet to be seen. The front appeared ordinary, but as I flipped to the second picture, and this is where it got interesting, the cargo box was transformed into a customized railroad apartment encased in quarter-inch thick transparent glass. And this box was fully furnished, with a transparent roof comprised of overlapping plastic pieces. The truck is about 8 to 9 feet tall, 8 feet wide, and between 20 to 26 feet long. It can carry up to 10,000 pounds of cargo.

"We have eight of them. Each will target a region in the US." explained *Special Skills, Facial Hair*.

Thinking to myself, *Eight!? But there are five regions. What are they going to do with the other three, crash'em into each other? Why would you need eight of them?*

"Oh, that makes sense," replying with no understanding whatsoever.

"We'll have you sign a non-disclosure," they said.

"Why?" I inquired.

"The product isn't on the market. The campaign starts the same day the drug is released to the public."

"Ok," I said.

The drug? Not a breakfast beverage, a video game system or a kissing booth on wheels.

I immediately pushed those thoughts out of my mind.

"Great, we will call you this afternoon to let you know," *Special Skills* said, and just like that, the second interview was over. The shortest interview I've ever had, like old friends planning an alumni breakfast.

Anna walked me to the door, "We'll call you later."

"Thanks for seeing me today. Tell the old man I said good-bye," I replied.

Back in Brooklyn, it was still morning, and I still wasn't sure if they were going to call me or not. They showed me pictures, revealing it as a campaign for a pharmaceutical drug set to be released in the new year. Despite this, my employment status remained unclear. I decided to make a pot of coffee and settled comfortably into the wooden rocking chair, facing the northwest wall by the phone. Flipping on the stereo, I waited... and waited. As the day grew long and the phone stayed silent, the realization crept in: *They must have passed on me.* It was time to let the whole thing go and seek a change of environment to clear my head.

At some point in my life, I made a conscious decision to walk away from everything I'd ever known and see what would happen. Sometimes it worked out and sometimes it didn't. Apparently, this time it didn't.

I grabbed my shoulder bag and house keys, slipped into my sneakers, and turned off the stereo. A change of scenery was in order. With the sun still hanging in the sky, I decided to venture out for a late afternoon coffee and some casual reading. It was time to let go of this. As I exited my building, I was only halfway down the first flight of stairs when...

Ring, ring.

"Hello," I answered.

"May I speak to Randolph Hubard?" the voice on the other end asked.

"This is he," I replied.

"Hi, it's Anna... we met today..."

"Yes, Yes, Yes! Hi," I responded.

"Hi," she said back.

"Yes, Hi, hello, very good," I said.

"Hi, just wanted to be the first to tell you, we would like to offer you the position."

"Oh, fantastic, that's just fantastic. I would love to do it!" I exclaimed, jumping up and down.

"Great, we really liked you, and we want you to do it. We are just finishing up a few things here, and I'll call you in a couple of days and give you more details... ok," her voice calm and soothing.

"Absolutely, that's fine, I'm excited," I said genuinely.

"Me too... welcome to the family."

"Ok, bye," I cried.

Hanging up the phone and sinking into that rocking chair, I wasn't sure if any blood was left in my legs. My mind was in a sea of delirium. This was amazing, unreal. This was absolutely marvelous. I got it! They called me and gave it to me. This guy who didn't have two dimes to rub together was going to travel across the United States in a *Glass Apartment on Wheels*. And then I thought, *Welcome to the family... What does that mean!?*

CHAPTER

Preparation and Hotel Accommodations

Phase III: Plane tickets and hotel accommodations were arranged for a week of training before kicking off the campaign in St. Louis, Missouri.

St. Louis was chosen because the company that built these *Apartments on Wheels* was based there, making it convenient for everyone to fly to their showrooms and work directly with the designers for any last-minute alterations. It was also an opportunity to meet with the team, learn the language associated with the promotion, organize the route, become familiar with our vehicle and gain insights into the drug.

By this point, we all had some knowledge of the drug central to the promotion: *Tamiflu* (oseltamivir phosphate). This marked the FDA educating the public simultaneously with the drug's release in prescription form. This was a new tactic, which marked a new direction in the marketing of pharmaceuticals. Every city *The Boxes* visited would be saturated with this campaign.

Full-page advertisements were taken out in local newspapers, radio and television commercials aired during viewing hours. High-profile personalities praised it based on personal experience. Even an episode of a gritty, high-stakes, and sexy medical drama, featuring fantastic haircuts, cutting-edge medical procedures, and set to a killer soundtrack, prominently showcased *Tamiflu*, with a character specifically asking for it by name. It even decorated a doctor's office wall in a Christmas classic about a man-child reconnecting with his long-lost father.

Tamiflu is a pill taken by mouth. An antiviral medication used to treat or more accurately, prevent influenza A and influenza B. Commonly known as the Flu. It is an inhibitor. The drug acts as a shield. It prohibits the virus from entering the lungs. It needs to be taken within 48 hours of (Flu) symptoms for it to work. This was a game-changer for the pharmaceutical industry, earning a spot on the *World Health Organization's List of Essential Medicines*. That was the science of it. We were the team acting as the face of the operation. But we were at the dawn of this journey. No one had ever done anything like this. No one had any idea what we were about to do. Let alone me.

We were slated just before Christmas to meet in St. Louis, Missouri, for an entire week. After that, we would have the holiday back at our respective homes and then gather in St. Louis, Missouri, at the beginning of the new year to start the tour. Mostly everyone flew from LaGuardia (LGA) in New York to St. Louis Lambert International Airport (STL) in St. Louis, Missouri, and arrived at the hotel, The Charles J. Hamshackle Inn (CJH). It's a business-friendly hotel right off Interstate 55 South. The front has a huge overpass, and a friendly, well-lit lobby awaits with the front desk to the left, sporting a small synthetic Christmas tree for the season.

The entire promotional team was already there, including the Heads of the Marketing Division, the Regional Office Managers, the Assistant Regional Office Managers, the Drug Liaisons, the Truck Drivers, the Vehicle Designers, the Tour Managers, the Assistant Tour Managers, the Publicity Managers, the Financial Officers, the Candlestick Makers, the Political Coaches, and the Actors, all present. It was a motley crew for sure.

While checking in, I noticed a small, unassuming, black marquee sign with white changeable lettering on the lobby wall that said, *Guest of the Week*. As I checked in under the registered name of *Randolph Hubbard*, I asked, "How does one become a Guest of the Week?"

"Oh, you have to be extraordinary in some capacity," replied the woman at the desk, peeking around the tiny plastic Christmas tree to see the marquee.

"Extraordinary capacity," I cried.

Thanking her, I grabbed my bags, room key, passed the marquee in the lobby, hit the elevator, and went to my room.

One of my favorite things in this world are hotels. Hotels, motels, lodges, extended stays, bed-and-breakfasts, log cabins—the entire industry excites me. And I knew I was about to spend many nights in them.

When you walk into a hotel room, the first thing you notice is that it's clean. The bed is made with fresh sheets carrying a faint scent of sodium hypochlorite, or as it's known on the street,

Javel water. Soaps and shampoos in fancy, differently colored bottles are neatly lined in the bathroom. Great literature, such as the names and numbers of the TV channels, the emergency escape route framed on the back of the door, and special notes just for you on plastic cards, say:

- TOWELS ON THE FLOOR WILL BE REPLACED.
- DO NOT DISTURB.
- LET US KNOW IF YOU WOULD LIKE YOUR LINENS CHANGED.

A copy of the Scriptures rests in the nightstand drawer. Ice machines and glass-front beverage vending machines are in small side rooms. You have to be a crackerjack and learn mind-bending codes like F-24 and K-06 to ensure you get the right chocolate bar and orange flavored soda pop. The downstairs lobby offers a morning meal consisting of cereal, fruit, small baked goods, toast or bagels, coffee, tea, orange juice, and sometimes a *Make-Your-Own Waffle Station*. With all the fixings, this is known as *The Continental Breakfast*. Some places have cookies in square, transparent plastic boxes at the front desk. You could seize one right after check-in and devour it, stuffing down your fear of being out of your comfort zone.

Most of these motels and hotels have 24-hour coffee and tea access. The coffee and hot water are usually in glass teardrop pots, with dark plastic handles. Or silver urns next to a special wooden box lined with red or green felt holding single serving wrapped tea bags. Blue, pink, and yellow tiny parcels of sweetener are stuffed into small stackable cubbies. Slender, stainless steel insulated carafes hold milk. Some chain hotels have an indoor pool and a hot tub, each with a set of universal rules:

1. NO LIFEGUARD ON DUTY.
2. NO RUNNING.
3. NO DIVING.
4. NO ALCOHOL.

And if you wanted anything, not just a wake-up call, at any time of day, you could just phone the front desk. The hallways are well-lit with gaudy patterned rugs. The lobbies have wide-open, inviting spaces with easy access private parking. The establishment's name is plastered somewhere on the front of the building, and they are in areas close to local businesses, restaurants, and groovy grocery stores. It's like a tiny college campus—everything you need in a simple, no-nonsense layout, in a clean and square space. That was a great luxury for me at the time, everything whittled down to a tin can with a boob tube. I had a television in Brooklyn, but I didn't have cable. But I did that night.

Every night, there are people in every room doing everything from bad business deals to proposing marriage to their young floozy secretaries. Most chain hotels have a bed (sometimes two), throw pillows, a bed runner (aka bed scarf), one or two telephones, a remote for the television, a television, an alarm clock, an ice bucket, two glasses, paper coasters for the glasses, a framed picture of a city or tropical landscape bolted to the wall, pleasant patterned beige(ish) wallpaper, child-proof safety windows, blackout curtains, a closet, hotel coat (aka anti-theft garment) hangers, a (folding) luggage rack, a jewelry safe under an extra pillow!, a plastic laundry bag, and a moldy hairdryer. A dresser, a mirror, some places have the full-body ones, a heavily oiled wood veneer desk with a side chair and some sort of cushion-stained sofa. If you get a suite with a glider chair, remember that room number for the future. Because those things are outta this world. A coffee maker or something like it, white styrofoam or paper cups, sugars, and a synthetic creamer substitute. A box of tissues inside a tissue holder (you know, a holder for the holder). Two small trash cans only big enough to hold a single sheet of paper, a mini-fridge, a climate control system, a magazine, or hard copy book about the hotspots in the town. Some of the older hotels have cigarette burns on the sink and nightstand. Some have letterhead stationery with the name and address of the hotel on it. You also have your five types of towels:

- WASHCLOTHS
- HAND TOWELS
- BATH MAT
- BATH TOWELS
- BATH ROBES

And finally, a floor lamp in the corner of the room you never use. This place had it all. It was high-brow, high time that night. I quickly kicked off my shoes, unpacked my dress pants and button-down long-sleeve shirt, made something from a brown packet on the dresser that said *Coffee* on it, put the *DO NOT DISTURB* sign on the outside door-handle, turned on the cable television, eased in the glider chair, took a sip of warm brown water in the white Styrofoam cup, and thought to myself, *Man, I made it.*

CHAPTER 4

The Rule Makers,
The Icebreakers,
and The Drivers Expectations

Phase IV: In a large, windowless meeting room is where we all met for the first day of training. There were several rows of white tables, topped with three-ring binders and name tags. I walked around until I found the one that said *Randolph Hubbard*. The room was filling up, and all persons working on the campaign slowly trickled in. I said hello to everyone I'd remembered from our first meeting, and everyone said hello to me that I forgot.

Ludan Wells came up to me, all smiles. She was at the conference table at The Coup de Foudre Aux Fraises Hotel (CdFAFH) back in New York. She stood about four feet tall and was a force on a mission, in constant movement, always doing something. If you needed to be in Cleveland on Tuesday, she would get you there yesterday. You could tell that she was once the lead singer in a garage rock band by the way she moved, and you could also see it in her eyes. You could never tell if she was working or playing. She was the living embodiment of living romance and the strategic planner for this project. She did everything for everyone as if she were doing it for herself. That morning, she was tasked with grabbing the last-minute travelers from the airport (STL). We exchanged quick hellos, and she darted off to the airport.

I did recognize two others. One was Anthony Emilia McAuliffe III. He was classically handsome, exuding playful leadership, and moved with a gentle, fatherlike quality. He was the type of guy you wanted to tell your stories of virtue to as you were cutting wood for a log cabin or pouring steel for the anchor of a cruise ship. He was a guy you wanted to do stuff with like, build a car or hunt a werewolf that was terrorizing the town folk. He was wearing headphones and listening to some groovy beats then, but today he already had the entire room eating out of the palm of his hand with his charm and wit. And any one of them could've been a werewolf.

And there was George Smythe. He was the other guy I remembered seeing back in New York. This guy was a bean sprout, with wavy blonde hair and dark, deep-set eyes. He was clever, like a substitute teacher that you never really knew if he had a

41

master's in teaching or if he just walked by a school one day, and the principal grabbed him off the street, yelling, *"History, you look like a History Teacher. Your first class is... right now!"*

Thin as a lath, fair-framed eyeglasses matched his hair, and he was wearing a strange necklace. Of the likes I've never seen before. It would be something we would have to discuss later. But this was not the time or the place to talk about jewelry. We all locked eyes for a moment, gave a friendly nod of recognition, and took our seats for the day.

This was a day for training, no-nonsense training. Coffee and danish already in the room training. Stand up and tell us a little bit about yourself icebreaker training. Large, windowless room training. And when you heard those conference room doors snap shut, you knew you were in it for real. There was some power behind this, and you could feel it.

Tensions were high. We had to be sharp. The money was watching. We started at the beginning and went over the heads of all the departments, your traveling team, and where you would be for the run of the campaign. My orders were to infiltrate the Midwest region. This was my route in random order: Illinois, Missouri, Indiana, Michigan, Wisconsin, Ohio, Minnesota, and of course, Nebraska, from January till April. Each team consists of five members. This was mine:

- REGIONAL TEAM LEADER / PATRICIA ARNOLD
- TOUR MANAGER / PETER NELSON
- ASSISTANT TOUR MANAGER / AMBER HARRIS
- TRUCK DRIVER / JOHNNY PRATTLER
- MAN IN THE CUBE / SPOKESMAN / RANDOLPH HUBARD

The regional team leaders had more than one team to oversee. But since no marketing company had ever tackled a campaign like this, from the home offices perspective everyone was on every team. Patricia Arnold was our leader. She introduced herself earlier that morning.

"You must be the one. The one they call Randolph?"

A young woman with strawberry blonde hair and summer blue eyes asked as she touched my shoulder.

"Yes, yes, I am. I'm sorry, who are you?" I asked.

"I'm Patricia Arnold. I'll be working with you. I'm on the Midwest team. I'm your team leader."

"Patricia, it's nice to meet you. I'll try to have my ducks in a row and not to call too much. I don't want to be a bother."

"That's too bad," she said.

Everyone was present that morning except one, Johnny Prattler. He was one of the few still in transition at the airport, and he was the driver of my *Box*. But we had to move forward with the icebreakers. You gotta break that ice early. We did it by the numbers. Each person, one by one, stood up, said their name, position, and something about themselves that they never told another human being before. It went something like this.

" Hello, my name is So-and-So. I'm one of the assistant tour managers. I am from Pahrump, Nevada. I enjoy avocado on toast, Rod Stewart, and long walks on the beach."

" Hello... do I say my name now? I'm So-and-So. I have driven trucks since I was a kid. I'm from South Carolina. I like fireworks. And I enjoy Danielle Steel novels."

" Hi, I'm So-and-So. Austin, Texas. Born and bred! I collect straws. I love roller skates. And I think this is awesome!"

Tamiflu (oseltamivir phosphate) was the name of the drug. The overhead projector gave us all that information. It's a capsule and only available in prescription form. Each drug on the market has a unique name and color scheme associated with its packaging. This was ours: yellow, white, and pastel green.

It broke down like this. Every team would take their *Cube* to fairs, festivals, and large social gatherings throughout the United States to bring awareness about this new drug. But also, we hit towns with high flu outbreaks. That meant we would also be flexible in our projected locations. At times, we would not know which towns we were going to until the *Flu-O-Meter* informed us. The data on (flu) outbreaks was gathered by local towns doctors and state healthcare professionals in white lab coats. They fed that information into the *Flu-O-Meter* supercomputer that was housed in North Carolina. Once that information was coded and calculated, it organized all the towns that had the highest flu outbreaks. Then we headed to those places to promote the tour. That meant some of our days would be more of a spur-of-the-moment or guerrilla-style approach. We had permits and permission to be on certain city streets and organized events, but we also winged it.

(Note: There is no such thing as a *Flu-O-Meter*.)

The Box, The Cube, or some called it *The Bubble*, or *The Apartment*, would have one individual inside during an event to give the impression, and I must stress this: the impression that they actually live inside it. And then just go about the day as if they were at home, unaware of the public viewing your every gesture and movement.

From all angles, even from office buildings above, you could see the message on the sides and through the glass witness everything happening. Events were planned to run four to twelve hours each day, depending on what was organized for the locations and the foot traffic of the area. Some event days we would be parked on the city streets. Other times lined in a row of an assortment of all different types of mobile marketing trucks and vendors. These would be at large social gatherings. These would be longer events. But the weather played a key role in the length of some days. Sporting events have a specific window for vendors. Parades and pageants have tighter schedules and specific locations for their events.

We also had a crew of sorts. These were locally hired individuals in each market we visited, circulating around *The Box*. The tour managers supervised four to six female models. These models were to dress up in light-colored khaki pants and a pastel green short-sleeve turn-down collared shirt (and a yellow winter jacket) with the *Tamiflu* logo on the front right side about two inches below the collar. The models also sported a short gray wig and wire-framed non-prescription reading glasses. Their responsibility was to walk around with pastel blue backpacks stuffed with packs of instant, high-sodium, chicken soup and small leaflets chock-full of information about the drug and hand these out to the public.

The models were to look like grandmothers giving out chicken soup. The drug was *not* actually in the soup. You can only get it with a prescription. The idea was someone you love and trust emotionally helping you through the flu season, providing you with chicken soup and educational information about *Tamiflu*. It's really a human zoo with young models disguised as your grandmother, handing out packets of salt. And to top everything off, each team had two wrapped Dodge Grand Caravan ES Plus LWB minivans with illuminating vanity mirrors and dimming lights. These vehicles had the same green and white color scheme and logos. Everything from the outfits to the minivans were color-coordinated.

A *Wrapped Minivan (Wrapped Vehicle)* is a colorful vinyl advertisement that partially or completely covers the original exterior paint of the vehicle. It looks like the advertisement is shrink-wrapped to the minivan, like a moving billboard in the third dimension. Each team had two of these wrapped minivans. Even the back window was wrapped in the advert, making it impossible to see out. The tour manager drove one, and the assistant tour manager drove the other. They also held supplies and the costume outfits for the models. They were an office on wheels, and they were to be your leisure vehicles as well.

We broke off from the main group for a while, and the truck driver for the Midwestern region (my team) slowly wandered in. Enter Johnny Prattler. He was not much older than twenty, falling out of his jeans and wearing his good white t-shirt with a mustard stain on the front. Sporting a sun-bleached red baseball cap that covered his buzz cut, but not the circles under his eyes. We all knew some people were still in transit from the airport, and I guessed this was Johnny. Everyone else introduced themselves during the intense icebreaker section, and the headcount for my team was missing one. This had to be Prattler. We bumped into each other and introduced ourselves.

"Hi, I'm Randolph," I said.

"Ya, (I'm) Johnny," he mumbled half-heartedly.

Just then, Ludan Wells zipped around the corner in her gray pant suit, Johnny raised his head and said to her, "I'm mad at you."

"Why?" Ludan asked with caution.

"Nobody picked me up. I slept at the airport all night."

"Why didn't you call me!?" Ludan cried.

I couldn't tell if her accent was from Sydney or Melbourne, Australia. It might've been Perth.

"I'm mad at you," Johnny said again with a low and muttered voice. I was actually surprised he could string that many words together.

Ludan straightened her shoulders, extended her hand, and said, "Let's start again; my name is Ludan."

At that point, I slowly and respectfully walked away. You could plainly see he was tired, confused, frustrated, and out of his depth. But I didn't understand why he didn't reach out to someone when he got to the airport. This was an unsolvable riddle. Besides, on a table to my left were three large urns filled with coffee, and they were not going to drink themselves!

CHAPTER

An Evening at King Callant & Skylarks,

The Plastic Space Action Figures,

The Mysterious Necklace,

and A Game of Giant Checkers

This was a long day; the meetings were done, the coffee urns were now bone dry, but it wasn't over yet. A big social brouhaha was planned at a place called King Callant & Skylarks, an adult amusement center that serves eats and drinks. It's a place where you can play carnival games, win colorful pulp tickets, and trade them in for a No. 2 pencil with a big purple eraser or a pink flamingo beach towel or a motorcycle. You can play pinball, old school arcade games, skee ball, and slug down a beer under a series of neon lights. It's a large square building with aluminum siding without a window in sight.

We were all to meet in the lobby in an hour right after the final meeting of the day. Just enough time to take a shower, change into blue jeans and blazer. We were all looking forward to this after the day we had.

After exiting the elevator, I wandered over to the young woman minding the front desk and asked,

"Is this outfit something a... Guest of the Week would wear?"

"Yes, something like that," she replied.

"Ok, at least I'm on the right track," I said.

It's tempting to spend the entire night playing skee ball, but I tapped out after an hour. I won enough scratchy yellow pulp tickets to get two fluorescent mini space dolls in the hopes to give them to my roommates for Christmas. A small group of people was hanging out at a table by the bar, and I joined them with my little space dolls proudly at my side. Something had been on my mind, a question, and this was the perfect time to ask.

"George, can I ask you something?"

"Sure," George replied.

"That necklace you got there. What's that all about?" I asked with childlike curiosity.

George smiled and said, "This is a prosthetic testicle."

I didn't know if I heard him correctly, but, most importantly, I didn't know how to continue this line of questioning. But since I started it; I better finish it.

"What?" I asked.

"It's a prosthetic replacement for men."

Around his neck was a black silk satin cord threaded through a small fish-eye screw. The screw was bolted into a white oval-shaped plastic part with a small yellow and blue sticker on it that said *Moonstruck Nanas.*

"What's the sticker for?" I asked.

"It's a banana sticker, you know... Banana Nut."

There were eight of us, and by this time, we all knew what region we would be traveling to. The guy who got the Southeastern region was already putting on sunscreen and ordering new golf balls. We all thought it was, or at least I thought it was, going to be one *Box* and we would take turns being inside, like shifts. We would be doing assigned tasks such as vacuuming, fixing the sink, or math. But we had free rein of what to do. I thought walking around in your underwear would be off-limits. It was nice to talk to the others about this; they were in the dark as much as I was. They hired eight totally different types of people for this. We were all different in personality, appearance, and character. One of the guys was a comic; one was a full-time office temp. One of them worked construction; one worked in the financial district. One wore an ascot; one worked in healthcare. And one of them used to play miniature golf professionally. His name was Mike Dugan (aka Miniature golf Mike). He always had a thousand stories about miniature golf and time he spent with the ladies.

We were pleased as punch to be getting out of New York for the winter. I already sublet my room, packed up all my belongings, and had my finances in order – well, at least for the next few months. And the big win for the night was the two plastic space dolls, so my Christmas shopping was done. The entire team blew a few more quarters on pinball, drank a couple of beers and ate another hamburger, and then at that point, we were ready to call it a night. We jumped into a van and headed back to the hotel.

In the lobby, I noticed the hotel had a checkerboard set. This was a rather large one; the checkers were the size of hockey pucks. The board was cloth with an off-white fringe along the sides. It was laid out on a round table about knee-high just next to the breakfast nook close to the main entrance. I didn't notice it when we checked in, but I noticed it now. I sat down and played a solo game. Just then, a young woman entered the lobby and noticed me sitting alone. She had eyes of green, blonde hair, and was wearing a black button-down shirt and lightly faded blue jeans. It was Amber Harris. She was the assistant tour manager for the Midwest region; she was on my team. She smiled and said, "Is this a solitaire game, or can anyone join in?"

"This is giant checkers. By law, it's a two-person game," I cried.

She sat down on the other side of the fringe and made her move. "These things are huge," she said.

"Yes, yes, I believe you're right. I've never seen checkers this size before. I've seen giant pencils before and my fair share of giant stuffed animals, and I've seen giant chess pieces. But never... never giant checkers. Never giant checkers," I exclaimed.

She didn't know if I was deadly serious or pulling her chain. She moved the conversation to something she was more comfortable with.

"We are going to have so much fun," Amber expressed.

"I agree," and I did.

"Some of us are meeting at the hot tub, why don't you come along?" she asked.

Then she stood up. At this point, I could tell she was done with giant checkers for the night.

"I think I'm going to call it a day," I said, feeling the novelty of the game had run its course.

"Alright, I'll see you tomorrow. Very excited about this thing; we're going to have so much fun," Amber said as we shared a smile.

She tilted her head, looked at the floor for a moment, then raised her eyes, slowly turned, and walked down the hallway. I remember seeing her blonde ponytail wave back and forth and hearing her heels clicking on the tile floor. I wish I had said something more meaningful to her. I hardly had a chance to speak to her at all that evening or even that day. As she slowly faded into the dimly lit hallway, I suddenly thought of something. Nothing of any importance. Nothing life changing. Just a playful story, something that we both could relate to. We were going to spend the next few months together and I wanted to say... I figured I'd just tell her in the morning. But that was the last time I ever saw Amber Harris.

I walked up to the front desk, half showing off the carnival dolls I'd won when I asked,

"Excuse me, have all the votes been counted?"

"Counted? Counted, what?"

"For Guest of the Week, of course."

She was caught off guard. You could feel a great sense of bewilderment emerging from her being.

"Oh, ah, I'm not sure. No one gave me a memo, but I'll leave a note that you asked about it. What's your name, sir?"

Standing completely still, composed in silence, holding two plastic fluorescent dolls. One in each hand, I spoke these words.

"It's Hubard, H-U-B as in bird, A-R-D as in diamond."

She grabbed a pen and paper, looked at me without blinking, and wrote down exactly what I said.

"I'll give it to, well, no problem. I'll relay the message to the proper... I'll take care of it," she stated. I thanked her and walked very slowly to the elevator.

In the room, I fell into bed and placed the fluorescent space men on the night stand. All three of us took turns reading a chapter from *Stephen King's Salem's Lot* till we fell asleep.

The next morning, the group were diced up into smaller rooms. The tour managers and the truck drivers had to pass a pre-planned obstacle course. A real one. Turn left, turn right, parallel park, fishtailing, donuts, jackknifing – things like that.

Then, the truck drivers had time carved out for going over their specific responsibilities when it came to the truck, as well as their daily log books or Hours of Service (HOS). Some of these guys had never driven a truck before.

One of the most common accidents for truck drivers is falling asleep while driving. To balance out fatigue, a truck driver is only allowed to drive a certain number of hours within a 24-hour period. That's why a lot of trucks are equipped with a truck sleeper (aka sleeper cab). It's a small room or sleeping chamber located behind the driver's seat where you could stretch out and sleep through the night.

Weigh Stations are located on highways where trucks are weighed to see if they fall under the weight guidelines, and sometimes drivers are asked to show their logbooks to ensure they are not burning the candle at both ends. For example, if you are driving from Clearwater, Florida, to Albuquerque, New Mexico, the weigh station attendant would know, by looking at the logbooks, if you stopped and slept or drove 26 hours straight.

CHAPTER

The Box-in The Third Dimension,
and The 1989 Batmobile

Phase V: Field trip to Craftsmen Industries, Inc. These guys physically produced *The Box* and are also responsible for, but not limited to, making versions of The Oscar Mayer Weinermobile and The Hershey's Kissmobile. If you ever wanted to see anything in vehicle form, these were the guys to call. We entered their facility and walked into this huge white skylight hanger that had three of the vehicles lined up, side-by-side, dead center in the hanger. Brand new, and they were staring back at us. And I thought to myself, *Oh, my God, they are going to crash them into each other!*

In the summer of 1989, MTV held a contest sponsored by Warner Bros. and Pepsi called *Steal the Batmobile*. It was a promotion for the most anticipated film of that year, *Batman*. On Sunday, June 18th, when they flashed the MTV *Batsignal*, sometime that day on their channel, you could call a (900) number to win an Anton Furst designed fiberglass prototype of the *Batmobile* (engine not included). Robert Wuhl, who played *Reporter, Alexander Knox* in the film, said, *"(He) will deliver it personally to your door,"* along with a check for $25,000. The winner of this contest was a college student from, and residing in, Richmond, Virginia. At that time, I was also residing in Richmond, Virginia. The gentleman who won the car displayed it that summer at The Science Museum of Virginia in the town of Richmond.

During that summer, I was working in a play festival, moonlighting as a carpenter. I built the set in the morning and rehearsed two of the plays in the evening. The set was a tilted circle deck with walk-around ramps on both sides, resembling two circles on top of each other. Lights were under the deck, bleeding through the spaces between the floorboards.

Smoke used for the entrance of God in one of the shows, a courtroom drama where the Alpha and the Omega was on trial. When the actor came to court, smoke billowed through his suit, and the lights under the deck reflected off the others in the courtroom. It was such a simple yet stunning effect to see live.

The day broke down into two parts: the mornings, working on the set, and the evenings, rehearsing. It's a great sensation to work on something you've built, but I had trouble traveling back and forth from the theater every day. I ended up staying with one of the producers that summer, and she lived downtown, just a hop, skip, and a jump away from the theatre.

All summer the whole city, nay the world, knew the *Batmobile* was at the museum, not far from where I was working. This was knowledge that I had. But I didn't have the time to go home that summer to take a shower, let alone wander through The Science Museum of Virginia and look at a car.

After dismantling the stage, concluding the festival and two bottles of champagne I embarked on a solo pilgrimage to the museum the next day, hoping to catch a glimpse of this thing. I entered the building and made my way through the great hall to the information desk, where, to my surprise, one of the actresses I had recently worked with was seated.

"Hey!" I exclaimed. "I didn't know you worked here."

"Yeah. What are you doing here?" she asked.

"I'm here to see the *Batmobile*."

"Randy, it's not on display anymore," she said.

My heart sank. I really wanted to see that thing. That film was reinventing the summer blockbuster, and it was exciting to be a part of... *"But it's still here. Do you want to see it?"* she offered. I looked at her and nodded yes.

"It's in the back. Go take a look."

"By myself!?" I exclaimed.

"Yeah, go ahead," she smiled with her perfect brown eyes.

I walked around the information desk and entered a long, dark hallway that led to a back room. It was littered with wooden crates, display signs, tools, and paint cans. It was a rather unimpressive grubby room—a wasteland of the museum's past displays. Things that were once shiny and new were now cold, gray, damaged, and covered with dust.

She said it was in here, somewhere in this room, I thought. But there was nothing here. I looked around the corner to another hollow hallway—an empty space. However, something in the distance caught my eye, just beyond the darkness hidden under the scaffolding. I cautiously walked into the next hallway, stepped over a series of thick black cable wires, and entered the area. Then paused. Something was there. I could feel that something was in this room with me.

Turning towards the mountain of pipes and pushing away the white, foggy, crackling polyurethane plastic sheet hanging from above, there it was—the *Batmobile*. The Anton Furst version. It looked like someone just parked it in that dingey old room. It was off its display, wheels on the ground. It was out of its cage. It looked like it was alive. It had breath. It looked like it could drive you clear across the River Styx. I was amazed. The room was void of any other carbon-based life form besides me. There were no barriers, no velvet ropes. Nothing was between me and it. I just stood there and stared. I placed my hand on its heart and then glided it over one of it's tailfins. I got goosebumps. *This thing shouldn't exist,* I thought to myself. It was electric. It was beautiful. It was awe-inspiring. It was otherworldly.

———————————————

That's how I felt when I saw *The Boxes* for the first time. We all stood there, gazing at them, like children meeting our hero for the first time. I don't think the paint had dried on them yet. They were just born out of an idea in a boardroom somewhere, and now they were in the third dimension right in front of us all. You could see them breathing, they were bursting with energy. I walked up to one and placed my palm on it. I could feel my fingers tingle. These things were from someplace else.

The designers were on-site to breakdown these crazy things. We referred to the units as *Cubes*. Top of the line vehicles! Straight out of the box, the cat's pajamas. We went over those strange vehicles inch by inch, from headlight to the taillight.

This next section isn't essential to the narrative.
If you'd like to skip the exposition, please continue on to Page 73.

THIS IS WHAT THEY WERE.

In the front, the driver's cab interior was gray – gray seats, gray dashboard, even the ceiling was gray. The exterior was white. On top of the cab was a fiberglass wind deflector (aka air deflector or air foil) with *Tamiflu* (oseltamivir phosphate) painted on it. Written on the cab doors were *Tamiflu*, the name of the company, and the State Address where it's located. The US DOT number and the Gross Vehicle Weight (GVW) were also displayed. The hood was secured on both sides with two black heavy-duty hood latches. To open the hood, you unlatched it and pulled it forward. We knew this because strawberry blonde, summer blue-eyed Patricia from the office jumped on the hood in her high heels like a spider monkey and pulled it open for us. A black gas tank also doubled as the step to the passenger cab entrance.

Behind the cab on the driver's side was a square door, the entrance to the *Cube* itself. A black metal ladder flipped out and rested against the side of the cab, attached to the floor inside. You would flip it down to get in, then flip it up to close the door. That's how you entered the *Cube*.

Directly inside to the left was a square Kubota (Three Phase) KJ-T180VX-50 (18 KVA) *Diesel* generator. It was orange with a black flat top and an ignition key hanging next to a couple of space-aged switches and knobs on the front side. A small door with a glass window protected the controls. I asked what all the buttons and switches were for, but I was told, *"Don't touch them."* I thought if I did, I might open a vortex to another dimension. The generator was bolted to the floor, serving as the power source for the *Cube*, solely for powering the *Apartment*.

Directly to the right were two ten-foot orange fiberglass ladders tucked in tightly at an angle to fit in the space between the generator and the wall. This was a small space lined with oriented strand board (OSB) walls. To the right was a door that led to *the Apartment*. Going through the door, you were now in *the Glass Apartment*. The door, the only door, consisted of two kitchen cabinet doors attached together, opening and closing as one piece. The lower cabinet door was about six feet high and a small cabinet right above. That was about two and a half feet tall. They were attached together to give enough head space for anyone taller than six feet to enter the apartment without bending over. It was a door disguised as two kitchen cabinets. From the street, it looked simply like a two-cabinet door. No one could figure out how you got inside. You would look like a ship in a bottle.

To the left, next to the cabinet door, was the kitchen area (aka kitchenette). A faucet, spray gun (decorative only), and a stainless-steel sink—brand new without a scratch on it. Velcro was attached to the plastic green and blue dish scrubbers that were placed on the lip of the sink towards the back wall. Two glass cabinets with a textured square-style glass design were right above the counter on the right side. They had white child safety latches inside. The safety latches were installed to keep the cabinets from flying open during the long drives and quick stops. These safety latches would allow the cabinet to open about a quarter of an inch, then you were to manually lift the latch to unlock. Then you could fully open the cabinets.

Two circular kitchen lights were hidden underneath the wood of the kitchen cabinet. That gave the countertops a good pool of light. There was no plumbing or water pressure, so the faucet didn't work. A round five-gallon plastic bucket fit securely into a custom-made metal circle in the cabinet directly below the drain. You could then pour liquid in the sink, and it would drop directly into the bucket. Later, you would pop out the bucket to empty it. You had to remember that you had liquid in that bucket before you drove away. A bump or sudden stop could force the liquid out of the bucket. In cold weather, it would freeze. It was important to remember that this was not a real functioning apartment, and you were in charge of maintenance. That included your own safety.

Above the counter were dishes in the glass cabinets tightly glued to the shelves. A single silverware drawer on the right of the counter had strips of black Velcro inside to keep it closed while the *Cube* was moving about. Secured on the counter was a metal rod paper towel holder and a small wooden dowel dish dryer. The dowel was used to hold napkins or small breakfast food items like protein bars—something I could have for a quick snack. The Mr. Coffee maker (that was free moving) and a Black + Decker white toaster oven, were both held down by strips of Velcro. A white controller panel for the heating/air conditioner unit was on the wall above the toaster oven.

The only things that functioned in the kitchenette were the toaster oven and the coffee maker. During conveyance, I would place the coffee maker in the sink, wrapped in a towel, to keep it from knocking about. The toaster oven was square and had its weight evenly distributed. That was held down by Velcro and needed nothing more. There was an outlet on the wall that powered both the coffee maker and the toaster oven.

Bolted to the wall on the left side of the sink against the cabinet was a one-inch-thick wooden checkerboard pattern cutting board. Above that was the intercom system used to communicate with the driver's cab (the driver cab only). Above the sink flat on the wall was a flat wooden knife holder where the knives were secured in place by means of a single strip of black Velcro. *Actual knives!* To the left of that above the sink was a thin horizontal metal rod, and bolted to that was a stainless-steel spatula, pot spoon, two-prong carving fork, spaghetti strainer spoon, and a ladle hanging from it. All items were glued to the wall.

Above them were two wooden shelves about two inches thick. On the first shelf was a round spice rack that held sixteen different spices. All the spices were in glass containers glued shut and affixed in the spice rack. A transparent plastic salt and pepper grinder set complemented them nicely. Eighteen spices in all (including salt and pepper). Above the salt and pepper grinders, on the wall, was a motion sensor alarm. Under the first shelf was another circular kitchen light-the width of a soda can-that illuminated the sink. And leaning against the wall to the right of the King and Queen of spices was a hardbound copy of *All Star Feast Cookbook*, compiled by Wendy Diamond.

Left on the top shelf were two transparent glass food containers with plastic-colored lids, one blue and one yellow, filled with big colorful gum balls. To the right of those was another wooden dowel dish dryer. The kitchenette walls were highlighted with gray grass-woven wallpaper.
(Note: I should have asked for an extra roll of the wallpaper.)

A white Cooaireford Breeze Bite Seven mini-fridge fit comfortably on the floor to the right of the sink. On the floor in front of the counter, on top of a red, orange, and light blue bull's-eye pattern round rug, was a high circular glass table. With four thin gray metal legs bolted to the floor through the rug. This had two gray thin metal-legged cushion chairs, with seven horizontal strips for back support. The legs of the chairs and tables were attached to each other by strips of black Velcro. By removing the Velcro, you could then move the chairs to the location of your desire.

Directly in front of the entrance, a few feet in facing you, were two light-colored wooden dressers sitting side by side with four drawers each. The top drawer had a transparent glass front, and the other three drawers had a dark blue front with a faux wooden top. A single gray knob opened each of them. On the top of the drawers was a small gray lamp with a round base and a frosted glass dome top, partnered by a silver-looking round two-handed clock that was firmly glued down. In the center of the dresser was a clear plastic circular tube that ran from the top of the dresser to the plastic ceiling of the *Cube*, acting as a support rod for the ceiling above. Otherwise, the ceiling would cave in under its own weight.

The ceiling was thinner plastic than that of the glass sides, composed of several pieces of square plastic that lined up like a shingle system on house rooves. It wasn't a single piece of plastic but several, supported in the center by the plastic transparent tube.

To give the *Cube* a connection to the outside world, it had a blue cordless Vtech 900 MHz desk phone. The phone (decorative only) had Velcro that connected the receiver to its base. The base was glued to the corner of the dresser facing the back. Although non-functional, I would often pretend to use the phone during times when it was most hilarious. I would answer the phone as I stared directly into someone's soul outside, making them uncomfortable as they slowly walked away to attend to their daily affairs.

The dressers were about waist high. Strips of Velcro lined inside the drawers to keep them closed, but that only worked in theory. They would pop open every time the truck made a stop, regardless of speed. Any kind of stop would force open the drawers, creating a somewhat haunted appearance at every stop sign as the drawers opened and closed intermittently. Something stronger would have to be used to secure them.

On the floor to the right was a fake potted plant that bridged the gap between the glass side of the *Cube* and the dresser. On the street, the floor of *The Box* and the potted plant could be seen at eye level.

The dresser drawers faced the entrance (kitchenette) of the apartment. If you kept moving towards the end of the apartment, to the left of the drawers after the glass kitchen table, there was a walkway between the dresser and the floor-to-ceiling window about three feet wide, leading to the other half of the *Cube*.

On the left side of the dresser next to the *small walkway* was a gray floor lamp with the base on the floor that ran up the side of the dresser with a bendable reading light attached. The bendable light could be focused on the area where the loveseat was stationed, providing a great glow for evening events or casual reading on a rainy day.

On the opposite side of the dressers, facing out the back window, was a white loveseat also bolted to the floor. White. *White!* This was a white loveseat, and I knew this would be the perfect time to quit grape juice altogether.

The loveseat and wooden dressers sat back-to-back, giving the illusion of dividing points into two different rooms. This loveseat doubled as a bed, and when fully opened was hard as a rock, stiff as a board, and white sheets were also provided. The two sleeping pillows for the bed were held in the bottom drawers of each dresser.

To open the bed, you had to move a wooden coffee table that was also bolted to the floor. This was a small space, and it had just enough room for a bed. I'll get to that in a second.

In the morning, you could pretend to be sleeping, then wake up, close the bed, and start the event. This loveseat also had two blue and two white throw pillows and a lap seatbelt. The seatbelt was double bolted to the floor, hidden under the cushions and could be easily buckled at a moment's notice. The seatbelt was to be used when driving down the road. We drove down the road while I was sitting on the loveseat, securely fastened, flying down the highway at speeds exceeding 55 mph, waving at all the people of the world. This would be the first time I had to be securely fastened in a loveseat before traveling.

On the floor in front of the loveseat was a small square rug with different colored horizontal stripes. Above the rug was the wooden coffee table with a glass top. The glass floated four inches above the table, supported by four gray rods on each corner, with four gray rubber industrial wheels two inches high on the bottom. Two long stainless-steel threaded rods attached to the bottom shelf of the coffee table ran the length of the rubber wheels and connected to the two floor bolts below. They were long bolts that attached the coffee table to the floor. They could be unscrewed, then the coffee table could roll around freely. The loveseat could then open without the coffee table in the way and become the bed.

Directly in front of the coffee table on the floor was *The Escape Hatch*. This was for security purposes only. Two small, flush, ring pull handles were on both sides of the hatch. By pulling them up, *The Escape Hatch* opened (unlocked). You could lift it and place it to the side, then exit through the floor and roll out from under the back of the truck. The hatch was painted manila, and it blended into the floor rather well (as much as it could). It opened easily in case of a fire or emergency. You were able to bolt the coffee table directly on the top of *The Escape Hatch*. There were two wing bolts, each about a foot long, that fed through the bottom of the coffee table and connected to screw points on the floor. There were two places where the coffee table could be bolted—one was directly on *The Escape Hatch*, and the other was about three feet further out. It provided just enough room for the end of the bed to touch the table, allowing sufficient space to open the bed. Alternatively, you could move it if you wanted more legroom. *The coffee table was on wheels!*

On the right, caddy-cornered at the back of the apartment was a 20" Panasonic PV-M2059 television VCR (videocassette recorder) combo. This had a black square bar that bolted it on a gray, question mark-shaped stand with a circular base that led to the floor. The television screen reflected the sunlight during the daytime. *In the second year a black metal plate was placed on top. It acted as a baseball cap to help prevent the glare.* A small, blue plastic oval trash can sat next to it, attached to the floor.

And to the caddy-cornered left in the back was a three-tiered glass display case with a wooden bottom and top shelf (five shelves in all) that was just about the entire height of the *Cube* inside. The display case had a glass door held shut by a double magnetic touch door latch. On the top wooden shelf of the glass case was a Ynoise (8-MC875M) five-disk carousel CD (compact disc) changer and a double tape deck player. The two square speakers were welded on the corners of the ceiling in the back, one above the glass case and the other above the television.

On the floor, in both corners, were two three-prong outlets serving as power plugs, one for the television on the right and the other for the stereo on the left. They were also used to power the vacuum cleaner that I used to clean the rugs and floors of the *Cube*. Power cords and wires from the electronics were well-hidden. The glass shelves held a picture frame on the top shelf, big enough for a postcard-sized picture, firmly attached to the glass.

The next shelf down had a tiny planter pot, accompanied by two transparent blue memo clip holder cube stands with alligator clasps for pictures. One on each side of the planter pot. The shelf below held two small, rustic green metal frogs standing upright, one holding a French horn, the other playing a fiddle. On the bottom shelf was a rotating globe of the earth, in case you forget what planet you were on.

The floor was sheet vinyl, light in color, in a hardwood patterned design, and it was also placed on top of *The Escape Hatch*, blending into the floor. All the wood was synthetic or veneer and light in color. Between the roof and the quarter inch glass siding was two feet of wall covered with the same gray grass wallpaper that was in the kitchenette. On the left side on the wallpaper section, about the halfway point of the apartment, above the glass, was a round white smoke detector. On the floor on both sides of the *Cube* was a set of three vents lined side by side, twelve vents in all, that pumped in the (heated/cooled) air. And that was *The Box*.

These things looked like die-cast metal toy trucks for adults. Did I mention a restroom? I didn't, because there wasn't one. That was my major concern, along with the large amount of glass and knives used in this operation—a large glass kitchen table, glass shelves, glass spice containers, glass cabinets, and a glass top coffee table on wheels! I was to be in extremely cold environments. And the *Cube, The Bubble, The Apartment, The Block, The Box*, whatever it was called, had no insulation.

Photo by Randolph Hubard

The Box, in its natural habitat.

It was time for a dry run. The generator had a key dangling from an ignition port, and an exhaust pipe that came straight through the roof. Once the generator was on, you could work the lights, the music, the television, the coffee maker, all the electrical outlets, and the air conditioning/heating unit.

When the generator was on, it produced a vibration in the *Cube* that was loud and almost unbearable. I knew I had to make peace with that sound real quick.

We took turns in each *Cube*—walking around, sitting in the seats, unbolting the coffee table, adjusting the air conditioning/heating unit, making toast, etc. Opening and closing the loveseat/bed.

I went straight to *The Emergency Hatch* and opened it. That was simple and easy to access. Then I did an external walk-around, kicking the tires—all six of them. It was a solid machine. The *Cube* sits on top of four back wheels, two on each side, so your eye level was a little above the person's feet inside.

This was the time to learn how many twists were needed to unbolt something, how wide your steps could be before you would knock the glass with your forehead, and where on the loveseat you could sit comfortably. Forming a relationship with the space. This was very different from anything else I had ever been in before. Nothing was simple. It would take two or three actions just to move a chair, and we had to make it look easy.

The outer shell of the *Cube* had metal siding covering the bottom, back wheels, and rear. A cubby hole was where the license plate was supposed to go. We never attached one to the back.

At the rear corners were two aluminum gauge flip weatherproof electrical outlets, painted white and located at the top of each side. These outlets allowed extension cords to be plugged directly into the back and provide power to anything outside.

A custom-made green tarp with a thin white mesh inner lining covered the entire *Glass Cube*. This is where the two fiberglass ladders came in. The green tarp was rolled up like a burrito, exposing what was inside, and then it fit firmly behind the cab. You had to tuck the tarp manually. The ladders were to be placed on both sides of the *Cube*, where the driver and I would climb up and flip the tarp over the glass and then over the generator exhaust pipe. Then secure it behind the driver's cab with black straps.

At the end of the event, you were to unroll it the length of the *Cube*, and it would fit perfectly on all corners. The bottom of the tarp was secured to the underside of the metal siding beneath the truck using button snaps.

This tarp covered the entire *Cube*, including the two circular brake lights located at the back of the vehicle. The tarp also covered all of the side marker, clearance, and signal lights. These lights help other drivers gauge the size, the position, and movement of the truck, reducing any risk of accidents, particularly at night, during lane changes, and extreme weather conditions. In the front you could see the signal lights, you could see the headlights. But all the external side and back lighting was covered by the tarp.

When the *Cube* was covered by the tarp, you could still enter via a square flap that was the same size as the entrance door by unzipping two black zippers on each side of the square. But there was a catch—the two black zippers ran vertically up, all the way to the top. The ladder to enter the back would be inside the door. There was no way anyone could unzip those on their own.

A tailored, four-foot, black metal rod was used to unzip the flap. On the *puller* or handle of every zipper, you will find a hole either in the shape of a square or a circle. That hole is most commonly used to thread a string or a synthetic lace to extend the grasp so you can easily unzip a backpack, jacket, or bag. These black zippers on this tarp had a hole the size of your fingernail.

The end of the black metal rod was to be secured in the hole, and then you would push the zipper up, extending your arm by means of the black rod, to the top of the *Cube*. That would unzip the zipper. To close it, you would use the black rod to find the hole at the top and secure the end of the black rod in the hole, then pull the zipper down. You needed to do that two times because there were two zippers. It was like trying to unlock a door with the key at the end of a four-foot black metal rod. And this was done in all conditions, including the cold, dark, merciless night.

The black rod was stored in the cab behind the driver's seat, and we only had one of these. After the zipper flap was opened and the side door was opened, you could then flip the black ladder out and climb into *The Box*. Then it was simply a matter of switching the *Diesel* generator on, going through the cabinet door, and once inside, you would prep for the day and have two individuals roll the tarp up and secure it. This series of actions would give the impression that someone was living inside, like unveiling a statue or looking inside a dollhouse.

Written on the top and bottom exterior sides of the glass and on the roof of the *Cube* was this message:

The Top of the Cube read:
This person's solution from the flu.

The Bottom of the Cube read:
For your flu solution, there's Tamiflu (oseltamivir phosphate) - your trusted choice.

And just behind the passenger side (on the right) and on the entrance to the *Cube* door (located on the left side of the truck) read this:

ABOUT THE PERSON IN THE CUBE:

Flu season is upon us, and this setup before you delivers one glaring truth: unless sealed off in a germ-free bubble, no one is truly safe from infection. If symptoms hit, it's time to act fast - get to the doctor and ask about Tamiflu. The antiviral pill, tailored to battle influenza, is a groundbreaking addition to a class of drugs called neuraminidase inhibitors. Unlike anything before it, it targets the virus at its core, curbing the illness from the inside out.

Timing is everything. To be effective, Tamiflu has to be started within two days of feeling that dreaded onset. However, Tamiflu isn't a preventive measure nor a vaccine substitute. Like all medications, it has its side effects. While most users handle it fine, about one in ten might face mild nausea or vomiting, which food can help mitigate. Other rare side effects include dizziness or bronchitis.

The idea is simple: spot the flu early, see your doctor, and let Tamiflu handle the rest. For further information, consult our brochures, our toll-free hotline, or the official Tamiflu website.

Or something to that effect.

On the sides of the green tarp in the center had the full name of the product *(Tamiflu)* written in white. The two minivans were to drive with the *Cube.*

One in the front and one behind, like a mini parade. The truck drivers were responsible for the care and maintenance of the exterior of the *Cube*, including the outside glass, the integrity of the vehicle, and the logos.

I was responsible for its interior, managing the inside of the glass, ensuring organization and cleanliness in *the Apartment*, and securing everything periodically throughout the day, especially at the end of the day.

THAT'S WHAT THEY WERE.

It was a wonderfully thought-out project that utilized every inch of that vehicle, and they looked distinguished. They were simply fun and just out of this world. Eight teams got two minivans and this beautiful, custom-made glass *Cube*.

The next day involved an intense focus on the language of the promotion. Each region had its own publicist setting up radio, newspaper, and television interviews. As Spokesmen we were equipped with the proper script and updated information. A political coach specializing in *bridging* worked with us, ensuring any question veering away from the main focus was bridged back to *The Box* or more so *Tamiflu*. The most asked question in every interview was,

"How do you go to the bathroom?"

This was a crash course, covering everything, including the kitchen sink, wrapped up neatly in a week. It was like inventing the textbook for this endeavor. We prepared to fly back home, making sure to have the three-ring binders with all the information. There were pages and pages of paperwork—a comprehensive college course to learn.

The morning before flying home, I discovered a single piece of paper by the hotel room door, notifying me that I had been knighted *Guest of the Week*. Finally.

On the first day of the new year, I arose before dawn, double-checked everything, and drank my morning coffee in the wooden rocking chair, facing the northwest wall, listening to *Ghost Riders in the Sky* by Johnny Cash as the sun slowly rose. Then, I heard the car horn outside, took my last gulp, turned off the stereo, and grabbed my bags. As I left my apartment, I glanced at the six-foot Fraser fir Christmas tree in the living room corner and said, *"I'll see you when I get back."*

Hopping into the car, I took the long, cold, hollow, lonely ride to the airport. Fortunately, I bumped into Anthony and Miniature golf Mike at the ticket counter, and we all boarded the plane together, promptly dozing off on the flight to St. Louis. The minimum age for flying alone on a commercial airline is 12 years. The first time I flew unaccompanied, I was one year shy of that. But the airline didn't know that. One can get away with it if you look like 30 when you turned 8. It was a flight to Norfolk International Airport (ORF). The flight from Newark (EWR), just under two hours, allowed me enough time to enjoy two orange soda pops and a bag of potato chips.

Since one was just knee-high to a grasshopper, I passed through security quickly, glided onto the plane first, and took the window seat on the right side, while a young couple took the other two. The woman took the aisle, and her male counterpart took the middle. After getting my bearings, I reached into my backpack and pulled out the casual reading material for this flight—a paperback copy of *Herbie Goes Bananas*.

Herbie, a Volkswagen Beetle, is a white racing car with the number 53 painted on the doors and front hood. Known for his playful personality and will of his own, *Herbie* was the central figure in a series of films and a short-lived television series. The book I was reading was the novelization of the fourth film in that series, *Herbie Goes Bananas*.

"*Is that Herbie Goes Bananas?*" the guy next to me asked.

"Yes, yes, it is," I replied.

The man then beamed with a wide smile and shared, "*You know, I'm the driver for Herbie.*"

What, I thought. *Who was this guy? Did I just hear him say he was the driver for Herbie?* I was utterly confused. *Herbie* is a haunted car. He drives himself. And this book wasn't a memoir; it was a fictional story.

"What do you mean?" I asked.

"*I'm the stunt driver. It (Herbie) has a steering wheel in the back, and that's how you drive it.*"

Just then, his girlfriend popped her head around him, smiled, and nodded to me, as if that's all the confirmation I needed to believe this turkey.

Then he started going into a speech about all the tricks and camera angles they used to give the illusion that the car could do all these crazy things on its own. I didn't understand what he was doing. Did all his friends grow tired of hearing about his

Herbie adventures? I didn't know why he was telling me this. I didn't want to know this; didn't ask for this. I just wanted to read my book and enjoy the adventures of a haunted automobile. I just wanted to pretend that this car could drive around by itself and pop wheelies. And suddenly, finding out that *Herbie*, my obsession at the time, wasn't real? On an airplane, from a complete stranger and his incredibly attractive girlfriend? I was 11 years old. I still wanted to believe this was real.

Once I put aside my fantasy, I could finally hear him. We talked about my love for *Herbie* and his real adventures with him. It was just a minute or two. I think he was just enjoying the fact that someone was a lover of *Herbie*, ultimately his work. He kept saying that the movies were trying to make it look like this car can do all these things by itself and that there were a lot of people, and he emphasized *a lot* of people working behind the scenes to give the illusion that this thing was real. I had no idea so many people worked so hard so that someone like me could enjoy a two-hour vacation from life watching an odd vehicle do strange things.

Now asleep on an airplane at the beginning of a new year, starting this adventure, going into a project where a lot of people worked behind the scenes on a vehicle to give the illusion that it was real, I suddenly realized how important everything was. I then awoke, opened my satchel, and looked inside for *Herbie Goes Bananas*, but I must have left it in my other bag.

It was the dawn of the new millennium as we headed back to The Charles J. Hamshackle (CJH). We had two days to kill before heading out, and our team wanted to stock up on some essentials. We took a trip to the local Mulligan & Applefield's and Major Fifty Sense to purchase bottled water, thick industrial paper towels, window cleaner, Uncle Pete's Used Sheets (aka rags in bulk), a purple compact vacuum cleaner, coffee filters, a handheld multi-tool, and a snow shovel.

We were given free rein in decorating the interior of the *Cube*. The inside was packed with brand-new furniture and fixtures, so it had not been lived in yet. I wanted to go subtle on the decor. But it needed something. I tried looking for something special in the Home and Garden Department, but it already had a synthetic potted plant. Then I tried the Furniture Department. The bean bag chairs were on sale, but we had more than enough furniture. Then the Art Department. But I decided against getting the velvet painting of a sunset on the beach or the eight-foot-tall stone statue of the Greek God *Kronos* devouring his children. Nothing was speaking to me.

Finally, I found a *Star Wars Episode 1: The Phantom Menace, Mace Windu* action figure and thought, *That would look great standing on the glass display case.* I grabbed a tube of industrial adhesive, a Samuel L. (Motherfucker) Jackson plastic figurine, and the box set of George Lucas's Widescreen Edition of *The Journal of the Whills* (aka *The Original Star Wars Trilogy*). Then we loaded up *The Box* with these supplies.

Because Amber was on the missing persons list, we were still short an assistant tour manager, so the plan was, once one was found, they would take the second minivan and catch up with us.

There was a nervous excitement the day we headed out. This was where the rubber hit the road. All systems were go! We spent hours going over every inch of this thing, studied dozens of safety protocols and procedures. Nothing could go wrong at this point. We were the experts now.

It's not as if one of the professional truck drivers did something foolish, like accidentally reversing a million-dollar, custom-built, brand-new *Glass Cube* into a lamppost. Imagine the entire quarter inch-thick glass wall shattering, with the shards raining down on the entire marketing team, the client standing in awe, becoming a silent witness to this unfortunate, gut-wrenching truth. But someone did!

CHAPTER 7

Chicago, Illinois, The Hooligans, and The Bitter Cold

It was only four hours and thirty minutes to our first Stay Quiet O' Bit Hotel (SQOBH) in Chicago, Illinois, but it took all afternoon to get there. Throughout this promotion, we stayed at a number of Stay Quiet O' Bits. These hotels are for guests who are remaining stationary in the same location for extended periods of time. The rooms have a kitchenette that is fully stocked with dishes, utensils, pots, and pans. There's a refrigerator and a stove/oven combo. A huge worktable with a thousand outlets for every electronic computer device ever created. Perfect for laying out and organizing documents, expense reports, or media press packages. And enough storage for all the leaflets and dehydrated packets of chicken soup. These hotels are designed to be accommodating for the modern-day American adventurer. They also have fully lit parking lots, outright wonderful for big rigs like *The Box.*

First day of the promotion. The temperature was well below freezing, and we wanted desperately to warm up *The Box* before we started. I got up early, packed a bag for the day, and grabbed a pound of coffee that traveled with me all the way from Brooklyn. Eager to brew in *The Box* for the first time, I was thinking two one-gallon jugs of water would be enough for an eight-hour day. I took a white coffee mug from the room, my *Tim Burton: An Unauthorized Biography of the Filmmaker* book, and my blue CD case filled with musical feelings that would complement the workday.

Out to the back parking area of the hotel, I went, thinking an hour would be enough time to set everything for the day before the team was to meet.

It was still dark outside when I noticed some hooligans had sliced an "L"-shaped cut in the tarp on the back window, clean across. We hadn't even broken in this thing, and the tarp was slashed. My blood was boiling. The best thing we could do was patch it up with some green duct tape. *Alright,* I thought, *we can pick that up today.*

I then grabbed the black metal rod behind the driver's cab, unzipped the side, unlocked the door, and entered *The Box.* Having a key to the side door and one for the generator was a great idea. The other generator key hung freely in the lock. I turned the key for the first time, and it roared to life. I crossed over the threshold and entered via the cabinet.

The tarp covered the entire *Cube*, except for the "L"-shaped cut in the back. *Those hooligans!* I thought. The white mesh layer hugged flat against the glass, giving the whole place an ominous green glow. To my sheer delight, nothing was visibly broken during our journey here. Everything seemed to be alright. The drawers on the dresser were wide open, Velcro wasn't holding them shut. Something stronger was needed to secure them. We did have bungee cords in the generator room, and that would secure them for now.

The television had a layer of frost on the front glass, and the heat on full blast. The temperature remained the same for the first 10 minutes, then 20 minutes, and finally, after 30 minutes, it hit me - the heating system didn't work. The lights worked, the mini-fridge worked, the coffee maker worked—I know because I was already on my second cup. I couldn't tell if the television worked; the cathode-ray tube was too cold to even power up. The carousel CD system worked. You could hear Juan Garcia Esquivel (aka Esquivel!) whistling *Mini Skirt*. We only tested three out of the eight *Cubes* in training. This one must have had a faulty heating unit. We had a full day planned, and the heat didn't work. The temperature was 18 degrees Fahrenheit inside.

I looked at Jackson's action figure now glued in the glass display case and said, *"Motherfucker."* The sun was starting to rise, and I decided to go into the lobby.

I left the generator on and the side door wide open in hopes that the heat fairy would come by and fix it while I was in the hotel. Peter Nelson and Johnny Prattler were already in the lobby, both in full uniform with bright yellow winter jackets displaying the logo. I approached Peter and said in a soft voice, "Peter, we have to go to DEFCON 4. The heating system doesn't work."

"How do you know?" he asked.

"It's been on for an hour, and nothing's happening."

"Alright, let's take a look."

We all nodded, understanding that this was our first day, and we had to look good. Peter, Johnny, and I climbed inside, looking at the heating control pad like three bumps on a log. It looked the same as it did when it was turned it on earlier. Peter went outside and checked under the truck, while Johnny stood there, shoulders up to his ears, staring at the floor. Peter re-entered *The Box*.

"I can't see anything under the truck; you think it will warm up in the sun?" he asked.

"I don't know," I replied.

"Does the heater work in the cab?"

"Yes," I responded. "But that's an entirely different system. I'm sorry, where are my manners... Would you gentlemen like some coffee?"

I picked up the steaming coffee pot, gesturing pouring a cup. Johnny moaned, something that I assumed was a no. Peter, using English, declined as well.

"Let me call the office," Peter said.

We all went back to the lobby to find out the plan for the day. I returned to my room, grabbed two blankets from the bed, and placed them in *The Box*. We were moving ahead with the day. I put the coffee maker in the sink, got the bungee cords, and locked the dresser drawers shut. Keeping the generator running, I climbed into the cab with Johnny, and we drove to our first location.

The *Grannies* arrived at the same time we did. Johnny sprang into action. We placed the two fiberglass ladders on both sides of *The Box*, climbed them, and started to roll the tarp back in burrito formation. Rolling the tarp in the cold was challenging. It was like crackling fruit leather.

"Johnny, you've got to fold it the same each time you flip it. Otherwise, it will bunch up and won't even out, Johnny, Damn it!" I cried.

"Fuck, it's cold. I don't have any leverage!" Johnny screamed.

"Use your core, you nimrod!" I cried.

"I'm going to stand on top!" Johnny said with great authority, rigor, and verv.

These step ladders had a yellow warning sticker on the side that said not to do what Johnny was about to do. He stood on the top step. Nothing happened. He looked at me for a moment. Then, slowly and with extreme caution, we rolled the rest of the tarp. The generator had an exhaust pipe behind the driver's cab sticking straight up to the heavens, close to where we were rolling the tarp.

Suddenly, Johnny slipped on his ladder, grabbing the only thing available - the exhaust pipe. Since the generator had been on for hours, Johnny scorched his hand. He lost his footing, the ladder fell from under him, crashing into the frozen ground. Now, he was hanging on the edge of the *Cube*.

"Peter, Johnny wounded his driving hand!" I yelled to Peter.

Peter seized the ladder, opened it, and Johnny got back on. Then he stumbled down. I acted quickly, got down, grabbed both ladders, and placed them in the generator room as Johnny muttered some colorful metaphors. The *Grannies* stood there dumbfounded, as grannies do in these types of circumstances.

Johnny, now wounded, retreated into himself, sat in the cab, licking his wound. We had just dealt with our second problem on our first day on the streets of the city of Chicago, and not a single person had walked by yet.

I was now inside under two blankets, wearing my winter coat, gloves, scarf, and hat. The *Grannies* were all around, smiling and waving as the snow started descending from the dark clouds above. All you had to do was look up and see each flake kiss the plastic roof.

Maybe five or six people walked by that day. I wish I could have done something besides trying not to become a human popsicle, but it was too cold to move. If I just had something like a couple of Wacky WallWalkers to throw on the windows—anything besides watching the snow fall and looking like a schmuck. The television didn't even thaw enough to work that day. The models had a better time than I did, they would take turns handing out the leaflets and chicken soup, then retreat into the minivan to warm up.

This was not what I had imagined at all. Miniature golf Mike was sunbathing in Florida right now and I was freezing in Chicago. We had to fix the hiccups before fully realizing the potential of this glass prism. It was going to be a bitter winter, and I had to chop my own firewood, metaphorically.

By the end of the event, I couldn't make a fist; my hands were so cold. I knew I couldn't endure another day like that. We had to do something and do it quickly. Johnny was still upset while we secured the tarp together. Then we drove back to the hotel through something called *Hubbard's Cave*—an underpass by the Kennedy Expressway with a series of overhead lights. Johnny uttered the longest sentence I'd ever heard him say. When we entered the tunnel, he saw the lights and exclaimed, *"Oh, stars! My stars are growing around the universe! Me like this. Blink, blink, blink, and blink."*

I couldn't tell if he had never seen lights in a tunnel before, if he had taken one too many painkillers for his burned hand, if I was suffering from hypothermia, or if I only imagined it.

When we returned to the hotel, Johnny parked the *Cube* in the back, and without speaking, Peter and I hopped in the minivan for a special trip to Mulligan & Applefield's. We bought a roll of green duct tape and two space heaters. The first one, long square and off-white, was placed on the floor above the vents for better heat distribution. The second, square, darker, and smaller, was placed on the opposite side on top of the kitchen counter.

Upon bringing them back, we entered the *Cube*, fired up the generator, and turned those heaters on. I then patched up the back of the tarp with the green duct tape. It didn't match very well. It just looked like duct tape on a tarp, but it was secure. We stood in silence, waiting to see if the space heaters would work. After 20 minutes, we could feel the heat. It wasn't a lot, but with a sweatshirt and some movement, you could stay somewhat warm. There was no way this thing would be fixed; the office said they would find someone who could fix it. I didn't hold my breath.

After those initial setbacks on day one, we stopped looking stupid. I would prepare *The Box,* turning on the space heaters an hour before leaving in the morning to warm it up. Then, using bungee cords, I secured the long square heater to the two ring pull handles on top of *The Escape Hatch* when we were in transit. The smaller one I would unplug and place in the sink with the coffee maker. When we were on-site, the first thing I did was turn the space heaters back on. Johnny learned to flip the tarp properly, then hide in the cab for the rest of the day.

We were parked on major streets in front of local businesses for the rest of the time we were in Chicago. One morning, in a little convenience store, while picking up the local paper and a pack of aniseed-flavored chewing gum, I came across a refrigerator magnet that said Chicago on it.

I'll get one for every town! I thought. And just for kicks, I'll go through this old rack of postcards next to the window in the front of the store. Find something simple like a *Wish you were here!* or something from long ago like a *Chicago 1998. Make it great!* I turned the rack a few times till it squeezed to a stop and then I saw it. It was right there on that old, rusted metal postcard rack. It was right there. On a cold winter's morning in a small bodega in the city of Chicago, I saw it. The best postcard I've ever seen!

I was starting to make *The Box* practical, livable, and, hopefully, comfortable. I already glued an action figure on the glass shelf, picked up the newspaper every day for the kitchen table. I vacuumed the two rugs and kept the glass sparkling like fine crystal. Always had a swashbuckling adventure or an oddball comedy playing on the idiot box. Though you could hardly hear it. The VCR volume was much softer than the one on the CD player. The generator produced vibrations so loud you could hardly hear anything at a low volume.

YEAR ONE: PRACTICAL, COMFORTABLE, LIVABLE.

We always worked with the same models, so this bred consistency. In the mornings in every new city, when the new flock of models arrived for the first time, they would see me outside before the day started, from time to time. I had to explain to them that I didn't actually live inside. I would get out of the truck or minivan, and I knew I had to talk to them. It was best if they heard it from me. Most of the conversations went like this:

"Wait, what! I thought you lived in there?" cried a future granny.

"No, I don't actually live in there. I spend the day in it and then go to the hotel at night."

Sometimes, models would arrive at different call times. And I would already be inside *The Box*.

"But I saw you in there."

"Yes, I am in there, but I don't actually live in it."

"I was here yesterday, and I saw you inside it... all day!"

"Yes, I was inside," I would reply.

"What are you doing outside of it now?" She would ask.

They were confused, even angry, that I didn't really live inside, but our interactions were far and few.

You can only imagine what Peter would say to the new batch each time we hit a different market. He spent days with them and could whip up any story he wanted. He could say I was a spy working for the government on a secret mission. He could tell them that I was the first human born from an egg, didn't have a bellybutton, or that I was dying from a mysterious illness, and that this was the only way I could see the country before passing on. And scientists created *The Box*, the entire campaign designed to avoid drawing unwanted attention to my condition and ultimately fulfill my final wish. Anything! He apparently told them I slept inside too. Said there was a shower right beyond the cabinet door. And they would absolutely, without a doubt believe him. And why wouldn't they?

They saw me inside that *glass apartment* right in front of them all day; they saw me calm and comfortable as if I was just milling about. It was plausible that someone could live inside this box. And they believed him. Then suddenly I would be on the street right in front of one of them, and they would question everything they ever experienced in their lives up to that moment, and you could see it in their eyes. I was standing in front of her, telling her the truth, and she wasn't having it. I thought she was going to slug me. I started looking for Peter, hoping he could save me from this before I told her that there was also a colorless Pepsi soda.

CHAPTER 8

First Interview

A Hubard on Hubbard Street

Now it was time to level up. We moved into the interview phase. This was our first one. The night before our first television interview, I was on the phone with the public relations representative. We had gone over all this information in St. Louis on how to craft the message they wanted us to convey, and the next day we had to do it for real.

"You have the press kit and know what to say?" The voice said with concern.

"Yes, I have it right here. No worries, we all know what to do." I assured the voice.

"Ok, ok. It is a live interview, just keep to the script. Call me right after!"

"Alright, it'll be a walk in the park. I'll call you right after." And I always called the voice afterwards.

We were scheduled the next afternoon to be downtown on a street called *West Hubbard St.* Not far away, there is another strip of road known as *Randolph Street*. I spent the early part of the day organizing the inside and making sure everything was gleaming. All the *Grannies* were in clean ironed shirts, as well as new gray wigs that had a nice Aqua Net sheen. We were all prepared on the outside, and well prepared on the inside. That afternoon the local news station arrived. They looked at us like we just found a UFO. These interviews worked in phases.

PHASE I - *Peter would be outside walking the site, acting as the guard at the gates. He would be the first smile they saw. Then he would escort the crew to the Cube.*

PHASE II - *I would be prepared for the visit but acted like it was a surprise when they arrived. I'd open the outside door and escort them in, and give them a tour. Then we would agree on the logistics and to shoot the interview.*

This promotion was a mobile happening. And we wanted everyone to know that.

PHASE III - *Kick 'em to da curb.*

If we were approached by a camera crew or reporter that we didn't have scheduled, Peter would do a quick pre-screen check and then let them in. The first year we had a Public Relations Department that planned all media.

The interviewer, the camera man, the sound guy, would all squeeze inside. Someone would mention the loud vibration of the generator. And a decision would be made on whether or not we should keep it on or turn it off. If we turned it off, none of the electronics would work. If we kept it on, it was difficult to hear anything over the hum of the generator.
(Note: I should've soundproofed the generator room myself.)

During day interviews, we would turn off the generator. We had the sunlight. Night interviews, we would keep it on. This first interview was in the evening. We decided to keep the generator on. We were located that evening on *Hubbard Street.*

And five... four... three... two...

We went live on the local Chicago evening news. They introduced me as... *Randolph Hubbard.* And written on the television screen below my person in white font also was the name... *Randolph Hubbard.* While we were doing the interview, I heard the sound guy say, *"Is that his real name?"* And we were off to the races. Four people are now inside, and my stomach was in knots. We made sure I had everything in working order, and all my focus was on listening to the questions of the interviewer. With all of us on top of each other, we had limited movement. The camera guy was trying to capture all the nooks and crannies inside. He then slowly pans to the glass shelving unit in the corner and focused directly on the picture frame, and in that frame was the postcard I had gotten earlier. It was this...

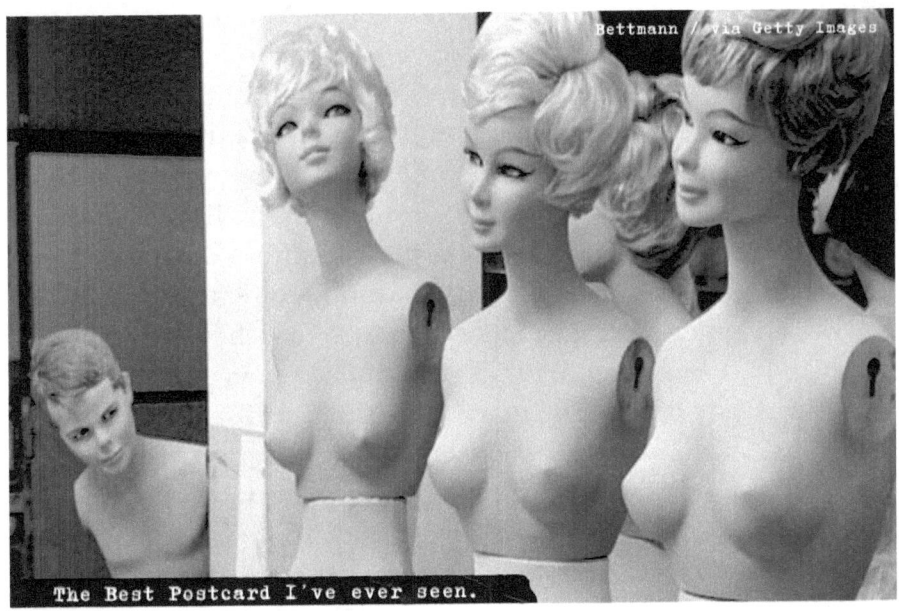

Bettmann / via Getty Images

The Best Postcard I've ever seen.

The sound guy started laughing so hard that he almost dropped his boom microphone. The whole thing was over in a flash. I stuck to the script. I talked about the *Cube*, my experience inside it. Then the product, what it does and where you could get it. And I made fun of myself a little bit. At the end of our segment the interviewer asked, "Are you guys going anywhere else while you're here?"

"Yes, we are going to the *Naval* Pier," I said with confidence.

"You mean the *Navy Pier*," he responded.

This whole exchange was on live television. Once they cut back to the newsroom, the sound guy had to put his boom-mic on the kitchen table because he was laughing so hard, he was gasping for air. I wasn't sure if he was laughing because he was nervous or thought my name was *Randolph Hubbard* or because I mispronounced *Navy Pier* or because they just showed a picture of four naked mannequins on live television. But that was it. They packed up and left.

I was twiddling my thumbs, thinking they were going to celebrate me as a hero or fire me as a fool. I didn't know. It wasn't as if they could see a Chicago broadcast in New York on the same day back then. The technology didn't exist! You had to wait until the office saw the interview. I had to sleep with that uncertainty, in my head for a couple of days. The station had to mail out a copy of the broadcast to office in New York. Ludan did call me when they finally saw the interview, and they were pleased as punch. Relief showered over me. I didn't know if they were going to like it. Didn't know if I had to talk more on the subject. Sometimes you only had 15 or 30 seconds to relay the message. No one had ever seen me under pressure like that before on live television. It was another risk they took when they hired us. But it was paying off. The office gave the thumbs up on my first interview. And I was relieved. We were getting great responses from all the interviews nationwide. This thing was something new and it was exciting to be a part of. And it showed. We were now all in every state. On every street. We were everywhere. The *Cubes* became the ultimate conversation starter, and we could take it from there. We had finished the week in Chicago, and more and more people were becoming curious about the promotion, not just in Chicago but everywhere. We had eight of these *Cubes* - 48 wheels spinning all around the country. And they were starting to roll.

CHAPTER 9

Greenbay, Wisconsin,
and The Loss of Another

We headed out to Green Bay, Wisconsin, late on a Thursday evening, with an event scheduled for that Saturday. We had a single day for ourselves in between.

Friday morning, I grabbed the keys to the minivan, ventured out into the snow-covered landscape, picked up some groceries, and found a quaint little coffee shop. It was something to do. I spent the day in the hotel looking at the snowstorm, killing time, and watching the New Zealand comedy troupe, *The Vestibule Runts* on television.

Slowly Saturday arrived, and it was just wicked cold. I jumped inside, made sure everything was secured for the day, and warmed up my office. We were parked almost directly in front of the lobby, so I waited outside, standing on the mound of snow by the front until my ears started to hurt. Then I went inside and waited in the lobby for Peter and Johnny. Peter popped in shortly after with dark circles under his eyes. We both enjoyed the rich and robust flavor of the motel lobby coffee. It was still pitch-black outside, and the inside had old, dark wood paneling and a blue, weathered formica table that held a coffee pot and two cardboard tubes. One was sugar, and the other was dehydrated creamer. Six paper cups were stacked next to it, and a single spoon lay flat on the table. It was the only spoon and had already been used.

"Johnny must be running late. Let me give him a call," Peter yawned.

He rang him from the lobby phone and left a message at his room. Fifteen minutes passed; we figured he must have slept through his alarm and didn't hear the phone ring. We went to his room and knocked on the door, but there was no response.

"Ok," Peter uttered with concern. We went back to the lobby, thinking Johnny might be there, but the lobby was completely empty.

"Maybe we got the room number wrong," I said. Peter went to the front desk and asked for Johnny's room. The guy on duty asked for Johnny's last name, tapped a few keys on his clunky computer, and said, *"Johnny Prattler? Oh, he already checked out.*" There was a long pause. Peter and I looked at each other. Someone had to break the silence, it might as well be me.

"I'm sorry, I'm having some trouble absorbing that information, could you repeat that?" I asked.

"*Yes, yesterday Johnny Prattler checked out.*" Johnny *left!* We had just received our first paycheck on Thursday, and Johnny skipped out on Friday. It was now Saturday. Peter and I were standing, dumbfounded, in the lobby of a hotel in Wisconsin. Then we realized that Johnny was the only one who had keys to the truck! We couldn't drive it anywhere. We were now just two schmucks in a lobby drinking bad coffee. Peter was immediately on the phone to the office. I turned off the generator and went back to my room.

About an hour later, Peter knocked on my door and said, "We are not doing anything today. The office is sending another set of keys (for the truck)."

"Alright. Let me know if you want to get something to eat later," I said. We both nodded to each other with understanding. That's the second member of our team that went missing in just under a month. Now it's just me and Peter. I closed the door, poured myself another cup of coffee, sat in an old, green armchair, and watched another rerun episode of *The Runts.*

I had time to stop and understand where I was and what I was doing for the first time. I had no responsibilities for that day. I didn't have to work or support anything. Didn't have to fix the drain in my apartment. Didn't have to carry the emotional weight of an individual, an idea, or a failing institution. Didn't have to scrap a few dollars together to have a meal. I was traveling across the United States in a *Glass Box* with a company that had a solid structure behind it. And that day, all I had to do was drink coffee. I grabbed one of the space opera action figures, a small thing I had slowly been collecting in each city, and placed it on top of the television.

We hung out in that room all day, doing nothing. I guess I had Johnny to thank for this because it was one of the best days I've ever had.

One day turned into two, and Peter and I were trying to find ways to pass the time while waiting for the keys. With so much snow on the ground, we felt as if we were trapped at the hotel. Although they didn't have a swimming pool, we stumbled into the hotel's game room. It was a white, windowless room with a pay-by-game pool table in the center, two arcade games in the corner, and a change machine. Two kids were huddled in the corner, taking turns blowing up aliens or something on one of the arcade games. We fished through our pockets trying to find quarters. It was two quarters for a single game of pool. At the same time, the boys in the corner just finished their game. I could tell by the music echoing from the machine.

"I'll have to break a single," I said to Peter, as I tried the change machine.

"It's broken; you've got to go to the front desk to get change," a voice said from the corner of the room.

Each game of pool cost fifty cents, and the front desk was on the other side of the building. I looked at the two kids and said,

"I'll tell you what, you break this for me, you can have half."

Before the sentence hit the period, one of them grabbed the dollar from my hand and ran to the front desk. He came back all smiles. The two kids played a round of space aliens something, and Peter and I played a round of pool. Then a second. Then a third, splitting the dollars equally.

"What are you guys doing here?" Peter asked.

"Our house burned down," one of the boys said.

"What!?" I mumbled.

"Our house burned down. We lost everything. We've been here for two weeks. They're doing an investigation."

They had just lost their home, and we had one in the parking lot.

Just then, a woman who had the weight of the world on her shoulders entered the game room. We assumed it was their mother. She had heavy bags under her eyes and could barely stand up. She said,

"You're not in here bothering these guys, are you?"

"Just playing some pool. They're fine," Peter said.

"Alright, boys, I think you've had enough shoot'em ups tonight," she said.

"Aaaaaaaaah! Just ten more minutes," they both moaned.

She snapped her fingers and commanded with authority, "Let's go!"

Both of them said, "Thanks for the quarters."

Then they all left, and you could hear the echo of the boys telling their mother about all the quarters they got and all the games they played as they walked down the hall.

At that point, I believe we were the only ones still awake in the entire hotel. It was an eerie feeling. We played a couple more games of pool. I provided the dollar. Peter went to the lobby and produced the change. We did get two copies of keys from the office the following day, and the first thing we did was make two extra sets at the local locksmith.

(Note: We should've gotten two sets of keys on day one.)

CHAPTER 10

Milwaukee, Wisconsin,
and Finally getting The Team Together

Now, keys to everything. I ended up driving the minivan as Peter drove the truck. We were now two people on a four-person gig. And as the skeleton crew that we were, next up was Milwaukee, Wisconsin. And there we would have a new truck driver and a new assistant tour manager. Two problems solved.

The makeshift heating system seemed to be holding out well. When the sun hit the *Cube*, it had a greenhouse effect. But when the sun went down, so did the temperature inside. Within minutes, the climate dropped. You couldn't predict the light because every day we were in a different spot. Some days it would be sunny skies till dusk. Other days, depending on where we parked, no direct light. Sunglasses were a must. The glare was so bright you couldn't see the image on the television. I also had to be aware of snow glare.

You needed sunscreen every day. But mostly, I needed to protect my arms and make sure they were covered. The light was uniquely intense. The sun reflected off the glass and off the snow on the ground. I couldn't get away from it. And don't be fooled if it was overcast. It will pierce through the clouds while simultaneously reflecting off them. No matter what, no matter how, the sun will find you.

Being in *The Box* surrounded by snow was the equivalent of being in a tanning machine for eight hours. When the sun went down, I had mixed emotions. I didn't have the glare, but I also lost the heat. And this happened in a matter of seconds. I would always wear long pants and long-sleeve shirts or sweatshirts. After a couple of moments, you could feel the sun and its intense reflection on you. And at the end of the day, it left you. Moving around inside was essential for all of those reasons. It was to dodge the sun.

Inside the *Cube*, the temperature would drop on a dime. And once the sun went down, you needed to be in pants. The most reliable thing was the coffee maker. It never let me down, no matter what the conditions were. It never let me down. But other things, things you would assume were strong, started to fail. When we were securing the tarp to go to Milwaukee,

I noticed some of the buttons under the truck that secured the tarp had started to rust off. *A few were already gone!* The external issue was that the salt from the roads had started to weather the truck. Now salt was the enemy, and I wondered how long it would be before it eats through the floor.

The tarp during long trips on the highway had its own unique problem. Once the truck hit speeds higher than 40 mph, the tarp would balloon out, expanding like a parachute. It looked like a green jellybean. From the passenger side point of view, you wouldn't be able to see anything in the side-view mirrors. The driver couldn't see anything either! In a truck, you only have side-view mirrors to witness anything behind you. There's no rear-view mirror. Everything behind you is a blind spot. There could be an elephant in polka-dot pajamas on roller skates holding a pinwheel singing *Yankees Doodles Dandelions*, and if it was in your blind spot, you couldn't see it. All eight trucks had this problem. The solution was to get two green ratchet straps with safety latch S-hooks and strap the tarp down horizontally in two places. The top of the *Cube* and the bottom. They held the tarp firmly against the glass so the driver could at least see via the side-view mirror. To this day, I still haven't seen an elephant in pajamas.

By the time we reached the hotel, the new assistant tour manager had arrived. She was traveling with her sister on this tour. This was also a common thing I found out about touring. Sometimes a plus-one would be associated with your tour by happenstance. It's a way to have all the benefits of traveling and no responsibility whatsoever.

Enter Antoinette Toggle and her younger sister Lakisha. Assistant tour manager problem solved. We just needed a driver. The four of us met in the lobby and got Antoinette up to speed on everything. Peter drove the truck, and Antoinette and Lakisha drove the minivans. Just before this, both Antoinette and Lakisha had finished a season as background dancers for a small amusement park somewhere out west. The park was a small, mom-and-pop-owned operation. They were also the choreographers for the three shows in the park. Then the day had finally come when the new driver arrived at the hotel.

Ladies and gentlemen, the great, the tall, and often confused Leonard (Len) Jones. Six feet, four inches. This guy could walk through a harp without touching a string. He was the final member, the last piece to that puzzle that you always had sitting on the kitchen table. And then someone finds the missing piece. We found the missing piece. We found a driver. We had a team now. Len was the real deal, a real truck driver. We all met in the lobby, shook hands, and then I gave him the ten-cent tour of *The Box*. After opening the side, we both climbed in. I'm not sure if his superiors explained exactly what this was because his jaw hit the floor when the generator fired up and he was shown what was behind the glass. First thing he did was try to move things around. But everything was secured and bolted down. Then he questioned his own sanity. He lost his understanding of reality somewhere in that parking lot.

"Does the television work?" Leonard asked.

"Yup."

"The coffee maker?! Does it make..."

"Yup."

"And the... you can listen to music!?"

"Yup."

"Does it have a seatbelt!?"

I walked over to the love seat, sat down, clicked the seatbelt across my waist, turned my head around towards Leonard, and said, "Yup."

"Heavens to Ms. April May June," he cried.

Leonard had been looking for work for some time, and then this job came along. Since he was a thousand feet tall, it was easy for him to help flip the tarp. We had five people on this gig now. Peter would take care of all the external activity, Antoinette and Lakisha would do the daily report paperwork and herd the *Grannies*. Lakisha wasn't working officially for us, but she just took the initiative to start. It was something to do. She was a direct contrast to Len who would just sit in the cab all day.

He didn't have anything to do once we were set up. He was the driver. That was his one true responsibility. Really, he was the getaway driver, so he had to be behind the wheel. His only responsibilities were transporting the *Cube* back and forth. He sat in the cab all day and would be bored to death. He would call me via the intercom every now and again and start talking. This was a typical conversation.

"Randolph?"

"Len? Do we have to move?" I asked him every time.

"No."

Then nothing from him for a good two minutes. But I could feel he wanted to talk.

"Randolph?"

"What's up?"

"Do you... do you believe in aliens?"

"Of course, I do Leonard."

"Have you ever seen one, an alien I mean?" he asked.

I would then press the talk button on the intercom and let him hear the hum of the generator and my breathing for a few seconds then release it. You could always hear a small *click* after you released the talk button. Then I would let him deal with that silence. I wouldn't answer him. He would ask me questions like that all the time. They just came out of the blue. Subjects we never talked about. We never had a previous conversation about aliens. I didn't know if he was serious or kidding around. But he said everything with a straight face and serious conviction. He would ask questions about time travel and doppelgängers. He talked with a slight lisp, and it made him sound like he wasn't all there. But he was. We would be at a restaurant, and he would look at the waiter completely stoned-faced and say, *"I'll have the wolf."* And I would look to see if they were serving wolf. I've never seen a menu that has ever served wolf!

He would wait a few minutes and call back.

"Randolph... have you ever seen one?" Leonard asked. Then *'click'*. I've never seen an alien, but he didn't know that.

"Leonard, I'm not allowed to talk about that," I responded.

You could feel his mind racing with a thousand questions. And then he said,

"Ok... ok." Pause, then *click.*

After that, I wouldn't hear anything from him for hours, sometimes not until the next day.

We would grind it out most of that winter, especially the brutally cold days. Some events would last four hours, and others twelve, from sunup till sundown. At the end of each day, you could gauge whether or not everyone wanted to go out or be left alone. If we had the next day off, everyone wanted to go out. If we had to drive to another town in the morning, everyone wanted to stay at the hotel. I'd understand completely when they wanted to just hide away in their pastel, colored rooms. We had two minivans, so it was just a matter of letting everyone know if they would be in the parking lot or in use.

A great pleasure for me was looking forward to the next hotel. Every chain that we went to looked similar. They all looked similar. The color palette and furniture would be the same, but the layout of the rooms would be different. The door would be on the right side in one hotel and the left in the next. Sometimes in the middle of the night when going to the bathroom, I would bump into the furniture because I had just memorized the placement of the room from the last hotel, and I was thinking I was still there, becoming disoriented and completely confused. Sometimes the rooms in each town would be the exact same, but the framed picture on the wall might be different. That would drive you crazy. The bigger hotel rooms were my favorite. It was the only time to be completely alone. And sometimes I thought I was still being watched.

Always asked for the higher floor rooms in the back so you could have a bird's eye view of the *Cube.* The minivans were parked in the front parking area because it was easier to access them. The *Cube* would be parked in the back.

Most evenings, I would cook in the kitchenette at the hotels and go out sometimes to pick up supplies or find something with sugar in it. You could just walk to the strip malls or the large truck fueling stations right off the highways close to the hotel, especially when it was snowing. You would be the first to leave footprints in the snow in parking lots or large flat fields. It would feel like you were on a quest in search of treasure.

The Truck Stop Marts have things like that. Truckers have an entire world of items made just for their profession. These are big things. They are on a larger scale, like enormous cup holders, industrial windshield wiper blades, beaded seat covers, thick rubber cart mats, quick mount car reflectors, replacement rearview mirrors, spill-proof cloth trash cans, snow tire chains, camouflage hunting vests, steering wheel tape, logbooks, road atlases, Texas belt buckles, bumper stickers, giant containers of beef jerky, racks of extra-large t-shirts, Styrofoam coolers, personalized license plate frames, double-barrel stainless steel exhaust pipes, custom-made gear shift knobs, semi-truck replacement batteries, boot brushes, 42-ounce-sized thermoses, multicolored windbreakers, first aid kits, rubber mallets, spanner sets, police-issued flashlights, fire extinguishers, X-shaped lug wrenches, sunglasses, gas cans, zip ties, boxes of road flares, bungee cords, tires, jumper cables twenty feet long, Lot Lizard stickers, air fresheners, shiny Mudflap Girl Decals, and snaplight glow sticks.

Lot Lizards are women who work as *"ladies of a certain understanding"* in truck stops. The (*Lot Lizard*) stickers are a picture of a female lizard, sometimes in a dress, with the red circle slash. These stickers are usually placed on the side windows on trucks indicating No sex workers. The term was popularized in the book *Sarah* by JT LeRoy.

Mudflap Girls a silhouette of a woman sitting on the ground leaning back. Bill Zinda created the design. It's not known who the image is based on. Leta Laroe and/or Rachel Ann Allen are two possibilities. But I can't confirm this. This image is often found on the mudflats of trucks. This is a popular pop culture image.

Road Flares, also known as a fusée, are small torches that are windproof as well as waterproof. Used as emergency signals on roads to alert other drivers of caution. They are tubes 8–12 inches long, burn bright, produce intense heat, and last fifteen to sixty minutes, weighing roughly 16 ounces. If you have ever witnessed a road accident, you've probably seen these.

Snap-light glow sticks, also known as chemlights or Cyalume, were created in 1971 by Michael M. Rauhut, Laszlo J. Bollyky, David Iba Sr., and Edwin A. Chandross. They are plastic tubes with two chemical compounds separated by a glass ampoule inside the plastic. When you bend the plastic, it breaks the glass, allowing the two compounds to marry by shaking the device. The chemicals then produce a glow that lasts a range of five minutes to twelve hours, fading over time. It's waterproof and does not produce heat. They are used for everything from emergency military lighting to rave party favors, and they come in a variety of colors, with green being the most popular.

CHAPTER 11

Making it a Science,
and The Elements

The best part of entering a new town was seeking out the coffee joints and ordering a slice of whatever the local pastry chef made that morning. I would always get a pound of coffee from one of the roasters. Sometimes we would be parked right in front of their establishments, and they would knock on the glass in the morning with a brown bag of their freshest roast. There were specific ways things were given to me while I was in *The Box*. Peter would open the side door and place the item (bag of coffee, the day's lunch, local newspapers, top secret documents, papers from the office, etc.) on the lip of the cabinet door, shut and lock the door. Then call me via the intercom system saying, *"It's in the cabinet."*

Then I'd wait five or so minutes, open the cabinet and retrieve the items. So, it always looked like we had everything in the cabinet. This magic cabinet. If it was coffee from a roaster, it would immediately be brewed and presented directly in front of the glass towards them, to thank them.

If we had a long day, say twelve hours, I would have three meals. And one of those meals, would be an event. I'd have placemats and silverware for each item and read the newspaper.

I pretended I was a single father raising two daughters—on a coal miner's salary—who weren't speaking to me because I wouldn't let them try out for the schools ice-skating team. That's because I was afraid, alright! Afraid that they would run away and join The National Ice Skaters Society of the USA (NISSOTU-SA), leaving me all alone. I raised these girls with morals and didn't want them gallivanting all over the world. I was afraid alright! Afraid of losing them the same way I lost their mother. They were all I had. And the only time we had any peace in this house was when we were eating at the kitchen table as a family, and I had the paper so I could read my stories.

I couldn't keep the water or any liquids in *The Box* overnight because they would be frozen solid by the next day. At one point there was a plastic bottle of dish soap on the counter, and it was all ice crystals by the next morning and stayed that way the entire winter. That year's winter was dark, cold, and very mean.

Jugs of water were stored in the hotel rooms and brought out every morning to brew coffee.

If Peter wanted a cup, I would have his portable mug available and make him a coffee and leave it on the lip of the cabinet door. For meals, we would have hand signals that meant different things. The consensus for all eight of us, on the inside of the glass, was to respectfully ignore people banging on the *Cube* to get our attention. We acted as if we were home alone.

If someone was doing jumping jacks or handstands, a simple wave of acknowledgment would do the trick. You could always see people craving attention in the corner of your eye. Women would flash me and then get upset when there was no reaction. Then I would look out the glass and give a slight nod, usually to someone else. That would always drive-'em crazy! I got flashed a lot. And it wasn't just women who would flash me. Small gestures worked great.

For my communication with Peter, it went like this: when I needed food, Peter would go get something. If he was leaving the site for any reason, he would pace back and forth twice at the back window. If he wanted a hot drink, he would come to the window and stand in a certain way. If he was freezing, he would wrap his arms around himself and shiver. I would then point to the portable heaters in *The Box*. And we never looked at each other.

If we had to move the vehicle, either Peter or Lenny would call via the intercom. Sometimes when the police came by everyone could see the patrol cars. Everyone knew when they were asking if we had our permits in order. If the event was done early, same thing. Talk with the intercom. After locking everything down, we would just glide back to the hotel. We had this down to a science.

One gentle evening, just after dark, it started snowing. Enough that you would notice a large amount accumulating on the ground. Then I remembered the top of *The Box* was plastic. I went outside to the parking lot and checked on the truck—a large amount of snow was accumulating on top. It started falling in larger flakes and then much faster. I headed back into the hotel, knocked on Leonard's hotel room door, and said, "Leonard, I need your help."

"What is it?"

"The snow, Leonard, we have to do something about the snow."

"You're right, Randolph... What do we have to do about it?"

"Get your gear on and meet me in the lobby."

"Ok, lobby, right!"

Leonard met me in the lobby 10 minutes later, and I was holding the snow shovel. "Leonard, we have to get the snow off the top of the *Cube*; otherwise, it will..."

"...cave in on itself. Right," Leonard remarked.

We exited the hotel into the parking lot, with the snow almost blinding we opened the side door to the generator room and took out the two orange fiberglass ladders. We climbed them and started to remove the mound of snow from the roof of the *Cube*. We only had one shovel, and it was difficult getting it from the center, but we managed. The truck was parked close to one of the hotel's mercury vapor lights, giving us a nice yellow gleam to work with. I didn't even think of this. If it snows more than four inches at night, it could cave in the roof. We kicked the excess snow off the ladders and neatly tucked them back into the *Cube*. The storm was starting to settle at that point. Now snow would be an element we needed to remember.

"Thank you, Leonard, we saved the world."

"Yes, we did, Randolph... yes, we did."

For the rest of the night, I kept looking out the window to make sure we would be alright. We were, and this became a discipline that we followed. *The Box* had a top speed of 65 or 70 mph on a good day. And that was if the weather was nice to us. But rain, snow or a combination of both put us in a different position. We started dealing with the weather as if it were a person. Its needs and desires would dictate our travel.

CHAPTER 10

St. Paul, Minnesota,

and The Inside Down-low,

Leaving The Medieval Motel,

Bloomington, Minnesota,

The Mall of America,

Two Chicken Dinners,

Battle Creek, Michigan,

A Box of Ricicles,

The 46 O'dinetin Video Game System,

and Ludan's Phone Call

St. Paul, Minnesota has two seasons: Winter and road repair. We visited during the winter. It was now February, at the St. Paul Winter Carnival, featuring ice sculptures, snow sculptures, and fancy snowmen with carrot noses in top hats striking poses. The area was a city of snow and ice, with small street vendors serving hot chocolate by the ladle, guys on homemade ice chairs playing accordions, and parents pulling their children on thin plastic sleds. It was a small, local event.

We took the liberty of securing (or stealing) some orange street cones and placed them on the ground in front and behind *The Box*, creating enough space for the minivans to pull in and park. This way, we had all three vehicles lined up like cans on a shelf, making it easier to secure parking. The stolen cones worked like a charm.

It was a cold afternoon, and the office decided to pay us a visit. There were about four of us in *The Box*, and I was educating Ludan on the makeshift heating system I concocted when it started to rain. Rain was the new problem—the leaking roof was the result. Just above the smoke detector was where the leak started, allowing just enough water to create a stream that traveled down the inside of the glass, sliding under the grass wallpaper, and then down the large right window to the floor. The best that could be done was simply to place a towel on the floor to absorb the liquid, then wring it out in the sink periodically throughout the day. We had a bunch of people inside that day. Since the office made the rule of only having one person in the *Cube*, they also could break that rule. It was like I invited the neighbors over for a housewarming party, and the roof started to leak. This was the first time I had people over and the roof leaked, you can imagine how embarrassed I was.

That was an easy fix; we just had to wait till it stopped, and a little bit of silicone sealant would do the trick. Replacing the damaged wallpaper was another matter. No one could see that spot, but I could. Once it dried, the wallpaper remained bubbled out. I was getting good at fixing these issues before they became major problems, like a homeowner. This was like repairing an actual apartment. We should've asked for a roll of that wallpaper before we left St. Louis.

The office was in town that week, excited to see the *Cube* in action. When they entered, everyone took a fancy to see the naked mannequin's postcard from the Chicago interview, and sure enough, it was still in its frame.

I spent my time getting the dirt, the tea, the down-low, the 411 on the other tours and what they were up to. Two people were already released from their positions. These were two of the guys inside *The Box*. Ascot (the one who wore it) was the first to go. He cursed out a hotel manager, doing so in their lobby, half-naked. He was irate because they didn't have a jacuzzi. Despite being informed the hotel had a jacuzzi, they only had a heated pool, and this revelation didn't sit well with him. The entire skirmish was captured on the hotel's security tapes, leading to his early release from the tour.

Then, on another occasion, the other guy who got let go took the *Cube* and parked it at a *Gentlemen's Club*, entered, got into an argument that escalated into a physical altercation with one of the entertainers. He even spat his gum at her. *Why would you be chewing bubble gum at that moment?* The situation involved the local police, and he got arrested. His team picked up the *Cube* and drove outta town the next morning, leaving him to fend for himself in jail. They dropped him like a hot potato. Other *Cubes* absorbed their events and details. I heard someone else stepped in as a substitute, like a second string, and took on their events.

On a bitter evening in February, after an event, when we returned to the hotel, just as I was winding down for the night, the hotel phone rang. Antoinette informed me that the office had sent new expense reports and asked if I could drop by her room and have a look-see. They must have brought them during the visit. Despite being in my shorts and t-shirt, reluctantly agreeing, and thinking it would be a quick exchange, I slipped into my jeans, glided into my sweatshirt, and slapped on my sneakers, expecting to see the new forms.

Upon reaching Antoinette's room, I found her and her sister Lakisha standing stone-faced in the doorway with their arms around each other. There were no new expense reports in sight. Then I noticed they were both wearing white face paint makeup. We all had just spent the day together, and I didn't recall any of this makeup. Then I noticed two red dots under their eyes above their cheekbones and a vertical strip of red lipstick on their bottom lip. Then it hit me. They were both made up to look like *Queen Padmé (Naberrie) Amidala* from *Star Wars: The Phantom Menace.*

"Happy Birthday Randolph!" they laughed.

———————————————

After the phone call with the New York police, my sleep was nonexistent that night. We rolled out of that airbrushed, 1970's style Medieval motel just before dawn on our way to Kansas City. I had a new type of adrenaline pumping through my body every time I went into *The Box* after that phone call with the fuzz. Realizing now every time I was in there, everyone could see me! Local cops, firemen, switchboard operators, single parents, elected officials, all had walked up to me on occasion wanting a picture. And without any reservation, I would always pose for them. Leonard would call me over the intercom and say, *"Randolph, Picture this!"*

That meant breaking the fourth wall for the local village municipality if they wanted a snapshot. And the fuzz could have cuffed and stuffed me at any moment. After the Medieval phone call, I made it a habit to always have Peter drive. When we went to the grocery store, out for supper, or anywhere, I'd bribe him with a bottle of anything he wanted, just for driving me to the site or get him his first beer of the night when we all went out to dinner. I couldn't tell anyone about this. One team already *left* one of their own in jail; I didn't want to be next.

Time to go shopping! The Mall of America (MOA), the seventh largest mall in the world, opened to the public on August 11th, 1992. It's a four-leveled mall, a marriage mixture of shopping, plant life, restaurants, and theme park rides, including roller coasters and merry-go-rounds. Essentially, it's a bio-dome where trees and plant life act as air purifiers. Instead of using pesticides, they employ ladybugs to control insect infections. Thousands of ladybugs can be found flying around the Mall of America.

Being a wanted man, I managed to work around Peter and Antoinette's schedules if I needed to go anywhere. Trying to stay close to the hotels, most of which were located just a few blocks from a supermarket, restaurant, or strip mall. However, sometimes we had to move to different hotels within the same town, affecting my routine, supply, and food needs.

In a new hotel far from any supermarkets or fancy hardware stores, I needed the minivan. It was a Saturday afternoon, and time was flying by when I realized I was out of supplies – no coffee, no water for tomorrow's event, and nothing to eat in the fridge. I called Peter to find out if he would be available to drive. He and the rest of the team had headed out earlier that day and had taken one of the minivans but left one behind. I did have keys but hesitated to drive, fearing I would get pulled over, *arrested, and expedited* back to New York. I gave Peter a call, but he, Len, Lakisha, and Antoinette were all at The Mall of America, enjoying the merry-go-round and collecting ladybugs!

I had the keys in my hand and sat inside the minivan for ten minutes before deciding to start the engine. I pulled out of the parking lot, and the roads were calm and clear, for the moment. Making the decision to use the back streets to get around and avoid the highway and any major intersections. I thought I could hide behind the mounds of snow and just slide by, disappear into the night. I made full stops at every stop sign, drove the statutory speed limit, and made it to Mulligan & Applefield's. I parked the minivan at the far end of the lot and walked toward the entrance.

Inside, I went about my business, getting bottled water, a roll of industrial paper towels, a bottle of window cleaner, some odds and ends, and a few other essentials. I paid with cash and walked to the restaurant next door, leaving the minivan parked at the edge of my sanity. I ordered two meals, kept looking out the window at the minivan in the far lot, and suddenly, the sun started setting. I sat down in the waiting area of the restaurant.

"Thank you, sir. Enjoy your supper," the cashier said. I grabbed the food, looked up, and it was night. I walked out of the restaurant and headed toward the minivan. It was spine-tingling cold, and now dark, as a police car approached me. We must have been moving at the same speed because I spent a long time looking at the grille of that car, thinking it was becoming self-aware. I swear I saw it blink. It passed me, circled around the lot, then exited onto the main road. I glided inside the minivan, started the engine, and exited the lot in the opposite direction, thinking I just dodged a bullet. I was about a half a mile away from the hotel when I saw that grille again, this time in my rearview mirror.

I was now in a minivan by myself with two chicken dinners, a warrant out for my arrest, and a policeman was right behind me. It didn't matter what they would pull me over for; I would end up being *arrested* and *expedited* back to New York. I was on the back roads thinking this situation would be avoided. There were no traffic lights or any other cars on the road. It was just the two of us. A stop sign was in the near distance. I knew it was coming up. I had to honor it. If I stopped too long or not long enough, he could pull me over. I had to stop; the sign was right in front of me. The brake was applied slowly. The minivan stopped completely, I turned on the blinker, and started shaking. Barely sitting still, I locked my eyes on the grille of that police car in my rearview mirror as I counted to twenty out loud without moving my lips, and then turned the steering wheel to the left. He came right up behind me and slowed to a complete stop. He waited, and waited, and waited. Then he turned right, and I saw him drive away in the opposite direction. I almost vomited. I knew this thing had to be taken care of before this thing took care of me.

Cereal City was a roadside attraction in the town of Battle Creek. It is home to The Kellogg's Cereal Company. The director of the Battle Creek Sanitarium, Dr. John Harvey Kellogg and his brother Will Keith Kellogg founded The Kellogg Company (as it's known today) in February of 1906. The company made pop culture cereals such as OJ's, Banana Frosted Flakes, Cinnamon Mini Buns and Kream Krunch. The museum had a beautiful red and blue sign with the words Cereal City written in blue cursive and Kellogg's in red. I grabbed one from the gift shop and popped it on the mini-fridge. The Breeze Bite Seven showed off all the magnets collected on this tour nicely. It was a perfect view for people to see where we had been. It was eye level from the street. We were at the museum and all I wished for was a box of Ricicles. But I knew I had to go to Ireland to get one.

It's a strange experience being in the box. You are fully aware of what you're doing, and you know people are staring at you all day. But every once in a while, you let go. You forget where you are and try to do something simple like move a chair, and remember it's secured to the legs of the table. And then you snap back, remembering what is going on.

Some days it would be calm and still. Then suddenly you hear *Ker-Splat!* and you notice a fully grown adult human being had just thrown themselves against the glass. As the entire *Cube* waddles back and forth. And you look at them. And they look at you and you can read their lips. And they all said the same thing... *"Made you look!"* Of course, I looked. People look out their windows when they hear a car honk its horn. A human being just hit the window at full force and shook my surroundings, what did they think I was going to do? If I was at home and a fully matured being threw itself against the window I would do more than just look. Being in that thing, you were treated as something different.

Later that week, during a lull, out of the corner of my eye I saw someone on the street holding a box and jumping up and down trying to get my attention. This individual was persistent. A manchild had thrown themselves against the *Cube* a couple of days prior, so I was not interested in giving anyone attention. I was just going about my day with the direction to pretend I was alone in my apartment and pay no mind to what was happening outside. Hoping this one would not jump against the glass.

Peter then called me on the intercom. "Randolph! Look outside the window." I looked up and realized it was *Special Skills, Facial Hair* waving a box in the air. I opened up the main entrance.

"Good afternoon, but we are not interested," I said as I closed the door on her.

"I was trying to get your attention and give this to you."

Special Skills handed me a shiny, new, black square box. It had weight, so I knew it was important and expensive – The 46 O'dinetin Video Game System with two new games: *Double Four: Off-road Redeemer: the 2nd Journey* and *eyeVenture: Golden Wheat Fields of Russia.*

"What is this?" I asked.

"We had a meeting with the Heads of O'dinetin, and they saw the *Cubes* and wanted their game systems in them. Everyone gets one. So here you go," *Special Skills* replied.

"This is a real treat!" I cried.

I don't know if this has ever happened to anyone before—someone knocks at your door and just hands you a brand-new gaming system. First time for me! Now, I had a brand-new video game system with two games. I had an entire arcade inside this black box. I attached it to the television and played *Double Four:* (ORR) for the rest of the afternoon. I shouldn't have this inside here; it was too much of a distraction, too much of an internal activity, and too isolating. It was too selfish to play inside the *Cube.*

I knew the commercial advantage of having multiple advertisements within an advertisement, and was fully aware of the need to strip labels and recognizable images off everything used inside the *Cube* – food wrappers, cleaning product labels – I put duct tape on names and logos. I even used mugs without any copyright issues. But now, a video game company wanted to partner with our little advertising adventure. This system stood out; it was neon yellow with a thin black stripe across the center. The controllers were neon orange and blue, and the wires—both those connecting to the controllers and the power cord—were neon pink. Initially, I displayed it proudly, but eventually, I moved it to the hotel room and played my games at the end of the day. It became too distracting visually and commanded too much of my attention. It was too much of an internal activity. *Wait, advertising a brand-new video game system!?*

Ring, ring, goes my cell phone.

"Hello."

"Hello, Randolph," Ludan asked.

"What's up, Ludan," I replied.

"What are you guys doing tonight?"

"I don't have a clue; I haven't seen anyone since we got back to the hotel," I said. Then the mood soured.

"Well, I just wanted to tell you that we are cutting the tour short."

My heart sank into a puddle on the floor. The controller dropped from my hands, and the pixelated vehicle stopped on the television.

"Why, what happened? Are the other clients upset I took the game system out of *The Box*!?" I asked.

"We hit every market ahead of schedule. The client is happy. They want to finish while we are ahead. This thing was gangbusters, it's not a bad thing. But I wanted you to hear it from me first. We are going to all meet back in St. Louis at the end of March."

That was gut wrenching to hear.

"That's too bad, I was just getting the hang of this thing,"

"You should be proud, Randolph."

"Thank you for telling me first," I said.

"No worries, Randolph. I'll talk to you later, bye."

"Bye."

We had to shift gears. March would be the end of this journey. The word got out that day that we would be ending the tour early. That meant everyone on the road had to find their next gig. Earlier than expected. Peter already had something book-ended to this, so he would just glide into his next job a bit early. The others didn't have anywhere to go. Lenny was going to stay in St. Louis for the month of April, as he had family there. He was going to find something else to do there. His last job was an exterminator for a chemical company, and he didn't want to go back to that.

The last week of the tour, I asked Hogarth to send me all the mail that had been piling up in Brooklyn so I could start paying off some of my invoices. Wanting the transition back to Brooklyn to be as smooth as possible. The last thing you want to see when you come home is a pile of reality on your desk.

CHAPTER 18

Omaha, Nebraska,
Fear of An Idea,
and The Perfect Party

We made it to Nebraska! About this time, we ran out of major events and started doing guerrilla events, maybe one reason we cut this thing short. We just didn't get any more permits or scheduled events. We would go out to a location, then move our operation. I would be brewing coffee, get the call, *"Randolph, we gotta move."* I'd gaze at the police officers, lock everything down, and as we drove away, wipe the nervous sweat from my brow, and come back to earth. I wasn't sure if my mind was slowing developing capiophobia; this warrant for my arrest needed to be taken care of, and soon.

Going from zero to sixty in fifteen seconds every time a police officer in uniform walked by. One of my concerns working at Wild Things! was encountering people with coulrophobia. It's a fear of clowns – the outfit or the idea, not necessarily the person wearing it. It's described as an abnormal fear, implying a normal agitation towards clowns or their outfits, in my case, a police officer's outfit. That's what would trigger me – the idea of authority. I didn't know what Officer Jenkins looked like, so, he was the physical manifestation of every cop we encountered. There was a thousand Jenkins in my mind. The fear of getting caught was much greater than any punishment.

Wanting desperately to stay grounded. I had a plan to take care of this once I got back to Brooklyn, in the meantime, I needed to keep both feet on the ground. As long as my mind didn't cross that line into imaginary fear, I was alright, I just needed to know where that line was. Jenkins was just a person doing his job. I was the one adding more to it.

When in clown costume and makeup, I was treated differently, not seen as a sovereign individual, but as a plaything, or a being of great terror. I was an idea.

When driving from clown gig to clown gig, I'd be in street clothes, a t-shirt and jeans, changing into the appropriate costumes before each party. No one batted an eye when I was in plain clothes. I had four or five t-shirts, changing often after each party due to large amount of sweating, releasing half my body weight. So, at times I looked normal. But when I had my face makeup on, I was treated differently.

White cake makeup with a red triangle around my lips and chin, three orange dots at each tip, two soft blue triangles under my eyes, and a small red circle at the point of my nose – a simple design for easy application and low maintenance during the day.

To get around, I drove the company car—an orange Chevrolet K5 Blazer, the second generation of that vehicle with a *Diesel* engine. Fueling this ancient creature required remembering it drank *leaded* gasoline. The Kubota generators in *The Box* also ran on *diesel* fuel. The refilling of the generator was always done by the truck drivers. But when you're a clown, you refuel on your own.

There were a couple of times I had the wrong pump in the gas tank but caught myself in the nick of time. Could you imagine what the gas clerk would think if he saw me in full makeup and costume and realized I got the wrong gasoline?

Since being constantly double booked, there were times where I wasn't able to change in and out of costume. Did I mention the company car didn't have air conditioning? When I was in full makeup, I was definitely in a different category of social acceptance. At red lights, you could feel people in the cars to the left staring at you. I would turn slowly without expression, pause, and slightly nod my head. Every single one of them would nod back, some smiling, others with a look of despair, as if I knew something they wanted desperately to forget.

This was simply the appropriate outfit for the job one was hired to do. The people who booked me knew that a clown was coming. They had contacted the agency, ordered the clown/costume character, and paid the deposit. I didn't just show up at their doorstep unannounced. Everyone always hoped for a smooth and pleasant experience. For me, a perfect party meant all involved would be excited to see me. No fear, no preconceptions about the immediate future. Just a series of events leading to a pleasant ending. Starting with turning into the driveway, having the kids jump out of the house, run up to the car, and mob me with questions like:

"Mr. Clown, do you have balloons?"
"Can we do face painting?"
"Are those your real shoes?"
"I can't eat wheat, sugar, or dairy?"
"Did you know it was my Birthday?"
"My dad's new girlfriend wants me to call her mom."
"Do you want some delicious red punch?"
"Are you from Clownville?"
"Remember me? I was at So and So's Birthday last week!"

Those were the things I heard all the time. I would check in with the client for any last-minute changes and then proceed with the party. I always started with balloons, followed by face painting, magic tricks, and a photo for each guest. We used an instant camera that produced a take-home image placed in a custom folding card with the company's logo on it. Everyone received a plastic derby party hat and a sticker also with the company's name. These were great novelties. And then, I would dance with the grandmother. If we were inside or in shaded areas that would be the icing on the cake. Shaded areas, work in shaded areas, I can't stress that enough.

That was a perfect party, ticking all the boxes. Then there were the *other* parties. The unplanned, just wing it parties. They would go something like this:

Every so often parents wouldn't tell their kids I was coming; it was a surprise. I would ring the bell, and the caretakers would announce, *"Look! (child's name), it's a clown! Surprise!"* The room would then erupt into screams, the kids running, hiding, and crying. It would backfire. The adults knew I was coming; it's not like a clown randomly showed up to their home. Terrified parents would then look to me for help, and I'd say to them, *"Surprise."* I had an hour, so, whether or not the children wanted to be involved, I had a party to do. I'd make balloons in an empty room because the kids ran away in fear, and sometimes they would protest by throwing them on the floor. Trying to paint a face in those conditions was a challenge. Paint doesn't stay on the face when it's crying. Sometimes, I would stand alone in a room for an hour and then leave. Now the parents were upset.

The big mistake they made, and this happened more times than I like to mention, was forcing a crying child to approach me for pictures. My suggestion always was to take the photos at the end so kids could ease into the situation, get a little more comfortable, and then decide for themselves whether or not they wanted a picture.

Parents stared blankly at this notion; they had their plan. They wanted to take photos to have as keepsakes forever. But the last thing you want on your mantle of memories is a series of pictures of your offspring, red-faced and crying, with clowns, Easter Bunnies, Santa Clauses, and grandparents. They wanted this to go as *they* imagined it.

Every one of my clients was a new parent; this was their *first* 8th birthday for their child, and they wanted a clown. They wanted it to be fun and exciting, with no tears. This was my *third* 8th birthday as a clown that day. I knew all possible outcomes. I've seen them firsthand. Between me and them, there was but one expert; they lacked a basis of comparison.

They treated these parties like boardroom meetings. First, we do this, then this, and we wrap it up by doing this. Not for the kids. This was the first time they ever saw a clown in their lives. You didn't tell them one was coming, and suddenly it was in their home!

Some events, kids conquered this fear, and were able to approach me, and we would navigate through the day. Some of the same birthday parties that started in terror would end with the kids saying,

"Do you have to go?"
"We were just starting to have fun."
"Can you come and live with us?"
"I have a dog named Jerry."
"Are you coming back tomorrow?"
"Mr. Clown, I love you."

Then we were all smiles for pictures, and that would be a great party!

Sometimes, there would be a kid so scared you thought they would be scarred for life; they hid during the entire event. This was one of those parties:

I was contracted to do the clown/character combo birthday. The first half-hour was a clown doing balloons, face painting, etc. The second half was the full body character. This party called for a purple and green dinosaur to come out and surprise the kids. The kids knew a clown was coming, but no idea about the dinosaur. Custom bags were made for these large characters. The head is the largest part of the whole bit. The width of the bag depended on the size of the head. They were fitted with a shoulder strap so you could carry them to each location. And you could always identify the bag because it had the company's logo embroidered on them. At some point, a private room would be needed to change into the character. I had done hundreds of these parties, changing in various spaces, from bar restrooms to parents' personal intimate chambers. Half-naked in someone's bedroom, there was always a curious knock at the door.

"Knock, knock."

"Are you alright... do you need help?" someone would ask.

"I'm alright, thanks. Be out in a minute," I would say, standing in my underwear trying to get into a full body costume looking out their bedroom window to make sure the neighbors weren't watching me.

For this party, there was a staircase in the back of the house leading to a bathroom at the top. The mother escorted me, and said the change could take place in there. The bathroom was big enough to switch in and out of costumes, and it had a nice-sized bathtub for the dinosaur. I placed the bagged character in the tub, closed the curtain, exited the bathroom, and shut the door behind me. I checked the stairs, ensuring they were wide enough for me to navigate in the character costume without tripping over myself. With a railing, I could safely guide myself down to the first floor.

You always tried to get a visual map of the places you went to in your head because you were on your own out there.

The kids were in the backyard, and I came out to say hello. Everyone was excited, except one little girl. Upon seeing me, she produced a sound I had never heard from a human being before or since. She darted inside and hid. She ran with the intention of never seeing her family and loved ones again, with the intention of leaving everything she knew behind.

The birthday boy was thrilled to see me, doing cartwheels and singing, *"It's a clown in my town. Mr. Clown, see you around. Mr. Clown... in my town!"*

I had a table all set up for me with a pineapple oilcloth that had a place card written in colored wax pencils saying, *Mr. Clown*. The birthday boy came up and shouted, *"This is your private table, Mr. Clown. My uncle Eugene tried to sit here earlier, and I said... No! You drink your beers somewhere else! This table is for Mr. Clown."*

After gracefully thanking him, I placed my face paints down, took out my balloons, and was ready. Attached to my hip was my trusty bug sprayer. We sprang into full-on party mode, doing balloons and face painting. You could see the girl poking her head out every once in a while, and then retreat back inside. At one point, her father picked her up and started walking toward me. She fought to get out of his arms, screaming. I made it a point not to look at her or do anything that might set her off – no sudden movements. All the other kids were having a blast, and I didn't have much time before I had to change.

The best standard balloons done for large groups, like this one, were swords for the boys and pink or red hearts for the girls. Swords were a snap. Hearts, you could take the balloon make a circle, bend the center inward, and it would hold the crease, resembling the outline of a heart. I would then look through the center and do *Sad Eyes*, handing it to the girls. That was my most requested balloon. Many times, the girls would bring back their mothers and say, *"Do the heart, with the sad eyes for my mom. Sad Eyes for my mom!"*

These were the easiest balloons to do. *Squeak, squeak, twist, twist, pull.* Instant balloon sword. *Squeak, twist, pull.* Instant balloon heart. The kids were loving it, and everything was going well.

I could do no wrong. Parents were laughing with the youngsters, Eugene was drinking his beers and telling me all about his pyramid scheme.

We were throwing high fives around like they were going out of style. *"You want one?"* Eugene said. *"You want one!"* one of the youngsters said. *"How about you? You want one!"* said the birthday boy to me. *"High fives for everyone."*

We were under a large oak tree that provided perfect shade. The afternoon sun was warm but not blazing hot. Then, we moved on to face painting. Everyone lined up patiently and politely in front of the table. We did small and simple designs on the cheeks like hearts, diamonds, pirate scars, and shooting stars. We took a couple of brilliant group pictures with everyone showing off their balloons, tall people in the back and shorter people in front. It was great. It was a flawless party.

Then, "Guys, I gotta go. Thanks for inviting me to your party. I had a blast!" I cried.

"Yay!"

"Awesomeness!"

"Great!"

"Thank you, Mr. Clown!"

"Mr. Clown in my town! He's in my town."

"See you around, Mr. Clown!"

Everyone thought that was the end of the party. But unbeknownst to them, the second half was to be inside. I said goodbye, gathered my things, and walked towards the house. The kids were to stay outside until I changed into the dinosaur, and then they were to come inside for the second part of the event. It was going to be simple. I was just going to slip into the full-body costume and act excited as they took pictures. I had done this a hundred times. So simple, so easy.

They were all over the backyard playing pirates and fairies with their balloon swords and hearts, with their painted-on scars and shooting stars. I went inside the house, and it was quiet and empty. Passing through the dining room and looking at the table, you could see all the beautifully wrapped gifts of all shapes and sizes, in stripes, polka dots, and solid colors. They had big bows and thin ribbons. Not to mention a series of bright and colorful goodie bags that the guests will be taking home with pride and joy. All were neatly packed with tissue paper, holding back the explosive array of small candy and plastic novelty items. These would be keepsakes for a lifetime. I hoped I didn't have to hand them out. The invoice didn't mention anything about having to do tasks in the full-body character suit. I wouldn't be able to hold any of these, especially not the thin string handles.

You had limited flexibility with your hands, and you couldn't see anything in those costumes. You couldn't hold onto anything. Sometimes parents would just give me a newborn, wanting a picture with a dinosaur and their three-month-old baby. You could not see a thing in those costumes. You would never know what they were handing you. Everyone knows you're in a suit, everyone knows you're a character, but everyone thinks you can do normal things. If you make a circle with your thumb and forefinger with both hands and looked through them towards your feet, that was as much as you could see out of that costume. You couldn't see anything, much less see where you were going. Then a person suddenly hands you something, and I would be like, "*Is this a child? Is this a child!?*"

All the excitement was happening outside in the backyard, and I took a moment to breathe. Those kids take a lot out of you. But no time for rest, another half-hour to go. I slowly started walking up the main to the bathroom at the top of the landing. It felt like climbing a mountain. Every step seemed like I was further and further away from that bathroom door. I finally got to the landing. At the top of those stairs, I let out a deep moan from the bottom of my gut. "*Ohhhhh!*"

The hallway to the right and the hallway to the left were empty and quiet. The whole house was quiet at that moment. I noticed the door to the bathroom was slightly ajar. I remembered quite clearly closing it earlier, but the lights were off. I knocked and asked if anyone was in. Silence, no response. Everyone was outside in the back, in sugar shock from all the cake and ice cream they were eating. I opened the door, switched on the light, and sitting on the toilet was the little girl.

CHAPTER

Heading Back to St. Louis,
and The Capper

We headed back to the CJH hotel in St. Louis and pulled *The Box* into the back parking lot right next to the other one that arrived the day before.

"We must be the second ones in," I said.

"That's right, Randolph, we get silver," Leonard responded.

We had a couple of days to kill before our final meetings were slated, and six more *Cubes* were on their way. We spent the majority of the day cleaning out all our belongings. Leonard and I unrolled the tarp and polished the exterior of *The Box*. Peter and Antoinette took the minivans to a local car wash. I did a final vacuuming and window cleanse inside. Looking at the space heaters, realizing we never did get that system to work. I locked everything down.

The day was growing short when Leonard asked if we should roll up the tarp. We agreed to wait until it's dry before we do that.

"Leonard, let's secure it tomorrow after it dries. In the meantime, we can break bread tonight."

"Sounds good, Randolph. Let's break that bread. Let's do that."

Leonard high-fived me and disappeared into the hotel. My hand outside my will turned the generator off for the last time, and the whole truck imploded into a deafening silence. The sun was setting as *Samuel L. Jackson* was taken off his glass shelf and gently laid in my bag, leaving *The Box* the same way I found it. I walked away from that glass object as it sat next to the other. We knew in a few days all eight would reunite in the parking lot of The CJH. And we knew they would have a thousand stories to tell each other. My time with them was done.

I went into my room, kicked off my shoes, hooked up my video game console to the television, poured myself a cup of coffee, sat in the glider chair and played road derby games for the rest of the night. And it was a sad event.

Photo by Randolph Hubard

Charles J. Hamshackle, parking lot.

I walked into the conference room early, and the entire promotional team was there, including, but not limited to, the Heads of the Marketing Division, the Regional Office Managers, the Assistant Regional Office Managers, the Drug Liaisons, the Truck Drivers, the Vehicle Designers, the Tour Managers, the Assistant Tour Managers, the Publicity Managers, the Financial Officers, and the Actors. It was buzzing with excitement, flabbergasted from the results of this thing, exceeding all expectations. It gelled to be a high-tech, extraordinary, madly inventive everyman campaign, with models dressed up like grandmothers – something for everyone.

All the office managers and heads of marketing saw every *Cube* on the road firsthand. We spent the next few days going over key points of the things that worked and discussed the elements that didn't. However, our *Box* was the only one that had the temperature issue. Miniature golf Mike in the Southeastern Region had no problem with the air conditioning or showing us his golden tan.

That night, I ended up at a table by the bar with the remaining actors. We all went back and forth discussing our *Plan B* means of employment for the month of April, but most everyone just wanted to get back to New York. As we were wrapping up the night, my head already back in Brooklyn, I bumped into a strawberry-blonde, summer-blue-eyed young woman named Patricia.

"Randolph, good job."

"You weren't too bad yourself," I replied.

"Thanks. Listen, I don't know if you would be interested in doing other promotions with us, nothing quite like this... but would you be interested?" she asked.

I turned to her, looked her in the eye, and said, "Absolutely."

CHAPTER

Year Two,
and The Climate Control System

I walked into The Charles J. Hamschackle Inn (CJH) and checked in at the front desk under the name Randolph Hubard.

"Good to see you again, Mr. Hubard," the woman behind the desk smiled.

"Thank you. It's good to see you, Alice," I replied.

I got my room card, passed the large checkerboard by the breakfast nook, and the *Guest of the Week* marquee on the wall. The elevator let me off at the second floor, and then entered a room not too far away. I was grateful they still had one for me. It was very late that night. I unpacked my button-down shirt, dress pants, and blazer, then sat down at the desk. I needed something to eat and something to wet my whistle. I opened the menu next to the phone and called the restaurant attached to the hotel. I ordered a T-bone steak with asparagus and fingerling potatoes, and a pitcher of beer. The bartender asked, *"What kind?"*

I cried, "Whatever you gots dats cold."

It was almost 10:30 pm, and we had missed the entire day. It was January 1st, and earlier that morning, I was at LaGuardia Airport (LGA) with Anthony, Miniature golf Mike, and Beatrix, waiting for our 9:00 am flight.

Just before Thanksgiving we found out we were going to do a second year. It was a surprise to be sure, but I was on board for a second year. It was *Year Two,* and the company decided to downsize, having four *Cubes* on the road rather than the original eight from *Year One.* We were doing this again. We all met the week before Christmas. This is how it went, and these were the players in the *Glass Box:*

-Anthony Emilia McAuliffe III / Returning player

-Michael Jason Dugan (Mini Golf Mike) / Returning player

-Beatrix Bianka Sykes / New player

-William Randolph Hubard Jr. / Returning player

We were the four. The New York office also flew out Cindy Collins, the new strategic planner for *Year Two*, and Helen Muse, one of the regional leaders working directly with Cindy. Beatrix was the new kid on the block. We all met the week before Christmas to go over that year's game plan. The *Cubes* were in storage for the summer and were revamped for the winter. The loveseat was reupholstered from white to gray. The logos were cleaned up. The fonts and colors were the same, but an entirely new tarp was made with stronger button snaps. This new tarp was the same in style, color, and design but thicker. It felt like two tarps ironed together and that meant it was much heavier. The idea was it wouldn't catch as much wind and billow out on the road if the material was heavier. I also made sure we had the C-straps in the unit from last year, just in case.

YEAR TWO: FASTER, STRONGER, BETTER.

Miniature golf Mike and Anthony claimed their *Cubes* from *Year One*. Only five were up to the challenge of hitting the road in Year Two. I didn't spend much time with Mike in *Year One*, but since we were a smaller group, I got a good listen to his stories.

Mike was a stocky, balding guy, with a scar that ran just under his right cheek. He said he got it when he was a kid, boxing a kangaroo. He had the gift of gab. He was a professional sportsman. I couldn't believe how many encounters he had with women just playing the game of miniature golf. There were two Mikes. One was the businessman, professional Mike. During the day he was on top of everything, eager and had a short funny story for everyone. And then there was Mike after dark (MAD). Once you were in a dimly lit room, he would tell you everything. Everything about the intense competitive game of miniature golf, and everything that went along with it. He was like a lawnmower. Once you pulled the cord, he cut loose and would talk your ear off for hours.

The Boxes were waiting in a warehouse just outside of town. Once we opened the door to those *Cubes*, it was like a tomb. The air was stale but not a speck of dust anywhere.

I jumped into the first of the five others available, and it was a train wreck. The reading lamp was broken and hanging off the side of the dresser, holding on only by the electric cord from inside it. The glass door to the display case was missing. The portable telephone was nowhere to be found. You could see the adhesive that was still on the dresser where it was once secured, but it wasn't in any of the drawers, cabinets, or under the sink. One can only assume it was taken for their real apartment. And the globe was gone—gone! *How do you pack a globe in your carry-on bag?* I can only imagine that the glass door must have shattered and collapsed on the globe, destroying it during last year's travel.

I didn't know how this glass would handle a second season of cold weather, or hot and cold climates before it expired. Or exploded. Every time we were in temperatures below freezing, I was always concerned the glass would pop. Not the windows. They were treated glass walls thick enough to handle extremes. But the thinner pieces, like the glass on the glass cabinet, or the tables, the lamps, the light bulbs, and the kitchen cabinets. That's why I always turned up the heat on the inside before we drove anywhere. I didn't want to be on-site and go inside only to find the floor covered in a sea of broken shards. And when we drove the highways in the loveseat, I didn't want anything to suddenly explode. I was always in a state of great concern when we hit a bump in the road. A bump in the right place at the right time could affect the glass coffee table, and that would be the end of it. It would start raining glass. But the glass in the coffee pot went from freezing to hot in a matter of seconds, and it never even squeaked. I judged the safety of the glass in that entire *Cube* on the strength of the coffee maker. The glass door to the shelving unit in this one must have been under the right conditions and just blew up.

Then the second one. This one appeared better. The original fixtures were still cherished and intact. The generator turned on with ease and sang rather nicely. It was smooth and rang identical to the one from last year. These *Cubes* were made in the same factory, by the same people, but there were slight differences. This one, the floor lamp might be a quarter of an inch closer to the left. The couch may be a fraction closer to *The Escape Hatch*. The television might be tilted 3 degrees higher. These were small differences, but you noticed them.

During the walkthrough, nothing seemed broken or bruised. Inside, I turned on the heating/air conditioning unit. First the heat. And it worked. The heating worked. Then I flipped it to the cool air, held my breath, and it became cool in a matter of seconds. It worked. Both the heat and the cooling air worked. I started jumping up and down. I walked up to the glass and started banging on it, looking at the others, and I cried, *"Both! Both! Do you understand what this means!? Booooth!"* The entire group had no idea what was happening. I must have looked like a madman in a glass prison. Excitement just ran over me that the system worked. *The entire system!* Both worked, and that was important. This time round we would be in warm and cold climates. I then focused on *The Escape Hatch*. It opened with a little force, but I chalked it up to being dormant for the past nine months. All the glass in this one was intact, and it was maintaining the desired temperature. The rugs were clean, and nothing was chipped, cracked or duct taped together. This was the one.

"Alright, I'll take this one. I would like it gift-wrapped," I said while exiting the *Cube*.

Beatrix had no idea why I suddenly turned into a detective and was examining every detail on them.

She asked, "What were you doing?"

"I'll tell you later."

Beatrix then jumped into each of the other four and started feeling them out for herself. With little effort and no prior knowledge of these things, she soon realized I was testing out the climate control system in each one.

Beatrix was an odd duck; she had told me earlier that week that she was only going to do the tour for a month and then quit.

She wanted to get out of New York for January and had another gig lined up for February. She was starting rehearsals for a show she wrote about a chicken farmer that finds jadeite on her land, and how the family deals with sudden riches the second week of February. I don't know why she told me that. I just met her two days before, and I was now in the showroom witnessing her pick out one of the *Cubes*. She was going to drop it like a hot potato in February to do her new chicken play. This was all on the down low. On the hush-hush. I had to keep that information under my hat. But now we were just excited that we got *Cubes* that had a fully functional heating/air conditioning.

Beatrix popped out of one, skipped up next to me, and said, "These looks good." I looked at the guys from Craftsmen and said, "We'll take these two." They replied, *"Great, we'll get these (four) ready."* Beatrix looked at everyone and then smiled at me. I smiled back because I think we were the only ones in that warehouse that knew she was going to throw dust in everyone's eyes come February.

We felt confident that the problems from last year had been solved. I also asked for multiple sets of keys to be made for each person to have with them. Someone said, *"You don't need all that."* I said calmly back, "I think it'd be a good idea, just in case."

We were finishing up in the showroom dealing with the *Cubes* when a small group of us decided to go out for dinner. It wasn't the entire company, maybe a dozen or so of us. We covered all the bases, crossed the t's, and dotted the i's for *Year Two* when it came to concerns about *The Boxes*. Since we secured our traveling glass apartments, we were just going to have a nice evening. As we were looking at the menu, I asked Beatrix what she wanted.

"What do you think looks good?" I asked.

"I don't know, I'm a vegetarian. So, something, I don't know," she said.

We all felt comfortable with each other by this time, and the wine was flowing freely that evening.

When it was time to order, I said to the waiter, "Tonight, I'm going to order for the lady." I looked directly at Beatrix, smiled, and said to the waiter, "She'll have the chicken."

Beatrix slowly laid her menu on the table, and through her long straight blonde hair, daggers shot out of her deep blue eyes.

For the rest of the time, we went over the same information from last year. Rinse and repeat. Meetings in large conference rooms and going over the specifics for that year. It was a shorter, condensed block of time. One of the changes in *Year Two* was we were our own public relations representatives. The campaign was consolidating positions. Now the regional team leaders set up the interviews, and we followed up on contacting the media to secure times and dates for interviews. We knew what we were doing at this point. We became our own PR reps. The tour managers set up locations and lodging and the daily operations. The truck driver drove. And now we were the spokesman and responsible for own own media. I was going to the Southwest and some parts of the Northwest.

And we had four *Cubes* on the road instead of eight. The regional team leaders would set last-minute changes if we were scheduled to be at a different event or if we were stuck in another town due to weather or some other unforeseen circumstance. We would be driving longer distances across multiple states, sometimes from event to event. This meant more time behind the wheel. The script was tweaked here and there. Instead of saying, *Ask your doctor... about Tamiflu.* We were now instructed to say, *Ask your Health Care Provider... about Tamiflu.* But everything else was the same.

Everything else was the same. The inside players were unchanged except for one minor detail. We all knew each other from *Year One.* Beatrix was a fast learner. Sharp as a tack, a bright bulb in a crystal chandelier. She caught on quickly, showing the wide eyes of excitement when she first saw the *Cubes* and posed the same questions, as we all had at first. This was going to be a challenge for her.

Now, we spoke directly to the guys who built these glass

machines themselves, at Craftsmen. We addressed the problems mentioned earlier, and with their fancy tools they fixed them. They were on top of their game, solving all of last year's problems. But finding a mechanic on the road to deal with any issue that came up was something else. You needed an auto repair guy, a HVACR technician, a carpenter, an electrician, and an interior designer to fix a problem. And try to get all of them in the same room at the same time after 5 o'clock on a Sunday.

As the week played out, we had our detailed route and logistics. We flew home, spent the holidays in New York, and returned at the beginning of the new year.

This was the first day of the new year and the first official day of *Year Two*.

It was late evening, and I was back in St. Louis at the beautiful Charles J. Hamschackle Inn (CJH), sitting in the glider chair when the phone rang.

Ring, ring, goes the telephone.

"Hello."

"*Randolph!?*" a voice said on the other end.

"This is he."

"*Man O' man. I'm so glad you made it. We were worried. But did you get something to eat?*"

"Yes, I'm dining right now."

"*Alright, good, you didn't miss anything. It's the same stuff from last time. We are going to meet with Craftsmen tomorrow, take a look at the vehicles one more time. What happened?*" The voice asked.

"Well, we were at the airport, and everything was dandy. Then they said the flight was delayed, and an hour later, it was delayed again. We could see the plane at the gate, but they wouldn't tell us why we were delayed; they just kept saying delayed. Another hour went by, and they said it was canceled. The airport didn't have any other flights going to St. Louis (STL). So, after searching for two hours, we found a flight leaving from

Newark (EWR). But not until the evening. We had to get our luggage off the plane, claim it, go to Jersey and wait for the evening flight to get here."

"Why did they cancel the flight?"

"Ready for this, the pilot never showed up. We figured he was still hung over from the night before," I said.

"Right... New Years!"

"Right, I've never heard of that before," I said.

"Alright, good enough. Glad you made it. Get some rest, I'll see you in the morning."

"Thanks, Goodnight."

"Goodnight."

We spent the last fourteen hours trying to get to St. Louis, and I sat down for my first meal of the day. I had a steak dinner with a tiny salt and pepper shaker set that looked like something from a dollhouse, and a plastic pitcher of beer that resembled something from a softball game celebration dinner.

The next day we had to play catch up with last-minute changes and new events scheduled. We had an entirely new road team. The players this time were:

- REGIONAL TEAM LEADER / HELEN MUSE
- TOUR MANAGER / DONOVAN HINDS
- ASSISTANT TOUR MANAGER / JERRY FITZPATRICK
- TRUCK DRIVER / KENNETH RABBIT
- MAN IN THE CUBE / SPOKESMAN / RANDOLPH HUBARD

Helen was from the New York office, and we met during our musical chair airplane event the day before. And our new driver. Enter Kenneth Rabbit, a truck driver by trade, a roly-poly guy with bushy hair, dark thick glasses, and I counted four teeth, but there could have been six. He wore the same brown safari hat and a hunting vest with fishhooks on the pockets, and green Kiki cargo pants. When we first met, he gave me his card:

Kenneth Rabbit
Professional Truck Driver

When you need things there fast,

Call the Rabbit.

480-555-7891
mikerabbit@loa.cmo

The tour managers, Donovan and Jerry, were partners in all things, pursuing mobile tours as a career. Donovan, the brains of the duo, had olive skin, bushy eyebrows, and was bald as an eagle. Jerry, a fair-skinned red-head with a row of freckles under each eye, complemented him. As professional Mobile Marketing Tour Managers, they transformed touring into a practical, livable, pleasant science. The trick was that if you were a couple on the road together, you only need one room, therefore pocketing the other per diem. We received a salary and a per diem. When negotiating contracts for mobile tours, your advantage was asking for a higher per diem rather than a higher salary.

Per-diem is something you keep if you don't spend it. You receive a salary for your specific position (tour manager, driver, brand mascot, etc.) and a per-diem. For instance, if your per-diem was $30 a day for food and $75 for lodging, and you were a couple, you would stay in the same room, then pocket the other $75. Both parties would make a profit of $37.50 each a day on top of their salary. I encountered many married couples on different promotions over the years who practiced the same principle.

Donovan and Jerry just bought a home from the tour profits off of per-diem alone. They had already mapped out our first lodging at a stylish bed-n-breakfast. This was the first of many.

We had four *Cubes* on the road this year, meaning we were here to cover more ground. Our first event was in Houston, Texas, but first, the tigers.

CHAPTER 16

Grosse Tete, Louisiana, and The Tiger

If you hop on Interstate (I-55) southbound and take a right on I-12 towards Baton Rouge, then hit I-10 West, you would find a place where you could get a soft drink, a hamburger sandwich, and a picture with a tiger. It was truck stop that had live tigers, and you could personally meet and get a snapshot with a Siberian-Bengal tiger named Tony. He was just six months old when I met him, and for $20, you could get your picture with him.

Kenneth and I discussed stopping at The Tiger Truck Stop in Grosse Tete, Louisiana on our way to Texas. It was a country store and the local tiger hangout. From the highway, a big purple pill-shaped sign announced *Tiger*. The restaurant was on the property, and out front a series of long cages with adult tigers inside passing back and forth. But in the store, walking around on its own, was a tiger cub. He was just six months old when we met. The twenty dollars was the asking price for that picture. It was to help with the expenses of raising Tony.

I payed the twenty, then the owner of the establishment, walked over to Tony, kneeled down, scratched his neck, and attached a leash to his collar and took all of us to a location I only assumed was the official photo studio. It was a small area set up for tourists. I was there, Kenneth was there, and the owner of the Truck Stop was there. And a tiger was there. Once the guy released him from his leash, Tony made a beeline straight towards me. He didn't run towards Kenneth. He didn't run out the door. He ran towards me. He was about the size of a golden retriever, no bigger. But he was a tiger.

Understand, I knew what I was doing. I paid money for this experience. I saw it walking around. It said *Tiger Truck Stop* on a plywood sign outside. I knew it was a tiger. But when I was standing in that country store and I saw him running towards me, I felt the angel of death calling my name. He jumped onto my chest, and both of his paws covered my entire torso. They were humongous. Each paw was the size of two human hands fully spread out. The owner said, *"Don't worry; he's just excited to see you."*

I was taken aback at how gentle and loving he was. He could have knocked me over, easy. This is a creature that was fully aware of his power and his abilities, but graceful and lighthearted in his execution. He was excited to see me. I was cautious and slow with him. I was scared at first, but I didn't want him to know that. I didn't want to frighten him or give him a reason to adjust his approach. He was declawed but he did have a full set of teeth, and we had just met.

"What do I do?" I asked.

"Grab his collar," the owner stated.

I was not about to do that. I stood frozen until he came over. I still didn't move until he handed the collar to me. I kneeled down and tenderly stroked the cub's back. He turned his head around and brushed his face against mine. *I guess we are friends now,* I thought. I looked towards Kenneth, who was having a field day with this, and the owner said, *"Goods, that's good."*

Then he took an instant picture of me and Tony, the living tiger. I then stroked the back of his head again and kindly released his collar. Tony turned around, jumped on my chest again, rubbed his face against mine, then skipped back into the aisles of the store and disappeared into the canned peas. My heart was pounding with a mixture of excitement, recognized danger, and compassion. This was the first time I met a tiger. I wanted to say goodbye to him. *But how do you do that?* I decided not to speak. He just took his umpteenth picture for the week with another random person he'll never see again and went about his day. That experience was something else. I got our picture and bought two t-shirts with their logos and colors on them. Pretty ugly stuff. Then I headed out.

Tony had come to live there just a couple of days before we met. He was one of the most photographed tigers ever to grace the earth. He passed away on Monday, October 16, 2017. Though brief, I hoped he remembered our time together because I'll never forget.

Photo by J. Whittlesworth

Year Two: Now with More Tiger.

CHAPTER 17

Texas,

Humphrey's House of Peaceful Siesta,

The Opal Room,

and Lost Highways

Houston, Texas is about twelve hours and twenty minutes away from St. Louis, but it took two days to get there. Donovan booked us at a place called Humphrey's House of Peaceful Siesta, just outside of the city. This was a ranch that was converted into a special events destination for weddings, large dinners, hootenannies, and reunions. It also doubled as a day spa and hair salon, with the spa/salon located in a separate building at the back. Two rooms directly above overlooked a heated pool in the courtyard. The walk to the front door featured six Christmas trees fully decorated with red and blue spotlights. The wooden fence had hand tied red bows on every post, half a dozen plastic flamingos with Santa hats in the hedges, and four wooden reindeers wearing Hawaiian shorts with artificial flower leis. Inside, two full-sized synthetic trees greeted guests—one hot pink and the other sapphire blue with shimmering silver tinsel and hand-blown glass ornaments. The entire ranch was finishing up its Christmas season, transitioning into its off-season.

Enter Donovan, the tour manager for *Year Two*, he loved making reservations at such places—independently owned and operated by individuals who invested their hearts and souls. He would say, *"Those rooms are going to be empty for that entire week. I can fill three of them for X, Y, and Z."* And he got rooms for the same price as a small, straight-off-the-highway motel. Todd Swartzman, the owner, greeted us at the door. He took time out of his day and gave us a tour of the entire ranch and asked us to choose which room we wanted.

"You must choose," Todd stated with a grand gesture. Donovan and Jerry had picked out their room prior to arrival and were already unpacked, sitting on the terrace of the Gardenia room (aka the Honeymoon suite). Kenneth got the Peacock room above the kitchen; I chose the Opal room above the hair salon overlooking the heated pool in the back.

The Box fit nicely on the dirt road next to several concrete statues of half-naked pixies in the garden out back, away from the main road. Even though you couldn't see it from my room, you knew it was well-guarded. The parking lot for the salon was adjacent to ours. A small, white gravel path led from the garden to the salon, hand-painted river rocks in gaudy designs of orange, blue, purple, yellow, black, pink, and white were sprinkled throughout. Two large truck tires were turned into flowerpots. These were the unique grounds of our stay.

When you open the door to the Opal room for the first time, you notice a huge difference in style from the usual chair hotels we had been staying in. The main walls were cerulean blue with fuchsia pink highlights, framed with several felt clip-on birds in and around plastic potted plants. Two gold-framed mirrors gave the illusion that the room was twice its size. The chandelier wrapped in white silk above the bed provided a nice overhead ambiance. Kenneth was in the Peacock room, so you can imagine my confusion when I saw the four purple vases filled with peafowl tail feathers in my quarters. The vases matched perfectly with the bed sheets on top of an ancient, queen-sized, mahogany wood-framed bed with six throw pillows of different colors, shapes, and sizes. Some had fringe, and some didn't.

On the console table by the door was an 8"x8" picture frame that looked like it once held sparkling stones embedded in the wood. The picture was an unfocused, black and white shot of a man and a woman in wedding attire from long ago. You could assume the frame was originally made from opals, and the couple once stayed in this room. I hoped they were no longer in the suite. This room was desirable because the terrace was right above the Kelpie statue next to the heated pool below. And you could see the steam rise beyond the roof.

This magical fortress also provided breakfast. It had a decent-sized kitchen, but since it was off-season, it didn't have the full staff of twelve. It had a staff of one.

Todd was up every morning before we were and made breakfast. The indoor banquet area had several modern paintings in glitter frames from local artists on white walls. Large, ceramic, glossy statues like giraffes and lions hid in corners and under consoles. Hanging spider plants and old, fish-eyed hubcap mirrors covered the wooden doorways. Handmade, barefoot gnomes with smiles that insinuated that they knew something you didn't were holding small, wrapped gifts, spices, and peppermint sticks. The glass dining table sat on a faux leopard skin rug. And transparent plastic bins were being filled up with Christmas decorations. The holidays were over. So much stuff was jam-packed into in that room you didn't know which end was up. There could be two or three other people in there, and you wouldn't know it unless someone started moving. Todd was packing up the holiday decorations and playing host at the same time.

When I came to breakfast, the first thing he said to me every morning was, "Would you like coffee?" And he provided a different mug every day. Sometimes it was a thick, heavy, diner-style mug from a gas station; other times it was a fragile teacup with the name of a retirement home across it. In a mismatched symphony, even the silverware looked like it was run over by a locomotive. Breakfast, meticulously plated, graced the table on family-owned, cracked and chipped China, sharing the stage with ancient, plastic, half melted fast-food trays. This was just breakfast, and it defined our stay at a place unlike any other.

It was time to see if Kenneth was up for the physical challenges ahead. We both had the responsibility of unveiling the tarp every day. Kenneth was an older gentleman who walked with a limp on a good day. The tarp was now twice the weight from last year's. This was going to be a problem.

On our first day, it took almost an hour to unroll the new tarp. We were in downtown Houston, and the weather was pleasant; both ladders were set up. Donovan and Jerry stood and watched Kenneth try to fold his section of the tarp. *The first flip, no problem, second flip, okay, third flip, ahhh, fourth flip, one more time... fourth flip.* That was it for Kenneth he tapped out. He had a bad leg and couldn't do any more than that. It was about halfway done.

I approached Donovan and Jerry and asked if they would help. "No!" they said. "That's your responsibility." They just stood there like two bumps on a log. I could feel the frustration seething through me. I got back on the ladder and flipped one side, got down, went up the other ladder and flipped the other side, and did it again and again until it reached the exhaust pipe. There was no way I would be able to flip that over the pipe on my own.

And the people that were there to help didn't want to help. I pulled both ends and tucked them as neatly as possible behind the cab and secured them with the black straps. Then I placed the ladders inside, cranked up the generator, and started the first day. I turned on the heating and it worked. That was what brought me back to sanity. I put on a pot of coffee, raised my arms, and shouted... *"The Box Rides Again!"*

This was a different Cube. The exact same design but a different one altogether. To my amazement, almost everything was in great shape after the drive. The glass table didn't shatter or crack. The loveseat was now a darker color and easier clean. The only thing that was different was *The Escape Hatch.* There are two small ring pull handles that held it shut. It was a Yale Night latch system that's fitted to the surface of the floor. But it didn't click shut.

Here's the thing: when we hit a bump in the road, *The Escape Hatch* would pop up and then suddenly slam shut. To stop *The Escape Hatch* from popping up all the time, I secured the coffee table on top. That provided a good amount of weight, and *The Escape Hatch* would stay shut. I discovered this on the ride back to The Ranch.

When Kenneth called me via the intercom and said, "We're moving out."

I would have to call him back periodically and remind him that time was needed to secure everything before we left the site. I would hear the engine turn over, and then he called me via the intercom and then would start moving. I had everything unlocked and free moving.

The first time he did this, I was standing up and was knocked over by the coffee table. The coffee table is on wheels, and it slammed into the back glass wall. I jumped on the loveseat and the dressers, hit the plastic support pipe with my shoulder, grabbed the chair next to the glass table (it wasn't secured to the table), and crashed to the floor. I got to the sink, pulled myself up, punched the intercom button and screamed... "Stop! Stop this thing right now!"

"I gotta move, Randolph. They said we gotta move," Kenneth stated this as he was still driving.

"Kenneth, STOP!" He pulled over.

"I need five minutes, a full five minutes to lock it down. When you call me and tell me we have to move. Five minutes is needed to lock this down before can move. Do you understand? Not thirty seconds, not three minutes, not four minutes. Five full minutes!"

"Can you call me when you are ready?" Kenneth replied.

"Kenneth... if I call you on the intercom, I have to then go back to the couch and strap myself in. That means I have to walk back to the couch as you are driving!"

"Can you call me when you are ready?!" Kenneth responded.

"No! Call me to let me know (we have to move)... wait five minutes then put it in drive and move out!"

"Are you ready now?" he asked.

"HAS IT BEEN FIVE MINUTES!?"

I realized that our understanding of the definition of five minutes was completely different. From the moment when the engine turned over, I knew Kenneth was about to move the vehicle. I then submitted to his understanding of five minutes.

If, for just a moment, you forgot that you were actually in a moving vehicle. If you truly thought you were just sitting on a small couch in a quiet place. And then, suddenly, the drawers opened by themselves. The coffee table started rolling around. The cabinets flung open—you would fully think the place was haunted.

After that day, I always secured the chairs back to the kitchen table every time I got up. And now, I would have to fear the driver.

When we were driving the *Cube*, I would be secured in the loveseat, and have the remotes to the television and to the CD carousel player in my lap. If it was evening and dark outside, I would put on the VCR and pretend to be insanely interested in the program and slightly wave at the cars honking at us. Otherwise, the CD carousel would be playing the song *Duel of the Fates* at full blast.

Duel of the Fates is a track on the soundtrack of *Star Wars: The Phantom Menace.* The choir is sung in Sanskrit against a ballet of string and woodwind instruments in the keys of E and G minor. It has a slow build to its climax. It is one of my favorite pieces of music, and it played at full capacity every time we zoomed down the highways.

You would only have a couple of minutes to experience that music or any other before hitting a pothole or a bump on the drive. A carousel CD player holds the CDs flat inside a drawer, and when we hit a bump or even a pebble in the road, it would spit them out, the CDs would then fly around like Frisbee's. When that happened, it was time for Plan B: turning on the television, the backup plan.

Everything was always secure when we were moving, but some things had a mind of their own. The glass door on the shelving unit would open, and *The Escape Hatch* on this *Cube* did that too. *The hatch* was loose; it didn't lock. It would jump about ten inches straight up, then crash back down into place. I had already discovered this. I was sitting tightly secured, snug as a bug in a rug on the loveseat, traveling at 55 mph down the highway, listening to *Duel of the Fates* on the CD player, waving and smiling at everyone. Then we hit a pothole, and in slow motion, I watched in horror as the CD carousel player ejected the CD at the same time *The Escape Hatch* popped open. Watching this with no power to stop it, the CD perfectly glided under the hatch as it snapped shut. I sat helplessly and just looked at the CD as it rolled away on the highway.

The solution to *The Escape Hatch* hiccup was to secure the coffee table on top. That way, the weight of the table would hold down *The Escape Hatch* every time we hit a bump. The solution to the CD problem was buy another one.

That was the only problem with this *Cube*. Everything else was great. The wallpaper didn't have water damage like the one from last year. And we were in warmer weather conditions. The *Grannies* didn't have to go to the minivans and warm up every half hour. It was a pleasant temperature most of the time. This also meant there were more people out and about. The nature of warm weather has people actively outside. And because of the warmer weather conditions, there were a lot more interactions.

Since we had four *Cubes* as opposed to eight this time around, the office came and saw us first. One of the regional managers came by our first week and stayed at The Ranch. He flew in the night before, and we all met for breakfast the next morning. Waking up that day, I wasn't feeling my best, and it wasn't a good time for me not to be at my best. I just wanted coffee in a strange and unusual mug, and I was planning on skipping the breakfast. I was trying to focus on everyone at the table and the morning conversation—talk about his flight into Texas the night before, keep it lighthearted and low key, but my gut was fading in and out of nausea. We had a full day planned with the eyes of the office on us, and we realized that. After a few sips of coffee and a glass of water, slowly, I started feeling better as I followed my plan and focused on everyone else at that breakfast.

I was just leveling out and feeling better when Todd placed a large portion of biscuits and gravy in front of me. As soon as I saw that plate, the oxygen ran out of my brain, my stomach flipped over, and I had to excuse myself. I calmly but briskly hustled back to the Opal room, dialed the porcelain phone, then laid on the bed under the chandelier, unable to move. Kenneth knocked on my door about an hour later.

"Randolph, are you alright?"

Trying to compose myself, I walked to the door. Opening it, the morning sunlight hit my being and almost knocked me over.

"I've been better."

"The guys want to know if you want to skip today's event."

"I think that might be best. I think that would be a good idea," I said as I faded in and out.

"We saw you turn as white as that plate," Kenneth laughed.

"I'm sorry, Kenneth, I don't think I can make it today," I mumbled.

Kenneth understood. He went downstairs, spoke on my behalf, and a few minutes later, the guy from the New York office called, asking if I was alright. I said I should be alright tomorrow, and he assured me everything was fine. I slept until the evening, and when I got up, everyone was gone. I was regaining my composure and went downstairs. Todd was sitting on a rocking chair, smoking a cigar in the front, and said everyone went into the city for the evening and would be back later. I walked to the garden, through the series of unusual statues, and noticed they left one of the minivans in the parking area. I was feeling better, better enough to drive. The eyes got their focus back, but the stomach was hollow. Not in any discomfort from the day - it just needed something to eat. I grabbed the minivan keys from my room and drove into Houston for the evening, by myself.

There are three major highways in Houston that I had trouble with:

1. US I-10
2. US I-45
3. US I-610

At the time, the minivan was not equipped with a GPS system, and that technology was not yet available on cell phones. I had the most recent *Rand McNally Road Atlas* of the entire United States in the passenger seat. Because I didn't bother to look at the Road Atlas, I thought there was only one route back, and that way was I-45 North. In reality there are three ways back to The Ranch.

We spent two weeks in Navasota, Texas, the entire time at The Ranch. Kenneth spent most of the time in his room at The Ranch, and Donovan and Jerry had one of the minivans. That left me with one of the minivans all to myself. In the evening and on days off, I would drive into Houston.

GETTING TO HOUSTON WASN'T A PROBLEM.
THIS IS HOW I WOULD GET BACK.

Interstate I-610 is a 38-mile loop around the inner sector of Houston and is divided into four sections: North, South, East, and West. The West Loop South runs into Texas 290, and that can be taken straight to The Ranch. At the time, I was unaware of that. The West Loop North goes to Buffalo Bayou and Highway 290. The North Loop East runs to I-45 and Highway 90. The East Loop North runs I-90 and I-10. The South Loop East runs Highway 225 and Highway 288. The North Loop West runs Highway 290 and I-45. North Loop East runs I-45 and Highway 90. Depending on where you were in Houston, you could pick up I-10 West or take I-610 and get on I-10 West or I-45 North. Or even just I-610 and loop around Houston. You could take Texas 290 West from I-610. If you missed your turnoff, you could double back or drive around the 38-mile circle and come right back to it. Simple right? These are very quick decisions you make as you are driving.

Manhattan is a walking town. It's a grid system. Traveling northbound, the street numbers increase: 14th Street, 15th Street, and so on. East to west, the avenues also increase in numbers: 5th Avenue, 6th Avenue, and so forth. Your destination is often a street number and an avenue number, where the two roads meet—it's called Finding the Cross Streets. In Lower Manhattan, the streets become a little more complex, some parts below SOHO get a little tricky. But it's relatively easy to maneuver around. It's a simple system for individuals to understand as they walk around and even simpler when driving.

In Houston, when I was trying to find The Gulf Freeway (aka I-45 North), it was a nightmare. First, I could not remember that I-45 North was the highway I wanted to take. Major Interstates have odd and even numbers. The odd numbers run north and south, and the even numbers run east and west. I learned that from Kenneth when we left Texas! I wasn't sure if I believed him, he didn't have an understanding of what five minutes meant. But I could take a highway back to The Ranch with an odd or even number, and US I-45 is an odd number running north. Every time I had to make the decision on which highway I wanted to take, I took the wrong one! I would be in the minivan and say to myself, *US I-10, that's the one.* I would take it, and it would be the wrong one, even though US I-10 could get me back to The Ranch. Then I would double back and get on The Inner Loop (aka I-610) and circle around Houston and come right back and take US I-10 again. On the third day in Houston, I was so angry making this mistake I started punching the roof and yelling, *"Aghhhhhh!"*

When we were working, I could never memorize the route because Kenneth could not flip the tarp closed, and Donovan and Jerry would not help. We kept it open the whole time we were in Texas. The inside was always exposed. That meant I had to be in it all the time. The whole point of the promotion was having someone living inside a *Glass Box.* We couldn't drive around with an empty box. When we traveled to and from The Ranch, I would sit in the loveseat, and Kenneth would drive the hour and a half back and forth. So, I would be looking out the back, and I couldn't see the streets or highway directions on the huge green highway signs explaining where everything was. All I could do was wave to all the cars honking and taking pictures of me. It was like I was the gunner in a two-seater Boulton Paul Defiant Interceptor, and Kenneth was the pilot. I could see everything at all angles behind us on the road but nothing in front of us.

When we reached The Ranch, we would pull into the back and drive right by the window to the hair salon. Then, we would park it next to the garden with all the gothic statues surrounding it. When I was shutting everything down for the night in *The Box*, there were always one or two women with tin foil or plastic, pink cotton candy curlers in their hair a short distance away, gawking at me.

The day before we headed out, everything had to be locked

down and secured. The two aluminum ladders seemed to be shifting during travel, and when I would open the door, sometimes they would slide right out. They were stored at an angle next to the generator and kept shifting about. Kenneth and I took the *Cube* to the local Hard & House Annex. I used to work for them in high school. Every time I pass by one of them, the intense purple colors on the buildings catch my eye. It is a dark purple color. It was on the building, on the aprons we wore, on the lockers, the break room tables, the shopping carts, and some of the floors were painted purple.

I worked in the Seasonal Department as a teenager, mostly moving large stones, bushes in pots, and bags of fertilizer. A short time later I transferred to hardware, stocking nails, bolts, thumb screws, and washers. The place was a madhouse, entirely unsupervised. Summer weekends were the worst, packed to the gills with people doing their home projects. One guy working with me would have his friends come by on busy days, and he would take things to their cars, totally unpaid for. He would just grab items like mini-fridges, stainless steel sinks, lawnmowers, and air conditioning units, walk out the front, load up their cars, and then they would drive off without a care in the world. He confessed this to me once, and every time I see the lavender logos on the buildings, I think of him.

After the lilac flashback standing in the parking lot, I went inside and walked straight to the wood section in the back, finding in a barrel of scrap a 6"x 8"x 3" piece of wood. Bought it for the price of a cup of coffee and walked back into the parking lot with a Phillips-head screwdriver, trying to bolt the wood down to the floor of the generator room as Kenneth limped around aimlessly. After I split the piece in two, I went back inside and got a slightly wider piece. I came back to the parking lot and checked on Kenneth mental state.

"Kenneth! Livin' the dream?" I shouted.

Kenneth looked at me in a half-daze. I apparently interrupted a conversation he was having, but he was the only one in the parking area. You would assume he did this in every parking lot he visited. I showed him the second piece like it was a nugget of gold, a piece of quartz crystal, or a chunk of jadeite found on a chicken farm, and he nodded back. He seemed to understand what I was trying to achieve but showed little interest in helping. The new piece of scrap wood was slowly hammered onto the floor. It worked, no splitting of this wood this time. The area now had a small lip to support and stop the ladders from shifting about. From then on, the bottom edge of both ladders rested against this small wooden trouble-saver. They were tightly secured, caddy-cornered in the generator room now. No more shifting about on short stints or long drives.

The dresser drawers also had an upgrade. They were now held shut by a new set of bungee cords I also just purchased, and the coffee maker was placed in the sink with a brand-new kitchen towel stolen from the hotel back in St. Louis just before traveling. The chairs were secured via new longer strips of black Velcro to the round kitchen table, and the coffee table found its new home (now and forever) bolted to *The Escape Hatch*. Happy with the new upgrades, we headed back to The Ranch, and I didn't have to worry about getting lost. Luckily for me, Kenneth was driving.

When checking out of The Ranch, there was an office room Todd had for taking care of the financial aspect of the arrangements. It was his office. It was right off the main lobby. It had a large window directly to the left of the door that looked out to the garden in the back. White walls and a humongous dark oak desk with a glass top. And matching bookshelves behind.

The shelves were filled with titles like *Ulysses, Gone with the Wind, Melmoth the Wanderer, Barry Stewardship Christmas Ornaments, Modern Man in Search of a Soul, Pride and Prejudice, Gothic Romance: For the Inter-designer in you, Eloise in Paris, Catch-22, The Joy of Cooking, The Elements of Style: A Practical Encyclopedia of Interior Architectural Details from 1485 to the Present, It's your Cake, now Decorate it!, The entire set (all 14 books) of *L. Frank Baum's Oz Series*, and a first edition hardcopy of the 1927 classic *Whispers of Death in the Opal Room*.

The office room was well organized, and nothing was on the desk except a fountain pen and a leather-bound day planner. The room was completed with two white leather swivel chairs in front and a red Persian rug underneath. In the corner were the two hot pink and sapphire blue Christmas trees that greeted guests, along with a few terror-stricken gnomes lying face down on the floor. These were the last things being packed up. This room was completely different in style and structure in every way from the rest of the place. It was almost monastery like with its colors and design. That was until I gave him my credit card. He then turned around, and behind him on the dark oak bookshelf, I noticed a black credit card terminal that had shaggy long pink fur surrounding it.

"Randolph, it was a pleasure to have you here," he said as he handed me back my credit card.

"No Mr. Swartzman, the pleasure was mine," I said, and I meant it.

It was time to move on to the next city. After checking out of the ranch I was in the back lot, taking the ladders out of the Cube, ready to flip the tarp by myself. As I set up the second ladder, I noticed in the corner of my eye Jerry was wandering aimlessly in the garden alone. We both stopped and looked at each other; then, without a word, he climbed one of the ladders and helped flip the tarp. Nodding to thank him, he went back inside The Ranch. I button-snapped the tarp to the bottom of the Cube, locked the side door, and zipped it shut with the black metal rod.

Donovan and Jerry then walked to the minivan with a small Tiffany lamp and a dark-colored rug wrapped in plastic. I pretended I didn't see them and acted as if I had something important on my mind, looking the other way towards the ladies in the salon. They were packing these things up at the last minute. I was hoping those goods weren't from the honeymoon suite.

Later that day, we headed out. This was a long drive. It's 775 miles from Navasota to Albuquerque. I didn't want to get lost, so I was going to follow Kenneth the whole way.

CHAPTER 18

Albuquerque, New Mexico,
and The Loch Ness Monster

New Mexico is a lot warmer in the winter compared to Chicago. We pulled into the parking lot that evening, while Donovan and Jerry arrived earlier that afternoon. We stayed at one of the local hotels this time, nothing exotic, no theme, no fancy-schmancy color scheme, just a regular good old hotel. We were only spending a couple of days in Albuquerque before we headed over to Phoenix. The place we were staying at was relatively new.

The lobby was painted mascarpone white with some local flair. A one-dimensional, rusted iron cowboy boot sculpture about four feet tall acted as a doorstop. It had a very tall and wide front desk to the right of the entrance. In the center of the left wall in the lobby was a huge, wooden framed picture of several saguaro cactuses painted in oil against an orange sky. Two cracked, brown leather chairs sat directly under it. Across the street was the desert, and I mean that in its entire definition. You could witness, from the lobby, sand as far as the eye could see. A silver teardrop camper and a couple of tents were sprinkled here and there. Some of the streets had one or two buildings, and then it was just desert. Some streets had sidewalks but nothing but flat land behind them. Just sand.

When we drove through the town, I kept seeing more and more of these tents in the sand. In the evening, when we were driving back to the hotel, you could see every star in the sky. And on the ground in that desert, you could see every lantern, every flashlight in each and every one of those tents, and a few small campfires glowing. It was quite seductive.

In the Scottish Highlands, there is a large body of freshwater about 23 miles long and a variation of depth anywhere from 744 to 889 feet or 124 fathoms (perhaps deeper). It is known as Loch Ness. It is the second deepest Loch right after Loch Morar and the second largest by surface to Loch Lomond. It is also known to hold a sea creature called The Loch Ness Monster, also known as *Nessie.* As early as the sixth century A.D., claims have been made that a large fishlike creature swims these waters.

In 1991, a gentleman named Steve Feltham made a life-changing decision. He quit his job, sold his house, and walked away from everything he had ever known in search for the monster full-time. He converted an old bookmobile into his home and started driving it around the Loch looking for it. To make money, he would sculpt little *Nessie* figurines out of molding clay, sitting on rocks he had collected from the shore, and sell them to tourists. After some years, the mobile library broke down, and he turned it into his permanent research facility/home, now located in the village of Dores. Steve was named Ambassador of the Year at the 2016 Highland and Islands Tourism Awards. He spends his days watching the shoreline and selling his colorful figures, looking for Nessie.

———————————————

When we drove by the tents and small campers in the desert, a part of me found the idea of living there quite inviting. The sand is dry and clean, and it judges nothing. For a moment, I wanted to take the *Cube* and park it right out there in the desert and live among all the ones there, live among those hiding in plain sight. I wanted to make little sand creatures from molding clay and sell them to drifters and the odd tourist that passes by. A part of me wanted to take that *Glass Box*, break it down, and make it my home.

I wanted to sit in that sand in the evening and watch all the campfires glowing in the darkness, hear the coyotes' cry every night, make that green tarp into a canopy, and block out the noon day sun.

A part of me wanted to disappear into that sand forever. These thoughts were powerful, more than I wanted to admit. I wanted to stay longer in Albuquerque, but we still had a long way to go before getting back home. Leaving part of me there in that sand, I got back in the game.

When solitude becomes a constant companion, especially inside *The Box*, peculiar pastimes are born to fill the void. I devised a method to unbolt framed pictures from the hotel walls.

It required some finesse, but you could manage to jimmy them off the wall, delicately open the frame, and lay inside on the picture a small image cut from a magazine or, at times, one of the pamphlets from the lobby detailing local attractions like haunted house tours, duck boat trips, or pirate themed seafood restaurants.

Strategically placing the image where it seamlessly blended into the framed picture, almost like hunting for a four-leaf clover in a patch of grass, you could then reframe it with the precision of a high school shop teacher. Slapping it to the wall, then imagining that someone revisiting the room would sense a subtle alteration without pinpointing it. Perhaps, one night, they would notice the change, and find the metaphorical clover in the framed picture of wild horses running on the beach above the bed. Or maybe not.

CHAPTER 19

Phoenix, Arizona,
and The Paradoxical Time Situation

It's a straight shot to Phoenix if you take I-40 West. Once we got out of Texas, it was much easier for me to understand the highways. Driving cross country is a straight shot, and this was no different. Early that morning Kenneth asked if I could help him move some stuff into a storage unit in Scottsdale. His back and leg were not in the best of shape, and he needed a hand. He was in between residences, and it wasn't that far out of our way. I said, "No problem." The others were halfway to Phoenix, and they would not know or care if we made a side trip. The concept of time on this gig, especially when traveling, was made up anyways. And Scottsdale is only 12 miles from Phoenix.

Kenneth had a dozen or so boxes to move from a house to a storage facility right outside of Scottsdale. I had moved boxes before, so this wasn't a problem. But I think he wanted someone else there just in case a certain lady showed up. That was neither here nor there. *Happy to help*. We pulled up to his gray single-level house that had a couple of red wooden shutters and an unkempt front lawn. There were no cars in the driveway, and you could tell Kenneth was relieved. It was a quiet street; a couple of the neighbors poked their heads out to see our little parade come in.

You couldn't get away from the constant advertising of driving the minivan. As for Kenneth, he had to drive the *Cube*. That was a top-heavy, wide machine you can't just parallel park in front of a supermarket or a strip club without some help. And then have to dodge the constant question of "*What are ya hauling?*" But his place was not too far from the main highway, and we found a nice spot to hide the *Cube*. This was just us moving boxes. This wouldn't take any time at all.

Anytime someone asks you for help when you are on the road, especially if you are dealing with storage facilities, vehicle maintenance, shipping pallets, new clients, or paperwork that needs signatures from two parties or more, they will always say, "*It's only gonna take 20 minutes.*" They're lying. Dealing with time, twenty minutes means it's going to take four hours. That's how I started dealing with blocks of time. Anything under four hours was a snap. I had enough mental strength for four hours, whether it's driving, flying, dealing with a shop manager, or a truck rental facility, or any unforeseen problem.

Four hours when dealing with unknown places. Everything is new for someone out of town. You don't know the shortcuts on the streets. You don't know the locations, traffic, or the distances between locations. And you don't know the groove of the area or the language of the land. You're the outsider. When some places say they are open till 5 pm, that means they close at 2 pm. Every day is like your first day at a new job. Anything outside of your planned route is going to be time-consuming. You had to be flexible, and when things weren't available or didn't go as planned, you had to be self-reliant. You had to pull yourself up by your bootstraps.

Everything over four hours you had to prepare for. When traveling over four hours, you needed enough sleep, food, water, caffeine, and an understanding of the day's expectations. Anything exceeding four hours is a workday. Driving over four hours is a workday. Flying over four hours is a workday. Watching a production of *The Iceman Cometh* is a workday. Four hours—that's how long it took to move a dozen single-wall double-face, half-filled cardboard boxes from Kenneth's house to a storage unit outside of Scottsdale and then drive the 12 miles to a hotel in Phoenix.

———————————————

One of the strangest aspects of being in *The Box* is that every time you looked out the large glass windows, the landscape was different. It's always interesting seeing something new, like when the seasons change and leaves start to fall, or when the flowers of spring are in full bloom. Or when your neighbor repaints his entire house in lime green or seeing a bright yellow Corvette parked on the corner with an airbrushed falcon on the hood for the first time. But I've never been anywhere, including home, and looked out the window and remembered seeing thick snowflakes falling with gray Rocky Mountains in the distance one day and seeing huge blue skies with marshmallow clouds and white desert sands that stretch for what seems like an eternity the next.

And the following week seeing busy city streets with bay-windowed bakeries filled with delightful sugar treats and orange-doored coffee houses brewing dark roast coffee. And then the next seeing something completely different. And different people. Sometimes they are in big puffy winter jackets and wool caps, and other times in cut-off shorts, monogram t-shirts, and flip-flops. Being inside that thing, you would be taking it all in—all the tall concrete and glass buildings, then the next day, rows of overgrown mossy trees and beds of spring flowers in a thousand colors.

During the nightlight events, all the interior lights were on, including the lamps and the kitchen cabinet lights, giving the place a bit of a spooky atmosphere. The television would be visible without glare from the sun. Looking out the bay windows, you could see a reflection of a reflection, then a reflection of yourself, the television screen, and the interior of the *Cube*. There could be a thousand people outside, and you couldn't see them unless they came close.

Sometimes, a group of individuals would come right up to the glass. In the darkness, sitting on the loveseat, I would suddenly see six sets of eyes looking back at me, making the hair on the back of my neck stand straight up. I had to play it off as if I were just in my apartment, enjoying the evening, watching an old rerun of *B.J. and the Bear*, and didn't just see faces in the dark.

Sometimes during daylight hours, you would sit on a mile of blacktop with food trucks parked to the left and right. In the desert, with all its wild, muted green sagebrush and big blue wax pencil skies, one of the things I noticed was the variety of cacti. As a kid, I always got the saguaro and the organ pipe cactus confused. Organ pipe cacti are cylinder-shaped, growing tall and upright with a semi-circular top. Saguaro cacti grow in a similar shape but like a tree, with branches turning upwards. Saguaro are the ones you see the most in pop culture, like neon signs, salt & pepper shakers, shower curtains, lamps, and T-shirts. They weigh a ton and have their built-in defense system. I was always getting the saguaro and the organ pipe cactus confused. It was like trying to remember the difference between stalactites and stalagmites.

The second thing that caught my attention was something called straw-bale construction, using hay bales for building houses as insulation. The bales are stacked and secured with a wire mesh, and then concrete, lime, or clay is plastered on top to prevent moisture from seeping in. It also gives a finished look to home. The hay acts as natural insulation and is an inexpensive building material. I saw many homes being built with this method, with bales of hay stacked in front yards and parking lots. These are the things that you think about when you are alone.

CHAPTER 20

Donovan & Jerry's Highway Robbery Heist?

We hardly saw Donovan and Jerry on this gig, but when we did, it went something like this. They handled all the lodging reservations, since that fell under their responsibilities. We saw them the most during check-ins and check-outs. However, they never drove with us when we traveled from city to city or state to state, and we found out why.

We were staying at a place that consisted of a series of small villas connected by a gravel path, resembling a dwelling for gnomes and urchins, similar to the ones Todd had at The Ranch. Circular or octagon-shaped units adorned with rubber rabbitbushes, dasylirion wheeleris, and krascheninnikovia lanatas (aka winterfats). I had been puzzled by the spacious accommodations they were getting, much larger than Kenneth's and mine.

One afternoon, Donovan informed us about changes in our route and invited Kenneth and me to his and Jerry's wickiup. We met at their door, but before we went in, I asked Kenneth, "Does anyone else know you're here?" He smiled, and we entered their lodging, walking down a small corridor leading to the bedroom.

The bedroom had a light, pastel pink color with brown highlights, resembling a small acorn pattern on the wallpaper. Clothes were sprawled over the bed—designer jeans, leather jackets, cardigans, and button-down shirts. Jerry was kneeling, sorting through the items, surrounded by about two dozen pairs of leather shoes in brown boxes. Two four-foot-tall matching brown teddy bears in vests sat in an armchair, and against the wall was the dark-colored rug still in its plastic bag, accompanied by the Tiffany lamp I saw them pack up in Texas. On the coffee table lay watches, bracelets, leather belts, sunglasses, and silver rings. Jerry said, "Come on in, and shut the door."

I turned to watch Kenneth slowly close the bedroom door. Jerry smiled at me while folding two matching white sailor uniforms, and Donovan, perched on a wicker chair to the right of the bed, raised his eyebrows, stating, "I talked to the office today, and we are now going to have to go to Washington (State). One of the actors - the one covering that region, just quit."

"Ohh," I said. "What happened?"

"I don't know. We are going to take the West Coast now. It's good Mother likes that area," Donovan said with conviction.

At that point, it got weird. I was fine with them taking the least amount of responsibility on this, okay with them not traveling with us, okay with the outrageous bed-n-breakfast places they found, okay with seeing teddy bears in matching vests. I was okay seeing sailor uniforms in the hands of civilians. I was even alright with them taking a lamp and a rug from The Ranch right outside of Houston. I mean, I've taken towels from hotels before. What's a rug but like four towels? I understand. And I was fine seeing all those stolen designer clothes, watches, and other things. I could handle that. But I had no idea who this *Mother* was. Did he mean his *Mother*? Or someone with the code name *Mother*? Or did he mean the *Mother* in his head or the *Mother* of all *Mothers*? And he said this as if we had a full understanding of what that meant and that we all agreed at some point in the past to call this individual *The Mother*. I did not agree to call anyone *Mother*.

"That's great. We can totally do Washington. You know a good bed-and-breakfast in that area?" I asked with the full understanding of my limitations in that room.

"I'll find something. I'm not staying in a cheap motel. That's beneath me," Jerry smiled as he folded another pair of jeans.

"What's with all the stuff?" I inquired.

I couldn't believe I just asked that. But I had more than two emotions struggling inside of me. I thought we were pawns in a cross-country robbery spree and didn't even know it until this very moment. *Like were the cops after us!?* I was trying to put this puzzle together and remain calm. I knew Beatrix was jumping ship, but I didn't know we would be talking her route. I certainly didn't know anything about all this loot. Or this so-called *Mother* character. I was about to ask where they got all this stuff when Jerry laughed, "Outlet Stores. Everything is on the cheap." Then I understood why they didn't travel with us. They just bought a home, and the reason, the only reason, they took this gig was to go to all the Outlet Stores all over the country to furnish their new place. The rug and lamp weren't stolen from The Ranch. They were bought in a shop somewhere in Houston. They always drove ahead of us so they could spend time shopping. Then I calmed down. They would get these big rooms to hold all the loot they picked up at all the Outlet Stores and what have you. Then pack it up and mail it to *Mother*.

Jerry was folding and boxing everything neatly. This was just another day for them. They didn't plan to meet with us about someone leaving the tour, it was just the only place for all of us to gather. Beatrix leaving was news to everyone. I just happened to know that piece of information in advance. Kenneth and I just happened to be in their room when they were organizing all that stuff. They had already shipped things like throw pillows, cat trees with hammocks, overstuffed ottomans, drapes, and whatnot. They wanted to get the rest of that stuff to *Mother*.

And now we were heading up the West Coast, and they could hit all of those Outlet Stores. I figured it out. But I still didn't know who this *Mother* was. Luckily, my phone rang. I said to the group, "Guys, I have to take this." And I exited the oubliette.

Ring, ring, goes my cellphone.

"Hello," I said with a great sense of gratitude.

"Hey," the voice on the other end said. It was Beatrix.

"I told them. I told them I had to leave" she cried.

"I know, I just heard."

"Yeah, I said my grandmother is sick, and I have to go," Beatrix said.

"That's a good... that's a good one. Yes grandmothers!... when do you start rehearsals for *The Chicken in the Bucket* play? Or is it *Bucket O' Chicken*? No, it's *Don't forget the Chicken*? No, that's not it. I forget what's it called again?" I laughed.

"Very funny. We start next Monday. I'm flying back to New York tomorrow."

"That gives you a few days to get your bearings. And it goes up in April?" I asked.

"Yes, are you going to come?" Beatrix asked.

"Of course, I am. I love chicken."

CHAPTER

Sacramento, California,
The Styrofoam Rooster,
and Attack of the Tumbleweeds

On the drive to Sacramento, we took I-10 West and found ourselves on I-5 North straight towards downtown. The average drive time is just under twelve hours. It ended up taking us three days.

On the way, I stopped at a small gas station just before California, not quite out of Arizona, somewhere in between. White sand covered the landscape, and the gas pumps were something left over from the Boom Generation. They were candy apple red with a circular light on top. The exterior of the station was also red with white highlights. Inside was something of a general store, with old barrels filled with oatmeal and nuts. Hanging upside down from the muntin bar behind the cash register was a series of blue Styrofoam roosters. The interior was made from styrofoam, covered with small blue feathers. Each had a set of talons made out of wire, buttons for eyes, and a plastic beak—all hanging upside down. At first, I thought they were real, but the wire claws gave it away.

I asked the young woman behind the register, "How much?" and pointed to the blue roosters just above her head. The man standing next to her quickly stated, *"Twenty dollars."* I looked at him, shook my head, and said, "Five." He nodded to the young woman, and she reached up and picked out a rooster for me. I paid cash for an orange soda, a green bag of chips, the blue rooster, the fuel, and then walked out of the store with a new co-pilot.

Now, we were taking on some of Beatrix's route. We had a major interview in Sacramento to hit, and we were going to appear on a morning talk show. After that, we were to head up to Portland, Oregon, and then to Seattle, Washington. Now we had a wider map of traveling ahead of us. We were on Interstate I-5 going North. This stretch of road you would have to find the radio frequency, and then it would fuzz out when you got out of the station's range. Music or talk, it didn't make a difference. I was driving by myself, but now I had the blue rooster to keep me company when the radio failed.

We were now in the Central Valley, and the area was quite dry. Donovan and Jerry were about four hours ahead, and Kenneth was about one hour behind me. Sand to the left of the road and sand to the right. There are stretches of road where there is nothing to see, and most of the time, no one was on the highway.

As another radio station fuzzed out of existence, I noticed the land moving. It was like small waves of land. Small circular pieces of land. Moving! It was rolling, and it was rolling into the highway. First, it was just a couple of them, then more and more. Then it looked like hundreds of them. They were bushes. Dead bushes. Tumbleweeds. And they were rolling like balls. The wind was picking up - and the tumbleweeds were pouring into the highway.

I'd never seen tumbleweeds before, and I started swerving the van around, dodging them. They were attacking me. One was the size of a garbage can, started rolling straight for me. I stopped. I dead stopped on Interstate I-5 and braced myself for impact. It came right up, and *Poof,* it bounced right off the front bumper. I got out of the minivan and looked to see the damage. There was none. I grabbed the tumbleweed. It was light as a feather, and I tossed it to the side. Then one hit me, and *Poof,* and then another, *Poof.* They were like cotton balls. Then I realized I was parked in the center of the road.

I got back in the minivan, as I was being bombarded by them. *Poof...Poof, Poof.* I pulled off onto the shoulder. And got hit by another. *Poof.*

I got out and grabbed another one slightly smaller this time so I could discover its detail. They were so big and had no weight to them. I thought, maybe I should take a couple and put one in the *Cube* and one in the driver's cab to scare Kenneth. I turned around, and *Poof,* another one hit me. Then I thought I better not. I better leave this one alone. They might really attack me. I didn't know how they would react if I took out one of their own. I would hate to wake up in Sacramento and look out the window and see two hundred of these in the parking lot below coming for me.

We checked into one of the Stay Quiet O'Bit Hotels (SQOBH) just outside of town. A modest place with a kitchenette—nothing too fancy—enough to make it feel comfortable, if only for a night. Life on the road had its moments of serenity, but they were fleeting. The time blurred together. We spent so many days in unfamiliar cities, navigating streets that never seemed to lead anywhere. There was no prize to be won. No ticker-tape parade with people yelling out your name in gratitude. There never had to be a destination to arrive at. You were already there.

You won't find understanding in the desert. You're not going to find peace in the mountains. You will not find silence in a meadow somewhere in a state where the sky is always blue and the sun shines all the time. You have to find that silence wherever you are. The best part of life is the struggle, not some arbitrary prize at the end of the tunnel. Having trophies doesn't mean you won at life. That's what the road is. It's the place where the rest of the world is searching for the same thing you are. People are looking for something outside of their daily lives to silence the chaos in their heads. Most people, if given the choice, would rather battle a dragon, save a town from destruction, and experience that brief rush of triumph than spend their entire lives in quiet solitude.

We had to stay grounded, keep our thoughts in check, and our feet firmly on the ground. This week had been busy. Our time was consumed by meetings, and now the last days were upon us. For February, the weather was surprisingly warm—a rare kindness from the road.

I received a call from the office about an upcoming interview at the end of the week. I tried my best to disengage, not wanting to let their worry seep into me. But Sacramento had everyone on edge. This wasn't going to be an ordinary interview. It was going to be a marathon.

Before the big event, we found ourselves stationed on the corner of 10th Street and N Street, right in front of the California State Capitol Building. It was a grand sight, surrounded by a park filled with over a hundred trees from all over the world.

Among them stood the Washington robusta palm, also called the Mexican Fan Palm. I had always assumed palm trees belonged in postcards, lining beaches or desert oases, never in the shadow of government buildings. But that's the thing about being on the road. You can stop for a moment and admire something new—or at least, new to you. You learn to let go of expectations. Both the order of nature and the chaos of life can exist right next to one another.

Having spent some years as a florist in my younger days, I noticed an odd plant in this California garden—the English Yew (Taxus baccata), which grew just like the ones back home in New Jersey tho it somehow survived here in the desert. It's just one of those little facts I've learned and tucked away in the files of my mind. I knew its berries were poisonous. You stayed away from them, but I had never feared them as a unique danger. You learn which things are dangerous and which ones only seem that way. But only by the act of doing. Of searching for yourself. I was never one to fear the wizard behind the curtain. He is only an illusion. An idea of danger rather than danger itself. The road teaches you that too. Which doors you should enter and which ones should best be left alone.

Not long ago, I had believed tumbleweeds could kill a man. That showing up for a newspaper interview and walking into a room might land you a job traveling the country. That life without a plan might be the best option. But I had come to understand something while I was on the road. Nothing outside myself was going to give me peace of mind. The road, with all its uncertainty, wasn't something that was going to push away the chaos. It was something to be embraced, but not something to take the place of anything.

And so, standing there, watching the palms sway gently in a place they didn't seem to belong, I realized—maybe none of us wanted to escape anything. Maybe we were just searching for silence in this world of chaos and a place to grow.

CHAPTER

Fifty Dollars Worth of Pastries
on A Good Day

This was a talk show. This was our longest interview, for a Sacramento morning talk show, slated for the full four-hour broadcast. The studio didn't interview us for the entire duration; I was introduced in the first hour. For the remaining three hours, the studio would cut back to us right before a commercial break for a 30-second snippet. Then, a long shot of me and the studio's personality inside the *Cube* followed. The morning talk show host, already with a fan club, engaged viewers daily with his crazy antics. He would dress up like a superhero on Halloween or help out at the local soup kitchen. The idea was for the host to discuss his direct observations from being inside the *Cube*. This was an opportunity to bridge the focus back to the campaign and its message.

The camera man had the task of finding interesting ways to shoot us outside in the rain before the commercial break. He then came back inside to rest between segments. While he could hear the broadcast from the studio in his headset, I heard nothing. We also had body mics that could pick up every sound. Without any rehearsal or planning, I had to switch off the generator after the camera guy signaled, they were about to cut to us or keep it running, depending on the shot they wanted.

Moreover, I had to keep the floors clean and dry between takes. This event extended beyond a typical four-hour workday. Around 5 am, in a large parking lot waiting for the crew to arrive, with rain already hitting us hard, I decided to get two boxes of coffee and pastries for the crew from a nearby Bustersteins Coffee. As I walked in, the manager's face was on the floor, asking, "What the hell is that?" he cried.

I explained, "It's a traveling campaign. It's a promotional vehicle."

"You drive around in that thing?"

"Yes."

He was either high on espresso or pulling my leg when he said, "When they invented raspberry ripple ice cream, I thought I'd seen it all."

"Or bubblegum ice cream," I replied.

"You're right. You're absolutely right! Bubbled gum iced cream! How do you even eat that? Crazy stuff."

They'd just opened for the morning, and with the sour weather, there was no one else around. I gave him the heads up about our morning show interview we were doing in the area, mentioning that we'd be in the lot for a while. And to my liking, he had just set out a tray of pastries and remarked, "Well, I guess we made this all for you."

All those buttery, sugar-coated, custard-stuffed kickshaws were fresh out of the oven, and I happened to be the first customer in the place.

I purchased a box of their Deep Dark External Voyage roast and a box of the Hazelnut Orange Ziggurat house blend. Three blueberry currant scones, two peanut butter brownies, three morning glory muffins, two orange-glazed cake donuts, two chocolate maple croissants, two granola brown butter blasters, four bananas, three vanilla chocolate chip cupcake balls, and two lady lemon squares. The barista at the register asked, "*Are you going to eat all of this?*"

"Oh, no. We are going to be here for a couple of hours; this is for the crew," I said with a reassuring tone.

Having nothing large enough to display all these goodies in the *Cube*, the manager generously gave me a large ceramic dish he had in the back, leftover from the holiday season, for everything I picked out. He also provided a half gallon of milk and a coffee mug with their black and orange colors and logo on it. Didn't charge me a dime for the extras. He didn't have to do that. Although we only had a brief conversation, I felt like I had met him before. He spoke with a full voice of understanding, as if he had experienced something similar in his own youth. Maybe not traveling in a *Glass Box*, but if he had told me he had been to Jupiter on a space mission, I would've believed him. He had a twinkle in his eye when he smiled, as if to say, "*Ah, yes. The adventures of the young, bold, and brave hearted continue!*"

I wanted to establish a rapport with the caffeine people because they had the only bathroom for miles, and we were planning to be there for a good five hours. This was simply a media day, and we didn't have any models on site. I hopped back into the *Cube* and set out the spread on the glass kitchen table. I hid the coffee boxes under the sink, placed the milk in the mini-fridge, and poured myself a cup of the Ziggurat, drinking it from the white mug I had taken... borrowed from the hotel in Chicago the year before. The mug that the coffee wizard gave me would go into my private coffee mug collection. We were only promoting *Tamiflu* that day, not the coffee shoppe.

Antsy and alone, I didn't want to burn out on jitter juice. My leg was starting to twitch, and I felt the need to talk. Kenneth was in the cab, the only one close by, so I called him on the intercom.

"Kenneth, you want a lemon square!?" I asked.

"I'm good, Randolph."

"Kenneth, I just want to make sure I heard you correctly. You're passing on the lemon square!?"

No response. About a half hour later, the morning show arrived. It was dark. It was bleak. It was rainy outside, and this was an empty parking lot. I opened up the side door, flipped out the black ladder, and threw down a towel on the lip of the cabinet to absorb the rainwater.

"Permission to come aboard?"

"Please, we've been expecting you," I cried.

They clumsily climbed the ladder, equipment and all, and stumbled in. The generator was on, and it was warm and cozy inside. I had just put on *The Flower Duet* from the opera *Lakmé* to set the mood. The crew consisted of four: the interviewer (host), the cameraman, the sound guy, and the producer. Introductions all around. We shook hands, and then I casually offered them the spread. Not one of them even acknowledged that I had fifty dollars worth of coffee and breakfast pastries carefully laid out for them.

We were five people in a glass container, and the place only had four seats. Once everyone was inside, the windows fogged right up. Each of us was producing about 110 watts of energy sitting still. We did have a squeegee, typically used for the exterior windows that year, and today we employed it for the interior windows. A subtle shift in temperature, just a few degrees, resolved the fogging issue.

The first part of the live interview involved a tour of the facility. The host half-heartedly lifted the plate of pastries and showed the viewers at home, then cut to commercial. After that, we all sat, except for one – the slowest one of the bunch remained standing because it was musical chairs in there, and you had to be quick. Another segment followed, and we played another round of finding a seat, with the sound guy finally getting one. I decided to stand this round and let him have the entire couch. I started asking the host a series of questions to pass the time, if nothing else. When the producer asked about a restroom, I mentioned Bustersteins (coffee) across the lot, and he exited the *Cube*, freeing up a seat for the time being.

"How long have you been hosting this show?" I asked.

"I don't know. It feels like I've always been hosting it," he replied.

"What was your craziest interview?" I asked.

"Legally I'm not allowed to talk about it," he said.

This was just small talk to pass the time, but he responded to it. I was glad he did; otherwise, it was going to be a long day. He was what he would expect from a host of a television show. He was tall, he was thin, his hair was slicked back – almost chalk white. But he had a youthful energy about him, and he was constantly smiling. He asked about the cities we visited and which ones we were going to next. Just talking relaxed the atmosphere a little. He was under his own pressure to host on-site, out of the studio, in unpredictable circumstances, making things like this seem exciting, fresh, personable, and interesting for his viewers.

And five... four... three... two...

I was extremely uncomfortable at the end of that day. We were doing a seat of our pants-type interview in this nutshell, breathing the same air for four hours straight and up each other's noses. It was more of a showcase of the *Cube* and the host than anything else, but we did it. Once they packed up and drove away in their van, I realized there was fifty dollars' worth of cold coffee and stale pastries to get rid of.

The other members of my team were lethargic from sitting inside the minivans all day. The talk show got what they needed and were off like a dirty shirt. It was still raining, and we were about to head out and call it a day. I was locking everything down and remembered I needed to ask Kenneth something. I called him on the intercom.

"Kenneth, can I offer you a lemon square?... Kenneth... Kenneth?"

CHAPTER

Portland, Oregon,

Mysterious People,

The Colonial Parkway Murders,

Billboards & Pylon Poles,

BBQ,

and Découpage

It was a ten-hour drive from Sacramento to Portland. That means it's two four-hour trips with a two-hour layover while driving. With three breaks for the restroom and one fueling session, meaning we would get there in three days. On long stretches like this, I would travel a short distance behind Kenneth. That way, I always had him in my sight in case he blew out a tire, and he always had me protecting his blind spot. If you have ever seen a truck blow out a tire in front of you on the highway, you know it's a religious experience. We would make stops to get fuel and highly salted foods at the large gas markets. These places were right off the highways with easy access roads and big concrete lots for the eighteen-wheelers to pull in and fill up. A lot of them give you free coffee if you filled up the big rigs. Sometimes these big stops had fireworks you could buy on the cheap. Gasoline and fireworks in the same place! The minivan held less fuel and filled up faster than the *Cube*. So, to save some time, I would take Kenneth's thermos inside and get him coffee while he was gassing up. I took a peek inside his thermos one day and saw a series of black caves and caverns. I think he hadn't cleaned that thing since 1994.

On this stretch of Interstate-5, we came across our first hitchhiker of the gig. On the side of the road with her thumb out, she was looking for a ride. She wasn't a day older than twenty, well-kept, and completely confident in her actions, thinking for a moment that I should stop and pick her up. I called Kenneth on his cell.

"Kenneth, did you see that girl we just passed?"

"Ya, what about it?" He asked.

"Ya, she... she looks like she could use a ride."

"Do you want to stop?"

He asked that. I had to think about it, and her image was growing smaller and smaller in my rearview mirror.

"It's probably not a good idea. It's best to let mysterious travels... travel alone. Forget I mentioned it."

"Roger that," he said.

Years ago, when I was just finishing up high school, two friends and I drove to Virginia Beach, just a two-hour drive from where we lived. We left in the morning, planning to return that evening after some big, dumb fun in the sun. The only reason I wanted to go was to get a box of saltwater taffy, so the three of us decided to make the trip.

On the drive home, the car stalled and then suddenly, without warning, died on the Chesapeake Bay Bridge. This bridge is almost four and a half miles long, made of concrete and steel, crossing it's namesake. It also goes under water giving the experience of travel to be seventeen and a half miles. We were driving on the bridge when we stopped. And when I say died, I mean died. It's an awful place to break down as there's no shoulder where we were, so we stopped right in the lane.

The police came to our aid quickly, towed us off the bridge, and then cut us loose. They were only going to tow us off the bridge because we were a hazard to other drivers, dropping us off at the end of the bridge. We were in a fix. We could hire a tow truck to take us to a mechanic if one was even open.

Then a small, unassuming gray car pulled off the shoulder, and someone exited, asking if we needed assistance. He was a short, bald man, pear-shaped, wearing a blue work shirt with a white name patch with red threading that read *Buck*. Buck asked, "Are you alright?"

We didn't know Buck. We had never met him before. I've never known anyone by the name of Buck. I realized this fact as the police tow truck was unhooking our car at the end of the bridge, and Buck started talking to us.

"Yes, we just died on the bridge," my friend, whose car had just been hauled to the edge of the bridge, said.

"Do you need a tow?" Buck asked.

All of us, including the cop, were completely stunned.

"That's very kind of you, but we are heading to Richmond," I said.

"Listen, I got a trailer at my shop. Why don't I give you fellas a lift to Richmond?" Buck said.

I couldn't believe what I just heard. We broke down, and suddenly, out of to the fabric of reality, someone we'd never met offered us a tow back to Richmond.

"Buck? May I have a moment with my friends here," I asked.

Buck nodded and walked over to the tow truck, chatting with the cop. The three of us huddled together.

"What do you think, guys? Should we get in a car with this Buck character?" I asked.

"Who the hell is this guy?" the owner of the broken-down car said.

"I have no idea who he is. But I do know this. I have four dollars and sixty-five cents in my pocket, and that's not going to get us anywhere," I said.

"I had ten dollars earlier, but I bought a box of saltwater taffy."

"I don't have any cash either," said the friend with no cash.

"It's your car. It's your call," I said to the owner of the broken-down car.

"Okay, but no one, I mean no one, falls asleep or drinks anything he gives you. Alright!"

We all nodded and walked over to Buck, accepting his offer. He drove off into the distance to get his trailer, and the three of us sat on the hood of the car as we watched the sun set over the Chesapeake Bay.

About an hour later, Buck returned with the trailer attached to the back of his car. Buck knew what he was doing as he locked our car on top of with ease. We were ready to drive to Richmond with a man we had never met before. I sat in the back seat with my cashless friend to my right, and the owner of the car sat in the front. He was the smartest of the three of us, furious that he didn't make valedictorian in high school, coming in second. This haunted him our entire senior year, and he talked about it non-stop. The game plan was, since he was the smartest person in our class (or the second smartest), he could keep Buck talking on a variety of subjects, including the subject of just missing the mark for valedictorian.

While I was the tallest, we decided that I would be the muscle and the quiet one. I sat directly behind Buck, and our cashless friend would play the dumb one, asking Buck to elaborate on what he was talking about on our journey towards home and peppering in a few *"Ahhh's"* and *"Ohhh's!"*

As soon as we started driving on I-64 West towards Richmond, *Second-place-valedictorian* started talking. Just simple stuff like how long Buck has been a mechanic, how long he has lived at the beach, and so forth. It was a pleasant start to the icebreaker session. But we all knew he'd never read a Danielle Steel novel.

Buck was forthcoming, talking about his recent retirement, but he said it was difficult letting go of work because he enjoyed it so much. He seemed happy tinkering at his shop as a mechanic.

We were taking I-64 straight to Richmond, and right before Williamsburg, we saw exit 242 B Colonial Parkway. Then Buck changed his tone and started talking seriously about the Colonial Parkway.

"Y'know, just off of here is the Colonial Parkway," Buck said.

"Is that right?" *Second-place* asked.

"Yeah, right off there."

We drove by the exit, and it said in white letters on a green back board, *East 199 Colonial Pkwy / Yorktown.*

"Yes, about three years ago. They found-'em. A young couple. They found them in the woods. Stabbed."

Nobody in the car said a word. It was quiet for a what seemed like an eternity.

"I think it was back in '86. Two from the Navy, I think. I believe it was over there."

Buck pointed into the shadow of the trees just off the highway.

We were all listening to every word he was saying with a great deal of concern.

"Couple of guys were hiking in the woods and found these two kids, just teenagers, stabbed. They had a search party looking for them, and the parents thought they went to the beach. They were missing, and then they found them."

We just came from the beach. People in our immediate lives think we are still at the beach. This guy seemed to know a lot about the murders that happened here, I thought to myself. I hoped I just thought it.

There is a name for these murders. They are known as the Colonial Parkway Murders. Eight people were killed around that area. Six were found dead, and two are still missing but are considered deceased.

(Note: If something has a name that means it's real!)

———

The Colonial Parkway spans 23 miles, linking Jamestown, Williamsburg, and Yorktown in a triad, intersecting I-64. Between 1986 and 1989, three couples were murdered along this route. Buck began discussing them once we passed the Parkway.

I've done some stupid stuff before. I've crossed railroad tracks when trains were coming, I've fare dodged before, I've jumped into waters at the bottom of man-made rock quarries that say *Do Not Enter* at their gates. Mispronounced the word *Navy* on live television. I've seen *The Beautician and the Beast* in the theater. I've eaten an entire chocolate cake in one sitting. I've even tried Zima. Getting into a strange car at the end of the Chesapeake Bay Bridge with someone I've never met before, listening to him talk about unsolved murders in the dark of night with and a box of saltwater taffy, was the stupidest thing I've ever done.

Unsolved murders. Why would you even bring something like that up with people you've just met? It might have just been something he wanted to talk about on the drive, but under the circumstances, from my perspective, starting a conversation about missing people and straight-up murder with three hitchhikers was the equivalent of watching *Jaws* at a pool party.

Someone had to start talking, someone had to take the ball. *Second-place valedictorian* managed to steer the conversation to something else (thank goodness I was friends with a smart one), and Buck followed. That seemed to be the end of it. But once we passed the New Kent Rest Stop, Buck said, "There... that's where they found one of the cars. It was a yellow Chevy Nova."

The relevance of the New Kent Rest Stop is that's where the car of one of the missing couples was found. It wasn't yellow, but it was gold.

Cashless was supposed to do his *"Oooh!"* but he seemed to forget to chime in because of the great amount of detail Buck knew about these murders.

"I used to have a Nova. 1963 Chevy Nova SS. Two door, hardtop. Red," Buck said.

"Ohh," I exclaimed. Buck was so calm, and he seemed like he didn't have a care in the world. He was just driving three teenagers two hours out of his way to their home, towing their broken-down car. Just three teenage boys he saw on the side of the road that he had never met before. And then decided to talk about unsolved murders. *Who does that?* I had my hand in a fist the entire ride to Richmond.

We pulled into the parking lot at *Second-place valedictorian's* apartment complex, and we were still alive! Buck was at the trailer unhooking the car as the three of us huddled together.

"Do you think we should pay him something?" *Second place valedictorian* asked.

I thought that was a good idea, but we asked him if we could do that during the ride, and he said no.

"Get his address, say... say we want to send him a thank you card (for not killing us), and we can just mail him two hundred dollars," I said.

"Two hundred dollars!?" *Cashless* cried.

Buck finished releasing the car, and we walked back to his trailer.

"Buck, we can't thank you enough. You are a scholar and a gentleman," I said as we shook hands.

"We would like to send you a thank you card. Give us the address to your shop," *Second-place-valedictorian* said, and then he grabbed a piece of paper and a pen from his dashboard and handed it to Buck. Buck smiled and wrote something on the paper, folded it, and handed it back.

"No problem, boys. It was a pleasure."

He hopped back into his car and drove away into the night. The three of us were astonished by the events of the evening.

We opened the paper Buck gave back to us, and it said,

Nice try boys. The pleasure was mine.
Take Care, BUCK

The better of me decided not to pick her up. I was driving an advertisement billboard of a minivan. She was alone on the highway and seemed to be dodging some serious stuff. It was like mixing peanut butter and nachos – awesome individually, but a weird combo. Besides, what were we going to talk about, the local unsolved murders?

It was time to fuel up, and we stopped at the next turnoff, one of the large fueling stations. I filled up the minivan, grabbed Kenneth's thermos of death while he was dealing with the *Cube*, and I went inside.

Snagging an orange soda pop and a protein bar, I moseyed on over to the register. Just then, she walked in the door. She was young, no older than 25, with long curly blonde hair and rich blue eyes. It was the girl from the highway. I found myself heading towards her and said, "I saw you on the highway."

"Why didn't you stop?" she quizzed.

I paused for a minute. She said that with such a full voice. Such confidence, such innocence. For a moment, even I was confused why I didn't pick her up. She asked the question like it was obvious, like, "*Why wouldn't you pick up a young blonde tart you've never seen before on the highway, simultaneously working for a major corporation that was advertising a new prescription drug that helps flu sufferers? Nothing could possibly go wrong.*"

"You don't have a father named Buck, do you?" I asked.

"What?"

"Nothing. I can't," I said back to her.

She smiled and disappeared into the aisle of potato chips and stuffed pretzels. I went about my business, paid for my snacks, and filled up Kenneth's thermos. As I walked across the lot towards the minivan, I saw her talking to a truck driver, convincing him to give her a lift to a destination unknown. Our eyes briefly met before she averted her gaze and moved on.

"Randolph!" Kenneth yelled from across the lot.

I turned to Kenneth and nodded, thermos in hand. When I looked back, she was climbing into an eighteen-wheeler rig. The cab door snapped shut, the engine turned over, and in less than a second, it drove off onto the freeway.

I could have given her a lift, maybe not to her final destination, but somewhere along the line. I could have given her a lift, and so many things could have happened.

Sometimes, when I wanted to take a break for an hour, I would call Kenneth on his cell and say, "Gonna drive ahead, and I'll catch up with you at X, Y, and Z." I would then pull ahead of him, create some distance between us, find a place to stop for an hour, and then meet back up sometime later on.

Being on the road you get a hankering for something different to eat, something that didn't come with a french fry. Kenneth had just filled up the *diesel* tank and his thermos, so I knew he would be alright. It was time to drive ahead and search for something besides the usual roadside eats.

When you are looking for food or a fueling station, a rest area, or your exit, all the highway information signs are green. Just green with white lettering. Everywhere. They are always green. I've never seen a purple or red highway sign saying, *Exit 205 Next Right* or *Food & Fuel Exit 5B.*

The reasoning for green is it's considered a soothing color. It's easy on the eye, and all the highway information advertisements are on green signboards. Logos for lodging and restaurants are advertised in small squares on green signboards. I've always associated it with the green traffic light. Green meaning go! You don't stop on highways; you are always moving forward. I suppose if the signs were red, I would constantly go bananas, stopping every time I saw one. Green became the standard color for highway signs in the early 1970s.

Billboards or pylon pole signs are also used to advertise on highways. Billboards usually have spotlights and are on mammoth poles that drivers can see for miles. And some are giant LED screens. They inform people about local attractions, radio stations playing the latest hits, lawyers working hard for you, restaurants, car dealerships, and so forth. Pylon poles do the same, reflecting the names, colors, and fonts associated with these establishments. They are often custom-made to advertise one franchise name and attract drivers on highways. It is plain and simple advertising. It's telling you exactly what it is.

I saw an unassuming, tall, square, black pylon pole with orange-painted flames and the letters BBQ on it. It wasn't quite a pylon pole, and it didn't exactly belong to the billboard family either. But it advertised something different from everything else I saw that day.

I took the next exit and circled back to the parking area of the BBQ joint, right off the exit and close to a gas station and some industrial buildings along the road. It was a one-story office that was converted into a restaurant, with a flat, white exterior wall and a small sign on the roof that said BBQ. I walked in and directly in front of the main entrance was a thick black drape, about five feet in from the door. Nothing else. No hostess or waiting area. Just a black drape. I found the slit, pushed it aside, and entered.

Crossing over, I found myself in a square room with a flat wall-to-wall red rug, six tables arranged in sets of two, each with dark blue soft-bottom office chairs. All four walls were covered from floor to ceiling in black drape, and the ceiling featured square fluorescent lights inside mineral fiber tiles, all painted black. It was a black box, and it was apparently a music-free zone. It was as quiet as a tomb. In the right corner was a man younger than springtime in a long-sleeve shirt and a blue-striped tie, sitting at one of the tables eating a salad alone. I asked him, "Is this the restaurant?"

"Yes, it is. Have a seat." I did as I was told.

Then, out of nowhere, a young woman in green dress pants, open-toe sandals, and a red and black plaid shirt dropped in through the drape on the other side of the restaurant. She suddenly and without warning appeared next to this man. With jet-black hair and an expressionless face, she walked up to me and placed a menu on the table. This woman said not a word, and then she disappeared back into the fabric. I looked at the menu, hoping they had racks of ribs or a good lunch special. I saw dishes titled Shrimp Scampi, Spaghetti alla Puttanesca, and Ravioli di Zucca.

I looked at the man in the corner and asked, "I thought this was a Bar B-Q place?"

"Oh no, that place was gone a long time ago."

"From the highway, it says BBQ," I stated.

"No. No. No. It's long gone, thank gawd. They just haven't changed the sign yet."

The young woman returned and stood lifeless next to the man. He said to her,

"Alright, let's do... the Lasagna Bolognese, yes, but first, I want to finish my greens."

And he then handed his menu to her. Again, the woman remained mute as she became a part of the background.

I had taken a seat at the first table by the door. I assumed the kitchen was right behind the man, and I knew she would be coming for me next. I wanted to make my departure the same way she did. Softly, quietly, expressionless, and without sudden movements.

I closed the menu, waited for twenty seconds, and rose to my feet. I began my escape by walking backward towards the exit. My eyes remained fixated on the area of the drape where the woman of great silence and understanding had materialized before, hoping she would not do so again.

The man was in the center of his own self, enjoying a plate of lettuce as I glided my hand above the thick, dark black cloth, trying to remember where the opening was. Finding it, I slid through. *Almost there*, I thought. The last few steps to the glass door and opening it were all I had to do.

The only thing that gave away my escape was the hanging bell above the door that chimed when the door opened. The sun was high in the sky, and it seemed much brighter than it was just minutes before. There were no other cars in the parking lot. Mine was the only one.

The feeling was like a vampire being released from a curse, seeing the dawn for the first time after spending a century in a tomb. It was almost too easy taking out the keys from my jeans and not looking back. I then got in the minivan, started the engine, did a loop around, and quickly got back on the highway. I decided to skip lunch that day and met up with Kenneth a bit earlier than we had planned.

Jerry met us as we pulled into the bed-and-breakfast just outside of Portland. We were surprised to see him, as we usually didn't encounter him on the same day we arrived at hotels. He stood on the street, mentioning that this particular place didn't have a television, which they hadn't known when booking it. Jerry offered to book us at a chain hotel closer to our event. Kenneth opted for the chain hotel due to better parking for the *Cube*, not to mention his desire for an idiot box to watch. I decided to stay at this location, embracing the television-less room. I just picked up the Stephen King novel, *The Girl who loved Tom Gordon*, giving me the perfect excuse to read.

This bed-and-breakfast, a converted house, featured small rooms covered in pink wallpaper, with an enormous bureau and a wicker hope chest taking up much of the space. A nice old cloth doll sat on top of neatly folded towels on the chest. Each room had a private bathroom with white semi-sheer half curtains and a casual weave. The queen-size bed had a few lumpy pillows, and the walls had sharp angles supporting the roof. Smooth jazz provided the ambiance for this quaint place. It was a cozy, but it did feel like someones home. Did I mention the doll sitting upright on the folded towels?

Our time in Portland was spent in the Pearl District, once railroad yards and warehouses. The highlight was Powell's Books: The World's Largest Independent Bookstore, located in downtown Portland on West Burnside Street. This well-lit warehouse offers a vast collection of new and used books, making it a haven for book enthusiasts and those interested in découpage alike. Like me.

Ever since I can remember I've been obsessed with découpage. I had been working with paper and cut-out images before, but I found a new love for the art—cutting out images and pasting them on anything and everything: postcards, Christmas ornaments, wood plaques, benches, boxes, hotel-framed pictures, you name it. This bookstore had picture books of space adventures dating back to the 1930s, and for pennies on the dollar, I must have gotten twenty books on fantasy spaceships and psychedelically strange aliens alone. Pulp magazines and Sci-Fi book covers from the 1950s, also cookbooks with circus-themed cake decorating from the 1970s, advertisements from the early 1940s—that was just the tip of the iceberg. All these wonderful images from the same bookstore, in the same place, created a visual treat.

Every day looking out those windows and seeing the snow-capped Mount Hood in the distance, it was captivating. Mount Hood has an elevation of 11,249 ft, and it's a volcano, specifically a Stratovolcano. It's considered an active volcano to this day, meaning it can still erupt anytime it pleases, and people buy real estate here! It looks like an oil painting against the sky, stunning and covered with snow. When you see it, or when I would see it, I always thought it was going to erupt. And wouldn't it be a hoot if it started to erupt while we were driving down the highway and all the class inside *The Box* exploded at the same time.

We seemed to fit right in there, snug as a bug in a rug. The landscape was old warehouses being transformed into living and workspaces. That's what we were—a truck converted into a new glass workspace.

Sitting at the kitchen table cutting away my space images, two women exited a tattoo parlor and stopped when they saw the *Cube*. I could see them talking amongst themselves. Moments later, one came over with an orange Post-it note, wrote something on it, slapped it on the glass window, then disappeared in the crowd. I waited a moment, then placed the coffee mug that the caffeine wizard in Sacramento gave me on the glass table. I put my scissors in the drawer, stepped toward the side, and bent down. On the note were the names of the two women and a phone number. Then *Ker-plat!* A large, bearded man in black jeans and a matching jacket fully face-planted himself against the glass, scaring the bejesus out of me! So much that I lost my balance and fell into the side of the loveseat. He walked away with a sense of pride and accomplishment. I got to my feet, regained my composure, and looked at the glass, and the note was gone. *That son of a bitch,* I thought.

CHAPTER

Seattle, Washington,
The Tugboat of Dreams,
The Anaconda Roller Coaster,
Pablo Picasso, Carles Casagemas,
and Holly

It's 174 miles to Seattle from Portland, and you take I-5 the whole time. You pass a handful of casinos right outside of Tacoma, and drive time is only a couple of hours. Kenneth liked the penny slots and wanted to lose some, so we pulled over, and I watched him gamble for a while. It got a little stuffy after a short time, so I stumbled outside and stared at the bright light signs of promised riches against the black night sky. He came out a little bit later and smiled; we didn't say a word. But I think he got rid of those bad pennies. We both got into our vehicles and continued on the road.

Seattle is known for the Grunge music movement that started there and in its neighboring towns. Grunge, meaning grime or dirt, is often considered a hybrid of metal and punk. Starting sometime in the 1980s and then exploding in the 1990s, bands like *Alice in Chains, Pearl Jam, Nirvana,* and *Soundgarden* originated from Seattle and its surrounding towns.

Seattle is also known as *Rain City, Emerald City, Jet City, Queen City, Gateway to Alaska, and The Coffee Capital of the World.* These nicknames come from its reputation for being a rainy city, a lush green landscape throughout the year, and, at the time, home to many aerospace industries. Queen City was voted to be the official nickname by Seattleites in 1982 for its promise of riches during the 1897 Klondike Gold Rush. Gateway to Alaska is due to its proximity to Alaska, and Coffee Capital for being the birthplace of Starbucks on March 30, 1971. It is also home to psychotherapist and radio host *Dr. Frasier Winslow Crane.*

The attractions in Seattle include Pike Place Market, the Experience Music Project, and the Space Needle. The first thing I wanted to do was go to the Space Needle. It had been on my bucket list. It clearly defines the city and is a defining image in pictures. Some of the oddities of the thing are:

1. HOGE SULLIVAN. FIRST MANAGER (AFRAID OF HEIGHTS).
2. SIX PEOPLE JUMPED FROM THE NEEDLE WITH PARACHUTES.
3. THREE PEOPLE HAVE JUMPED WITHOUT PARACHUTES.
4. NIRVANA & PEARL JAM HAVE PERFORMED ON THE NEEDLE.
5. ONCE HAD A TORCH THAT COULD BE SEEN AT NIGHT.

Absolutely excited to be in Seattle, when we drove into town, you could see the Space Needle in the sky, shooting straight up to the heavens. It was truly awesome to see. The first thing I did was call the restaurant to see if I could get a reservation, but they were closed for renovations the entire time were in Seattle. Disappointment ran over me. I couldn't kick the bucket.

The other place was the Experience Music Project. Unfortunately, due to our schedule, we didn't get a chance to go there either. Two strikes against me in Seattle. Then I found out that Dr. Crane wasn't taking any new patients!

We did manage to get down to Pike Place Market, home to some of the local fishmongers, dozens of restaurants, and local shops, spending most of our days in that location. But the accommodations Donovan and Jerry found in Seattle took first prize for the best lodgings on this entire project. It wasn't a ranch, an old ladies' home converted into a bed-n-breakfast, or anything I've ever stayed at. It was a tugboat.

A real *Diesel*-engined tugboat floating in the water in the city of Seattle. Right on Elliott Bay, docked on the pier, was a tugboat bed-n-breakfast. It was a real hard-nosed tugboat that was converted into five overnight rooms. The captain slept on the boat also, six rooms including the captain's quarters.

The tugboat Lightweight Paperweight was an orange and white TP Class tugboat run by a retired couple, Captain Teddy Cottonwood and Martha Elizabeth Cottonwood. We got a call from Jerry saying everyone would be staying on a boat, but there were some circumstances we had to agree to first. The pier had a locked gate, and we were given the code to enter. Around the gate was a series of fencing and barbed wire to keep hooligans from climbing around and entering the pier. We punched in the code, entered the wooden, salt-weathered pier and met Donovan, Jerry, and Captain Cottonwood at the boat. It was easy to find; it stuck out like a sore thumb.

"What do you think?" Jerry asked both Kenneth and me.

"This is fantastic," I said. Kenneth showed no enthusiasm and was not the least bit interested in staying here.

"Good afternoon, I'm Captain Cottonwood. But you can call me Ted."

I wanted to call him Captain Cottonwood. He was in his early fifties and didn't look like much of a Captain, with short brown hair and a bit on the stocky side. He wore blue jeans and a t-shirt celebrating a drinking festival at one of the local pubs. And one of his thumbs was missing from the nail up. He took us on board and showed us the boat, then the rooms. They were small. Two of the rooms had bunk beds, and the captain's quarters had a full bed located towards the bow on the second level, the most expensive room on the tugboat.

Donovan and Jerry chose the first mate's chamber. Captain Cottonwood asked if one of us would mind transferring rooms because he overbooked for the week we were there. These were the circumstances we had to agree to if we wanted to stay on the boat. He mentioned that as compensation for one of the nights, he would provide the captain's quarters. I eagerly accepted, expressing no issue with changing rooms. The first two nights was in the Hippocampus room, a bunk bedroom with two porthole windows, wood paneling, a small wooden desk and chair. There was only one bathroom on the boat, and it did have a shower.

The center of the boat was gutted out and made into a common room with three couches, an armchair, and a television located on the stern facing the bow. The cockpit was turned into a seating area with a fridge next to the wooden shellacked steering wheel. A long table was placed in the center for entertaining guests. The wood floor was now carpeted with an off-white runner. It looked like your crazy uncle's summer home. Kenneth decided to stay on the boat, so we had to find alternative parking for the *Cube*. He found a spot not too far away in an empty lot. We dropped the *Cube* in the lot at the end of the day, and drove out there in the morning.

The tugboat had no kitchen, meaning all meals outside of work were to be consumed in restaurants, and only one bathroom. I thoroughly enjoyed it; it felt like indulging in the fantasy of being the captain of my own ship, and we had the privilege for a whole week!

One of the great fantasies of being on the road is that you could eat whatever you wanted, and the calories wouldn't count. Every new town we went to or passed through had a small specialty apple fritter Pub. Or a place that served fresh banana flips. Or a joint where you could get a slice of *The Best Strawberry Rhubarb Pie in the State*. Or a restaurant that had been serving the same oil cake recipe since World War II. Want to try something different like a key lime cake? You would find it and so much more. Kenneth introduced me to that one.

I would cook most of my evenings in the hotel kitchenette. But every now and then, I would stumble upon one of these gems and indulge in a full-out dining experience.

On *Year Two* we ate out most of the time. The first bed-n-breakfast we stayed in only provided the morning meal, and the tugboat had no kitchen at all. I did the occasional dine out with Kenneth. But mostly by myself, donning my black blazer, dark jeans, leather shoes, and dark button-down shirt, I would venture out to enjoy a three-course meal. Every now and again, someone in town would recognize me with a look of bewilderment on their faces. They would lean over and whisper something to their spouse or friends, then they all would all look at me like, *"He looks like the guy in the Cube, but doesn't he live in there? This guy is here, walking among us... in a blazer."*

One night in a restaurant somewhere in side streets of Seattle a young woman slowly advanced towards me, and as soon as I locked eyes with her, I knew exactly why she was approaching. She stopped, paused for a moment, mustered up the courage and asked...

"Hi, I don't normally do this but, didn't I see you... Are you the guy... in that truck thing, with the glass walls, the television, and the furniture and what not?"

———————————————————————

When I was a teen, I did a commercial for a local amusement park called Kings Dominion. At the time, it was owned by Kings Entertainment Company (KECO). The commercial was for their new Anaconda Roller Coaster, designed by Ron Toomer, who also designed *Motorcycle Chase* and *Runaway Mine Train*.

The commercial featured a bunch of kids, including me at seventeen, having a grand ol' time at the park riding the new roller coaster. At the end, when the coaster returned to the station, the kids had aged forty-some odd years, with a big booming voiceover saying,

"How amazing would it be to take a ride on the New Anaconda Roller Coaster at Kings Dominion? Let's just say it might be so crazy it takes a few years off your life." Or something to that effect. It sounded stoic, ominous, and regal.

Photo by Mel Turmount

Anaconda, roller coaster commercial.

During the shoot, we were locked in the roller coaster seats for two days with an over-the-shoulder harness securing us inside. The green fiberglass car we were sitting in had the words Kings Dominion in white lettering on top. The coaster was just off the assembly line, without a smudge on it. We couldn't even touch it without someone coming to wipe off the fingerprints.

The first six kids in the initial six seats, me included, were replaced at the end by six similar-looking gray-haired adults – older versions of us. The idea was that the roller coaster was so intense it would age you, by forty years. When we were on the set at the amusement park, our younger versions ran into our older versions. Each of us stood in front of our other selves, and I said,

"We should all go out to the highway and wave down a car and say... *There is something wrong with the Time-Space Continuum... You have to help us!*"

It was a once-in-a-lifetime experience because I couldn't ride a rollercoaster that intensely ever again. It was a shot in the arm for me at the time, finishing up my third year of high school. One day between classes, a young woman with bright red hair, fair-skinned, freckled-faced, and almost six feet in height, named Bandie, approached me—similar in demeanor to the woman in that side street Seattle eatery—and quietly asked,

"Hey Randy, did you have fun doing that (roller coaster) commercial?"

"I did, I had a great time," I replied.

"How long did it take to do it?" Bandie asked.

"It took two days; we actually rode it forty-two times," I said.

"Really?"

"Yes, we were locked in the seats the whole time."

"You were locked in the seats for... two days straight?"

"Yes, when we had breaks the director would ask... You guys want to go again!?

And we would go around again, and again, and again!

"Really, two days, um...

How did you go to the bathroom?" Bandie asked.

It had been a long day; I was very tired just finishing up my coffee, about to leave the restaurant and go back to the tugboat of my dreams when she asked that question, "Are you the guy... in that truck thing, the glass and furniture and what not?"

"Yes," I said. "I am," I cried softly to her.

She approached me sitting alone in a Seattle restaurant, lit only by candlelight, two thousand, eight hundred and fifty-seven miles away from home, in a town that was alien to me. I had never seen this woman before in my life. She made a conscious and deliberate decision to approach me, a stranger. She could've picked a thousand different things to talk about; she could've questioned me about anything. She looked at me with all the innocence in the world and asked,

"How do you go to the bathroom?"

"I don't."

Every night when returning to the tugboat Lightweight Paperweight, you would walk down the long pier and catch a glimpse into everyone's boat. A lot of people lived on their boats. You could see the flicker of the television through the portholes or see them sitting with a group of friends having a beer or a wine cooler. And when you got to the tugboat itself, the party never stopped. Captain Cottonwood, Ted, was entertaining, almost every night. Since the rooms were small, I would spend the evenings in the common room watching a television program about homemade robots fighting one another. And Captain Cottonwood would have two or three friends in the cockpit with a bottle or two of red wine.

One cool evening I came in, and Ted was three sheets to the wind, and he said, "Rander, Randolph, come on in here and have a drink with us," Captain said.

"I'm good, Ted. Just had dinner and an interesting conversation with a stranger. I think I just want to veg out for a while," I said.

"Alright. But I'll get you one night."

I grabbed the remote, lay on the green and blue flowered couch, and turned-on *Homemade Robots Running Amuck*. Captain Cottonwood and his friends were enjoying themselves when a young fair-skinned woman with gray eyes, who was in the cockpit, crossed the threshold and entered the common room, asking, "Why don't you have a drink with us?"

She was about my age, dark-haired; I assumed she was the daughter of one of the gentlemen in the tugboat's cockpit.

"It's ok. I just want to relax for a while then hit the hay," I said.

"Are you sure? Come have a drink," she asked.

"I just want to watch my fighting robots destroy things. But thank you."

She nodded her head in disappointment and returned to the party. I think she just needed someone else in that room because she probably heard all of Captain Cottonwood's stories a thousand times. But the fighting robots were on, and there was nothing left in me.

The next room was the Vodyanoy room. Similar to the Hippocampus, but larger. This had a single bed against the white wall, and had a square window that looked out to the pier. The room was at the other side of the boat, and I had to walk past all the others to use the washroom.

That evening, I awoke around 3:30 am to use the bathroom. It's an odd sensation waking up in the dead of night on a boat. We were docked at the pier all the time but for the first few moments, you believe in your heart of hearts you are at sea and have no idea how you got there. Tugboats are powerful things. Their purpose is to pull ships. It's a small ship that moves a larger ship. They are small and they have two massive cycloidal propellers located under the hull. The first-ever tugboat was called the Charlotte Dundas. We were staying on its distant cousin, the tugboat Lightweight Paperweight. All the rooms had names of sea creatures.

1. THE HIPPOCAMPUS ROOM.
2. THE VODYANOY ROOM.
3. THE DRY MOLLUSK ROOM.
4. HOLLY'S ROOM.
5. THE CAPTAIN'S QUARTERS.

Hippocampus is a cross between a horse and a fish, also called a seahorse.

Vodyanoy is a cross between an elderly man and a frog. He is considered an angry creature, often destroying man-made water-based structures like dams and water mills. He swims alone, kidnaps individuals, and brings them to his underwater lair to be his slaves.

Mollusk refers to some shellfish, like snails or squids, having a soft body with a shell. Squids belong to the family of mollusks, known as cephalopods. The room, titled *Dry*, used to house the captain's collection of mollusks displayed on the walls.

Holly is the name given to a female siren, a creature that is half woman and half fish. The legend of sirens is rooted in mythology, portraying them as enchanting creatures capable of luring sailors to their doom. Their songs were so intoxicating that men would abandon logic and reason, jumping off their ships to swim towards these mesmerizing beings of sound and beauty. Despite sirens typically not having legs, she apparently did.
(Note: Apparently Captain Cottonwood encountered her in his youth. It is unclear whether he met her at sea. It is unclear if she took his thumb. It is unclear if she still walks among us.)

The Captain's Quarters is the room where the captain originally slept, but he no longer enters that room, and the reasons for this are unknown.

The boat had the captain's history displayed everywhere: black and white, hardly in-focus pictures of him holding giant fishes, and him looking into the abyss of the ocean during sunsets at various ages. It featured an unusual 3D display frame showcasing various sailor knots, alongside a store-bought, hand-weathered wooden sign that read, *Life is better on a Tugboat.* Such little quotes were scattered about, perhaps to deceive or ease the edges of his hardship. Yet, his presence permeated every room and corner of that boat.

At the turn of the century, a museum in the city had a two-part retrospective on Art in the 20th century. The first part was art from 1900–1949, and the second part was art from 1950–1999. The exhibition was extended in an almost crossover two-part event.

These works were a collection of what the museum could get on loan from other museums and private collectors for the exhibit. The second part of this retrospective is what interested me the most, mostly because the boom of pop art happened during that time, and some of Andy Warhol's work would be there.

A gentleman named Pablo Picasso also had some of his work on display. His works were in the first part of the exhibit (1900–1949), but they were also on display in the museum during the second part (1950–1999).

Pablo Picasso, considered one of the most, if not the most, influential artist(s) of the 20th century. He is credited as one of the founders of the Cubism movement. This movement was divided into two different periods or phases: the Analytic and the Synthetic. The first phase shows work as the mind would perceive the image rather than the eye. Soft facial features were replaced with squares and other sharp shapes to represent an idea of a face, rather than what is seen in everyday life. The second phase featured simple forms and objects in a bold and brash color scheme. Picasso painted a series of works where his color scheme reflected moods of blue. These works are known as Picasso's Blue Period. It was during a painful rhythm in his life when his friend and fellow artist, Carles Casagemas, took his own life. The first painting in this series is *Casagemas in his Coffin* (1901).

Some of the paintings from this Blue Period were on display. I had never met this man, had limited knowledge of his personal life, seen his works reproduced in magazines and in pop culture. But I'd never seen one of his works in person. The museum had a room for him; a room for his paintings. As soon as I entered into that room, my entire body flipped inside out. My head started to spin, and my stomach tied itself in knots. I had to leave the room; leave the museum entirely. Those paintings were alive. Picasso had died before I was born, but you could feel him in that room. He was alive in these paintings. The man was a lightning bolt in a human body, and you could experience that electricity of sorrow and loss in his work. For a moment, you were standing in the center of one man's pain. He was in that room. His paintings were bursting off the canvas. You could feel his frustration with the world. The weight of his life was bouncing off the walls. The explosive dynamite of his work went right through me.

Captain Cottonwood's tugboat had shadows of that same darkness in all its corners. That night, as I was stumbling through his boat, I passed Captain Cottonwood's room and saw him fully clothed, lying face down on the floor in the doorway. *My God, he must be dead!* I thought to myself. *The captain is dead!* He wasn't moving at all. His bed was only six feet away from the door. He must have tripped on the carpet and broken his neck on the fall. I stood there for a moment trying to figure out what to do. His wife hadn't been on the boat at all. And she wasn't here now. I never even met her. I didn't know if I should wake the others, call her, or throw him overboard. *I should've had that drink with him! He's dead, and I could've had a drink with him before he died*, I thought. Then I bent down to see if I could find a pulse but whispered first, "Captain Ted? Are you alright?!"

He turned his head towards me and said, "Ya," then laid face down on the floor. He wasn't dead! I felt relieved. I didn't have to look for Holly, call the coroner, or tell his wife that I found him face-planted on the floor of the tugboat, Lightweight Paperweight, dead as a doornail. I was planning on doing it in a letter or in one of my decoupage postcards. But he was alive. Captain Ted said, *"Ya."* Dead men don't say that. He said it as if I was disturbing him. Like it was Wednesday night, and the captain always sleeps fully clothed face-planted on the floor in the doorway. I had to step over him to go to the bathroom. I had to step over him twice! The next day, he didn't mention anything about sleeping on the floor, and neither did I.

After my disappointment of not finding a dead body on a boat and the Needle being closed, I did take a trip to the well-known coffee house, The Starbucks, where it still had its original store. The original location was 2000 Western Ave., and it later moved to 1912 Pike Place in 1976. Technically it's the second store location but recognized as the first official store. It sits on a block of stores between Virginia Street and Stewart Street. I managed to take a wander inside. It still had that 1970s warehouse feel and the original, brown circle logo with the double-tailed siren, fully naked from the waist up. Wasn't sure if I could show that image on live television.

Since we had to eat out every night, I would sometimes dine with Kenneth. He was in bad shape that night. Kenneth had backed up and hit a concrete block in the parking area where we were that day. It was the underbelly in the back. There's a thin metal siding that is above the tires, and he ended up bending it as he hit the concrete. He was an emotional wreck. He didn't want to tell the office or even me for that matter. I had to coax him into spilling the beans on what was bothering him. He made me promise not to tell the office. He was going to take it to a body shop and pay for the damage himself. He didn't want to have this on his conscience.

He really liked the company and wanted to work for them again in the future. He thought if he destroyed the truck, he wouldn't be hired again. He showed me what he had done. It wasn't destroyed beyond recognition or anything like that, it was just bent a little. I told him something worse happened to another driver on the first day of the campaign last year. "Mum's the word," I said. And he found a way to get it fixed.

That was a strange day. That same morning, one of the *Grannies* was freaking out because her old dealer was hanging out in the area, and she didn't want to run into him. It was freezing cold that day. She showed up in jeans and a sweatshirt, shivering to her core. I gave her my winter gloves and assured her that no one would recognize her in the wig and glasses. She told me she was trying to straighten out her life and didn't want to see this guy. It was the dead of winter, and she was freezing because she didn't have a winter coat. I walked over to Starbucks and got coffee for all the models that morning. I gave her the first one. She drank it like it was the first cup of coffee she ever had. She worked for us the entire week without running into her old friend. I noticed her every morning in the corner of my eye when I was in the *Cube*. On the last day, I handed her one of our winter jackets and said, "Here, take this. And if Donovan or Jerry gives you any lip, you tell them to talk to me."

She smiled and walked away with the coat and the gloves I gave her earlier. And I think one of the gray wigs.

When we were there, Seattle had its largest snowfall since 1990. Back at the boat it was time for the final room Ted promised me on the tugboat Lightweight Paperweight – the Captain's Quarters. This room was on the second level right above the cockpit, with two huge windows looking out to Elliott Bay. The bed was much bigger and was in the center of the room. The whole thing was wood with an old rotary phone next to the door. On either side of the bed were the Sidelights – red and green lights that signal passing boats, allowing them to know where you are approaching. The red light signals the left, or Port side, and the green signals the right, or Starboard side. These lights were in brass fixtures on both sides of the bed. You could turn on one or both to illuminate the room. These lights had a dull inner glow to them. It was snowing like crazy that night, and I turned on both Port and Starboard lights and watched the snow fall like pebbles from the sky and completely disappear on the Bay.

It was time to move on. The day we left the pier, Captain Cottonwood was on deck and thanked us for choosing his boat for our stay in Seattle.

"I want to thank you, gentlemen, for staying here," he said.

"Thank you, Captain. We wouldn't have wanted to stay anywhere else," I replied.

"Thank you."

Captain Cottonwood smiled and shook our hands.

"If you ever find yourselves in Elliot Bay, you're always welcome here. I always have room."

We smiled, grabbed our bags, and strolled along the pier toward the road. Taking in the boats for the last time, the only sound was the clicking of luggage wheels on the pressure-treated wooden baseboards. Then, a final question crossed my mind, and I turned to Ted.

"By the way, Captain, who was that young woman that was here the other night?" I shouted.

"Oh, that's Holly!" Captain Cottonwood cried.

CHAPTER 25

Jitterbugs,
Tommy Tune,
and Just Another Tuesday Night
at The Angry Cobbler

If we went any more north, we would hit the Canadian border. So, we headed south on I-5, back to Arizona. The four of us spent the most time apart on this stretch of road. We didn't even stay at the same motels during this part of the tour.

On the second day of our southbound journey, it was getting late, my eyes were growing heavy, when I spotted a Jubilee Cottage Hotel (JCH) sign glowing in the distance, making the decision that this would be the place to to stop for the evening. Speaking to Kenneth earlier, we planned to meet up for breakfast at a place he was familiar with.
(Note: Kenneth - truck driver by trade, knew all the restaurants.)

It was just after 9:30 pm when I wandered into The Angry Cobbler bar, an unassuming place attached to the hotel, hosting live music that night. The marquee read, *Flatfeet Dance Nite: This Tuesday. Featuring: Davie Henshaw and The Tranquil Jitterbugs. LIVE!* No, it wasn't a dancing magician with an oversized bug circus. No, it wasn't a tall, lanky tap-dancing man with reflective shoes. It was as the marquee stated. My understanding of what a Jitterbug was had changed over the years.

When I was living in New Jersey, a gentleman named Tommy Tune performed a one-man show called, *A Salute to Fred Astaire*. With a dance background and a towering height of six feet and six inches, the entire night was all about him, just him and his dancing.

The show took place in an off-off-off Broadway theater at Montclair State College (aka Montclair State University). Before the final number, he sat down on a chair center stage, talking directly to the audience as he changed his shoes.

The first thing he said was, *"This is my Upper Montclair debut."* The shoes he laced on were probably a size 24, adorned with tiny reflective mirrors or crystals covering the tops of both tap shoes. He exclaimed, *"Don't you just love these shoes!"*

A beam of light hit a hundred tiny mirrors as he stood up.

The stage, dark except for the light reflecting off his shoes, made the chair vanish, and he somehow morphed into some type of bug. Wires suddenly appeared out of the back of his jacket with red feathers at the end.

This was his final number of the evening. It was called, *Jitterbug*. Whether it was his unique dance style, his towering height, or the footwear, he became a contrast to his own self, separating in style, movement, and appearance. He transformed into a Jitterbug.

———————————————

My newfound understanding of what a Jitterbug is and could be unfolded at The Angry Cobbler hotel bar on the western side of the United States, a land I had yet traveled extensively. I ordered a chicken sandwich and fried cheese, sitting at a small round table in front of a large wooden dance floor, awaiting The Tranquil Jitterbugs.

The place was rather full, and you were lucky to secure a spot. The crowd was soft and mellow. Slowly, on an unassuming stage, three young, hourglass-shaped, black-haired women appeared, each in a short white polka dot dress. One wore green, one red, and one black. All three donned white tights and Mary Jane shoes, with eyelash extensions and ruby red lipstick.

They began playing easy Big Band and light jazz numbers, nothing too wild—just slow and easy tunes. The kick drum displayed the name *The Tranquil Jitterbugs* in dangerous green and black font. The drummer, in the black dress with white polka dots, showcased a green and black dragon tattoo on her right arm, extending from shoulder to wrist.

Besides the drums, there was a dark purple cello, a trumpet, a fiddle, a black banjo, a saxophone, an electronic guitar with wood paneling, and a French horn. All instruments were lined up on or against a red wooden shelf to the right of the drummer. The three ladies swam in a pool of red and green light.

The woman in green played the cello, the woman in red handled the fiddle, and the woman in black manned the drums.

They didn't utter a word; they just played. Thomas James Tune was the only human I associated with a Jitterbug until I witnessed these Jitterbugs on the other side of the country.

And then, without warning, the mood of the place changed. The lady on trumpet played a fanfare and then stopped. They all halted, and the room fell silent. Each of the girls slowly changed positions and instruments. The one in black took the cello, the one in green took the drums, and the one in red took the saxophone. The lights shifted from red and green to purple, and Davie Henshaw took the stage.

Enter Davie Henshaw, a thin, tall man with dark hair, dressed in a green and black striped, double-breasted suit with red and black striped pants. He wore wing-tipped shoes in white and brown, and sported a dark pencil mustache. Exploding onto the stage, he grabbed his guitar and stood at the edge of the floor. The lights dimmed once more, and a spotlight illuminated Henshaw.

Then, out of nowhere, twenty people made their way to the dance area, and everyone, every single one, started swing dancing. The East Coast Swing, the Lindy Hop, the Balboa—everything except the Dinky One Step. There was a guy who had to weigh at least 300 pounds, and he was tossing girls in the air like they were tissues. They all executed a series of moves, then switched partners. I had never seen an entire room start swing dancing like that before. The Tranquil Jitterbugs bewitched an entire crowd of people. Turning to the couple sitting next to me, I exclaimed, "This is incredible. I've never seen anything like this!"

I was absolutely amazed. They all knew how to swing. It was like someone buttered the floor, and every one of them was poised and graceful in their maneuvers. It was a wonderland of sound, style, and movement—either the room dancing or The Ladies of Jitterbugs playing, Henshaw singing, or perhaps it was the fried cheese. But it was spectacular.

The woman at the table next to me leaned over and shouted, *"They're in a swing class. They take lessons just down the road and then come here on Tuesdays!"*

CHAPTER

Interstate 10,
and The Thing on It

Interstate 5 is 1,381 miles long, and in the state of California alone, its length is 796 miles. It runs from Mexico to Canada, and I found myself spending a lot of time on this stretch of road. It was the place where I first battled tumbleweeds, adopted a blue rooster, saw the concrete dinosaurs at The Cabazon Dinosaurs, and witnessed the the talents of the Jitterbugs.

One of the spots on my list was the Cabazon Dinosaurs, recognized as the World's Biggest Dinosaurs, despite not being genuine dinosaurs but rather constructed from concrete. We passed them twice during this journey – once heading up to Seattle and once on the return. Most of the joints along the stretch felt like they were at the edge of the world, with minimalistic surroundings, a couple of truckers, and a young woman or two with their newborn children sitting at a roadside dinner. Mostly watching the small television barely hanging on the counter and observing the local weather updates. Snow was on the menu, and lots of it.

Interstate 5 became the longest stretch of road I had ever traveled alone, but there are many things on this highway that can catch your eye. This was one of them. I ended up passing this a few times before deciding to see it.

Interstate 10, Exit 322: you will find the one of the largest billboard advertisements in the United States. Florida has the most billboards per state. I am referring to the number of billboards used to advertise a single attraction—more than 200 of them. South of the Border in South Carolina is a close second with 175 billboards advertisements for a single destination.

It's wonderful seeing these billboards when driving the desolate highway, and it gets you instantly interested about the place in the coming miles. Lots of them tell you exactly what you're in for: The Cabazon Dinosaurs are exactly that, The World's Largest Ball of Twine is precisely that.

The Thing roadside attraction is another place entirely. The billboards glowed in bright yellow, proclaiming *The Thing?* in a purplish-blue font. The taglines echoed a sense of uncertainty: *Mystery of the Desert, What is It?* and *It's a Wonder.* That was all that was written on the signs. Sure, there are variations of that theme on different billboards throughout, but that was it.

Thing is a name of the nameless.

Some things have names specific to what they are, like hot dogs, hair dryers, and flying cars. Then there are things that exist without a clear definition. The Thing, a roadside attraction, falls into the latter category.

One becomes curious when first spotting these billboards. And right off of Interstate 10, you can go and see it. I wasn't sure what The Thing on Interstate 10 was. My understanding of what it was came from the American monster movie. And people use that word all the time. They say, *"Go get me that Thing."* and *"Come on, we have to meet grandma at the Thing in fifteen minutes."* It can mean anything from a tool to a place. The Thing (roadside attraction) had no other information about what it was on the billboards. It's really an idea, and I got sucked into it.

Exit 322 leads to the parking area right in front of the yellow sign that spanned the width of this one-story warehouse. It read: Souvenirs, T-Shirts, Jewelry, Gifts, Museum, and *The Thing?* in all its yellow and purplish-blue color boldface lettering. The word *ENTRANCE* was painted in yellow with a red square somewhere on the compound. A petroleum fuel station is in front, and *The Thing* is somewhere close by. It's in the middle of the desert in the center of nowhere.

Inside, various items with *The Thing?* stamped all over them were for sale, but no pictures or even hints at what it was. The entrance led to a small labyrinth with a false rock doorway adorned with the yellow sign above, and admission was only $1. Initially, it felt like you had just walked out the back door, but then the realization hit that you were in a compound. Following a concrete walkway marked by faded yellow footprints, you reached the final room housing *The Thing*. A low chain-link fence provided a sense of walking between people's backyards as you entered a sequence of buildings.

The first held mannequins in cages and one of Adolf Hitler's cars. The second displayed an assortment of old items, from rifles and wood carvings to driftwood sculptures and ancient kitchen devices. Native American art was scattered throughout in glass cases with driftwood on top.

This collection left me confused, as it seemed like a mishmash of seemingly unrelated objects. I dashed through all of this, eager to see the main event. It felt as if the wool had been pulled over my eyes. It is like if someone asked you over for dinner, and when you got there, it turned out to be their aunt's bridge night, and you had to hear stories about their vacation on a discount cruise.

It was a hodgepodge of things that had no meaning in relation to each other, featuring large plywood cutouts of people, more yellow signs with vague statements about life and questionable facts, and a lack of thematic consistency. *Why was there a yellow-fringed-topped surrey? Why were there mannequins in black iron medieval cages in this apparent lack of connection among the kitchen appliances and driftwood assortments? What did all this mean? And what was Hitler's car doing in the desert?*

After beelining it to the end, and finally making it to the warehouse where the prize was kept, the only way you knew it was the end was because there was the final yellow sign that stated, *Here in this room lies The Thing*, metaphorically speaking.

It was in a long hanger with transparent green corrugated panels that let in the sunlight in. But the green panels were on the side of the hanger. The roof had an aluminum triangle design held up by metal beams, giving everything inside a green tint. A square, chain-link fence separated you from the items, giving the place an old-school field trip feeling but without the tour guide. At the end, in a cylinder block case four blocks high on the floor with the top covered in glass, was *The Thing*. It was under a sheet of glass, and I looked at it with curiosity, the same way all the people had been looking at me behind my sheet of glass. And then, with no answers to any questions I left the exhibit. But I saw *The Thing*.

I walked out of the museum, checked the experience off my list of places to go and things to see, hopped back into the *Tamiflu* minivan, and drove away.

CHAPTER

27

End of Year Two,
and A Bottle of Caffeine Pills

The four *Cubes* returned to the back parking lot of The CJH, and we gutted everything out clean and neat. Kenneth headed back home to deal with his living situation, while Donavan and Jerry were going to see *Mother*. They had a house full of goods they accumulated and were ready to decorate.

We spent a few final days at the hotel, and we knew for sure this would be the last time we were going to be doing this gig. The office had new management close us out. This was the exit interview and the wrap-up.

We didn't recognize her from any of the meetings or anything we did before, and no one had never seen her in the New York office. She took the podium with the confidence and passion of a new CEO of the company that you had worked for your whole life and you had never even heard of this person, and suddenly, they are congratulating you on your life's work and saying things like, *"We knew you were a great asset to the team since the first day we met you"* and *"Throughout the years, we had seen some rough times, but we did it together."* Like going to a class reunion, and every single person there was a stranger.

She talked about the accolades and the surpassing of expectations on this campaign. She mentioned the awards they took home last year: The PRO Awards for Best Overall Promotion & Most Innovative Communication Strategy and the APMA Globes Award for First Place in Most Innovative Communication Strategy- Global. Even the sales were beyond what they had projected. Everyone was hopping around saying, *"We beat The Brown Beverage Brewing Company."* These awards were given to the campaign the previous year, and they were still celebrating, which is understandable. If you are going to celebrate, you might as well do the whole year.

There wasn't much for her to do for a climax. She wasn't going to pop out of a birthday cake or anything. She presented the end like a book report.

On game shows, you have a great prize awaiting you at the end of the journey through a bizarre, physical task of great skill or a complex mathematical riddle, like a Caribbean cruise, a wicker chaise lounge set, a new car, or a billy goat.

As for our great prize, the bonus, the celebration for exceeding projected expectations, cutting production costs down by half, and covering twice as much ground, all the while working in strange and unpredictable lands, we received a *Road Atlas* and a bottle of Snap N'Awake pills – a bottle of caffeine pills.

Sitting at a table during the wrap-up of one of the greatest campaigns the company had ever created, I listened to the accolades, awards won, and the boasting about beating The Brown Beverage Brewing Company. Sales had skyrocketed, exceeding expectations on every level, and the luck of getting the green light to do this thing twice. And I got a road map and a bottle of pep pills as a bonus. I tuned the rest of the meeting out.

In my mind the next logical step was to dismantle *The Boxes*, and sell all the interior furniture and fixtures. Perhaps you'd find the salt and pepper grinders in a thrift shop, unaware they were once plastic statues in the *Cube*.

Maybe they'd donate or give the trucks away to delivery companies or orphanages. I thought I might come across a repainted, restructured truck hauling orange soda pop, or ball point pens, or tube socks, never realizing it was the skeleton of the *glass apartment* I traveled across the country in.

Or I'd walk down the street, gaze through a bay window at a freshly baked strawberry rhubarb pie or key lime cake, never realizing it was the same window I looked out of and saw a thousand different landscapes. You definitely had that last day feeling. There was no way, no way in the world they would do this again. This was lightning striking twice, and it would never strike a third time. I knew that.

CHAPTER

Year One Upshot,

The Outstanding Warrant,

Southern Living,

SoloMarÉ-Tech,

and The Alf Coloring Book Fiasco

After spending *Year One* in the cold, often harsh, winter of the Midwest, it was time to get back to New York. The flowers were blooming, and the air was sweet. Spring in New York City is the best place to be. My body landed in Brooklyn, but my head was still in the clouds. Knowing that I needed a few days to crash, crash hard I did.

After a high-flying adventure on the road, the best thing to do is get to a quiet place, get your house in order, get hydrated, and get some sleep—about three days of sleep.

Unpack everything from your clothes to the colorful, strange, and unusual keepsakes you picked up along the way. Wash the dirt off and remind yourself where you are at that moment. You just had a strange and beautiful romance with the places you visited, something you'll never have again.

It's time to go home. Keep the things you need and get rid of the things you don't. It's best to do it at the same time in the same day.

Then, when you start to feel yourself fall off that high, you can fully implode. Don't make any major decisions until you level out. Just sit tight. Have some space operas ready for casual viewing, and make sure you are fully stocked on coffee.

But there was one little thing that needed to be taken care of – the warrant out for my arrest. I also considered the possibility that Officer Jenkins could still come and get me, as he had my home address.

Returning to my apartment in a time of transition, the two people I was living with were moving on to greener pastures, leaving me with two beds to fill.

Enter Hogarth Del Monte. We had known each other for a number of years. He was subletting my room that winter, and I was in a position to offer him first refusal for the apartment as his residence.

At one point, we were living together in a house converted into five living units. It was small, holding no beds, and it had a makeshift plastic shower. We both slept on the floor.

Hogarth is tall, about six feet four inches, with dark hair and wide eyes that hold an old soul. We met when we were lads at art school, and you would believe he had already lived a thousand lifetimes.

Calm and clear in his actions, he speaks with a mastery of all things cultural. If you were looking for a logical, smart, and grounded way to solve a series of complex problems, he was your go-to man.

At that time, Hogarth was the only teenager I had ever known who looked at home reading *The New York Times Sunday Edition* in his pajamas.

We found that tiny, North Carolina apartment because we were dealing with the bureaucracy of getting approval to live off-campus as full-time students. The university had a certain number of living quarters and beds to fill, providing out-of-state students a housing fee for those beds. In-state scholars had the opportunity to dodge that by-law entirely.

We wanted to meet those requirements and bypass the housing fee. To do that, we had to go in front of the housing board and state our case. The heart of our argument was that the facilities provided to students by the university were not adequate for the growing demands of our capital venture. These inadequacies were hindering our projections for our quarterly growth and ultimately our success. We needed to live and store our equipment off-campus for our growing business to thrive. Hogarth and I had started a business. And we had to sound legit.

We embarked on our first business venture together at the age of 19. The company was called Clowns N' Syndicate, A Party Clown Company. Although we worked events and generated revenue, the business served as a front, a red herring, for our primary goal: establishing residency in the state of North Carolina.

To become a resident, we needed a permanent address. Once secured, the next step was obtaining a North Carolina driver's license. The law required us to live at that address for twelve consecutive months and have employment in the state to pay taxes. As we crunched the numbers, we also sought additional employment, aiming for an hourly salary in a North Carolina trade to bridge the tax gap.

During that summer, I worked as a midnight telemarketer for SoloMarÉ-Tech, a company specializing in 21st-century technology for people living in the 20th century. The office was housed in a tan, stucco building near the downtown business district, and had a lower level dedicated to research and development.

I ventured onto their office one afternoon, where all the employees wore white lab coats and had laminated keycards displaying their picture, rank, and security code. Two different worlds – we were upstairs in casual attire, working with old technology, and had a plastic plate on our door that said SoloMarÉ-Tech, while downstairs, they had up-to-date software, leather shoes, and a brass plate by the front door that said SoloMarÉ Advancement of Science and Future Center (SMASFC). Important work done by important people.

Working on the second floor at the Telemarketing Call Center (SMTCC), we cold-called the West Coast, attempting to sign individuals up for a low-interest credit card over the telephone. We never saw the people we called; we were on the telephone with them all night, but it they were in a different time zone.

The two floors couldn't have been more different. Starting our day at 4 pm, we worked an eight-hour shift, getting off just after midnight. The first-floor employees worked all hours of the day. After work, we would sit on a lawn chair on the concrete slab right outside my apartment, enjoying some ice-cold beverages and sampling some of North Carolina's finest tobacco. The three tiki torches, lent to me by a neighboring couple who used them in their wedding ceremony, would provide light at night.

In that back apartment, there were three of us: me, Hogarth, and a young dancer named Nora, who was in between housing arrangements for the summer. The three of us slept side by side on the floor with the door open all night due to the heat of North Carolina summers. Did I mention we didn't have air conditioning? Hogarth had some eccentricities—he didn't want to shower in our bathroom because he didn't like the sound of water hitting the plastic sides. Additionally, he insisted on living only by natural light, avoiding any artificial lighting once the sun went down. For three months, we didn't touch a light switch, and a handful of candles illuminated the apartment, creating an atmosphere enhanced by marital torches flickering on the lawn. Southern alien like insects were the only sounds you could hear. Candlelight was the only light seen inside. Reading by that dim flicker added a fresh layer of meaning to the summer novel of choice: *Mary Shelley's Frankenstein.*

That summer, I was the only one working the straight and narrow. We were in our early twenties, contemplating whether to return to art school in the fall. It was a time of reflection and a decision of what kind of people we wanted to be in the world. For the first time, I was with my generation who were asking questions about morality, death, and taxes. For the first time, I realized we weren't children anymore; we were in the world now.

My focus that summer was to make enough money to pay the state income tax, a goal that kept my mind busy. It was a wonderful time to be lost, with a low overhead, a convenience store that sold beer on the cheap, and the laundromat a few blocks away. We knew the local bodega owner by name. There were two bodegas, right across the street from each other. One of them was very popular; the other one, not so much. The owner of that one got out of the game by blowing it up. And I mean quite literally, he blew up his own store.

Every night, something was always happening in that closet of an apartment. We would sit on those lawn chairs, and Nora would dance in the backyard to the music in her head. A few drifters would find themselves sitting on that concrete slab, drinking beer, pondering our existence. Some were neighbors, some were teachers, some were religious fanatics, and one was a drummer for a local rock band that was gaining popularity. He found joy in listening to the soothing yet oddly uneasy sounds of Enya. *Ah, he likes the Enya,* I thought, or I hope I just thought it.

We would then fade into the night like the motley crew that we were, at peace in the center of our own chaos, unsure of the future and wanting nothing more.

It was quite a juxtaposition between my work and residence during that time. In the mornings, drenched in sweat, I would peel myself off the floor, walk a few feet to the open door, and wave to my neighbor tending her flower garden.

"Good morning, Ms. Saunders. The black-eyed Susans look fantastic."

"Oh, thank you, Randy. They do look rather sweet, don't they."

She had a variety of flowers—heartleaf foam flowers, dwarf crested irises, daylilies, sunflowers—and she grew blueberries and corn.

"Don't sell yourself short; they look beautiful."

"Thank you. Oh, Randy, I just made a blueberry cobbler. Would you like some for your important work tonight?"

"I would love some."

Ms. Saunders would always call the fuzz when our late-night evenings got too loud. I would compliment her flowers the next day, and she would feel guilty about disrupting our midnight carouse and make it up to me with her homemade blueberry cobbler in a used Cool Whip container. It was a little game we played. The cops came by so often that we knew their first names. They would say the same thing every time.

"Randy someone called, said that things were getting a little rambunctious."

It was just the three of us with a few odd ducks dropping by, just a couple of scalawags hanging out on a concrete slab drinking beer by torchlight. My landlord thought that we were having naked parties every night. The only thing he ever asked of me was to invite him to one. Never to mow the yard or shovel the snow off the walk in the winter, just invite him to this made-up idea in his head of the naked orgies we were throwing at one of his properties. He was the only man I ever met that broke a sweat changing a fuse. The entire time we were living in that house, we never had a naked party.

Ms. Saunders lived alone, and she would always find a reason to go to her garden when I was outside. She would do things like move her watering can or pick up her spade. I believe she just wanted someone to compliment her flower garden every day. She knew I disappeared in the afternoon and got home after midnight. We shared a driveway, and her door was about thirty feet from mine. We knew each other's habits and patterns. She would be in her garden most afternoons in *that* heat. I don't know how she did it. I would find great comfort going to the office for a couple of hours just because they had air conditioning. I would pack up the cobbler she made with my lunch, wave to Ms. Saunders in her bonnet, and head out to the office.

Even though the town was small, I rarely saw anyone from the office, except one. Only because we lived on the same street. He was an older gentleman with white hair and the voice of a thousand saints, and he could sell a low-interest credit card to the same family twice. All the telemarketers were on the same floor, and after a while, you could recognize everyone's mood by the sound of their voice. You always knew when he had a sale; he would go up an octave when he got one.

I drove a light blue 1984 Toyota Tercel hatchback and passed by his house on my way to work, coincidentally catching him heading to his car. Every day his son would run to him and hug him as if it was the last time he was going to see him, and his wife would give him his brown bag lunch. I would see him eat it in the break room every night. I never knew families like that existed. He worked hard every night cold-calling complete strangers, selling them credit cards, and went home to a family that loved him. And he wanted nothing more than that.

My work there was for the purpose of paying state income tax. I couldn't think any further into the future. Someone else's grandmother was making me blueberry cobbler, and I was sleeping on the floor with two other people. I was just excited to have some walk around money. I would pull into the office parking lot just before 4 pm, park in the back next to an oak tree that gave great shade to my car. Then, I'd strike a match and have a honey-toasted tobacco cigarette right under the oak, looking forward to midnight. I had a job, a car, an apartment, and a cigarette in my hand, I thought to myself, *It doesn't get any better than this.*

THIS WAS MY IMPORTANT WORK AT SOLOMARÉ-TECH.

Each telemarketer had their cubicle, and you would be stationed at this cubicle all night. Each one had a telephone connected to a headset via a long black curly cord and a personal computer. A supercomputer located on the first floor would dial up the home telephone numbers of people residing on the West Coast of the United States at lightning speed. Once they picked up their home phone, the call would be transferred to your phone line. Your computer screen would light up in orange text with the name of the person you needed to speak to. Then you would start your pitch. After the sale or dropped call (hang-up), you would receive another connection within 30 seconds. And every 30 seconds after that call and after that. You had half of a minute between the end of each call to interact with everyone at work. It was just enough time to say *hello,* stretch your back, or compliment someone's new haircut. If you wanted to take a break, you had to pretend you needed to use the facilities. That meant you would take your headset off and whisper to the four managers sitting at the control center that was four feet above everyone's desk, *"I have to go to the bathroom."* Then at the speed of molasses walk to the bathroom, sit in the stall for a moment, regain your composure, then walk back to your workstation.

The office had two shifts: the morning group working 8 am to 4 pm and the evening group working 4 pm till midnight. The phone and computer were also shared with your morning counterpart. The gentleman I shared the space with would clear out all his paperwork and personal items at 4 pm. He was well-organized but had a habit of leaving his caramel cream candy wrappers on the floor. After my shift, I would clear out all of my work, personal items, and coffee cups, tidying it up for the morning. So, every night, we brought in our paperwork and some decorations to spruce up the wall of the light blue cubicle.

The telephone was attached to a small computer. The computer gave you only the barebones of information on the individuals you were calling: the first and last name of the resident and the home address. The paperwork was a specific, well-crafted, simple series of legal mumbo-jumbo stating the rules, guidelines, and responsibilities for accepting the card with bullet points of information relayed in a casual coffee shop conversation-like concerned best friend style of speech. Besides the computer and telephone, the desk was bare. You were allowed to bring personal items of your choice, like a suction cup basketball net or your favorite ball point pen. Many employees had pictures of their kids tacked up on the small walls next to their scripts.

To spruce up my cubicle and add a touch of familiarity to the office setting, I decided on the only obvious solution – tack up a page from an old Alf coloring book that someone sent me in a recent care package.

Care packages are boxes filled with odd stuff you would randomly find in your attic or basement. You would slap them in a box and mail them to friends with a note saying something like, *Just found these odd and ends and I thought you could use them on your journey through life.* This coloring book was one item that was in the last care package I received.
(Note: Alf was a sitcom about an alien from another planet that comes to earth and lives with a family in the suburbs.)

I playfully colored it outside the lines with wax pencils, wrote in black above the picture, *Dad, I love you,* slipped it into my paperwork, brought it to work, and casually tacked it up on the cubicle next to my script.

268

All the young women would walk by during their breaks, turning their eye to the colorful coloring book picture, and the note, then gleefully ask me, "You have a kid!?"

I didn't have a kid, but they didn't know that.

I would smile and respond, "Yes, I have a son."

"How old?" they asked.

"He's 12," I would say back with a sense of pride. Confused, they would ask, "How old are you?"

"I'm 19."

Then suddenly another call would be automatically transferred to my phone by the SoloMarÉ-Tech S-2847 Supercomputer. I would shift my focus to the call, and they would either catch the riddle or believe in their hearts that I had a son. The rumor bounced around the office that I had a *kid*. People were talking about it at the water cooler. Sooner or later, it was going to bite me in the ass.

It was a warm Tuesday evening around 9pm. I had just gotten a diet orange soda from the vending machine and was standing at my desk during the pause between calls. *Ker-snap!* goes the aluminum tab. The air briefly carried the scent of orange cleaner. Suddenly, one of the young women working the phones approached me. We had spoken to each other just about every night, discussing what we did over weekend and her choice footwear. Just friendly banter, chit-chat, nothing special. She couldn't have been a day older than twenty, with long brown hair. One night, right on the office floor under the spying eyes of the control center and a thousand, non-flattering, fluorescent lights, she asked me point-blank if I would go out with her. This was out of the blue; she never gave an inkling that she was interested in my companionship. I only assumed she thought I had a son and put something together in her mind that I was a good father! She asked, "Randy, do you have a girlfriend?"

"No, not at this juncture in my life," I replied.

"Would you like to go out sometime?" she asked.

Our eyes met and she smiled.

I mumbled something in response, unsure of how to handle this, I noticed my hands were moving. I had my headset on, in the middle of a call, and apparently, she thought I was this *Father of the Year*. I wasn't expecting my night to go this way. This was just another shift of tedious work when suddenly someone asked a very personal question. She kept looking at me with those sparkling brown, smiling eyes, but I kept dodging them. I could only look at the dictators in the control center, those sterile beings of merciless compassion. Finding no comfort in them, I didn't know what to say.

She could feel me pulling away, yet she asked me a direct question with her whole heart in a fully lit room, surrounded by people selling low-interest credit cards to strangers on the other side of the country. She wasn't nervous; she didn't shift her weight. She stood her ground and waited for an answer. Trapped and completely wired to my computer, I was looking for an escape. We both turned our heads and stared at the wax-colored picture hanging two feet away, directly above the phone. It said, *Dad, I love you.* No denying that. She sensed at that moment I wasn't interested. With my headset on, I anxiously awaited the supercomputer to send me another call, but I would've settled for an earthquake.

Then she asked, "Is it because I'm pregnant?"

———————————————————

With the salary from SoloMaré-Tech making up the difference, within the year, I became a resident of the state, dropping the tuition drastically. In the simplest terms, our argument was that the housing on campus had two individuals in a single room, and it was limited in the amount of storage space needed for our stuff, including, but not limited to, our invoice files, balloons, face paints, props, and most of all, our costumes and clown shoes. Our argument was solid. We were now a legitimate company. We filed for a business name, a sales and use permit, and opened a bank account. We had business cards and and checks with the slogan that said, *You make 'em cry. We make 'em laugh.*

Once our paperwork was in order, we were granted permission by the University's Housing Board to have a residence off campus. We met with them five times, and when all the paperwork came in, we got the thumbs up. The odd thing was the apartment we could afford was half the size of the housing on campus. At one point, we had a third naked person living there.

We only had two costumes, but the Housing Board didn't know that. Every costume and prop we used, we borrowed from the Costume Department on campus. They had thousands of costumes from old shows. All we had to do was request a series of costumes in writing and then sign them out, then return them in the same shape and condition they were lent to us after our event. It was a dream scenario. These were hand-made costumes of the highest quality. We did a huge wedding that spring at the Forsyth Country Club. It was a 16th-century gothic-themed event. Tapered candles, mercury wine glasses, silver trays of grapes on stems, the works. We hired four other guys as models to dress up in the clothing of the period using the University's costumes from a prior production of *William Shakespeare's, The Merchant of Venice.*

We worked the company for about six months, and then closed its doors for the last time after Hogarth decided to depart from school to gallivant his way around Europe using only his appeal, intelligence, and wits. I was granted residency in the state after a year at that address and working a telemarketing job on the side. The company dissolved after we stopped making a profit. I paid tax in its name for the last time, closed the company bank account, and sold the remaining assets.
(Note: We didn't have any assets.)

We made just enough to get by. It was getting to be a full-time job. At one point, we were acting as agents for stand-up comics and talking with a local nightclub that wanted us to book their Thursday Night Line-Up. They wanted five to eight comics. We were in meetings with the owner, and at one point, we looked at each other and said, *"What the hell are we doing!?"* We were a Party Clown company; we only started this so we could get off campus to become residents of the state of North Carolina, and somehow, we became agents for stand-up comics. Hogarth and I met up again in Brooklyn a few years later, and he was now my flatmate.

It was the end of *Year One*, and time to face the music. I had the address that Officer Jenkins gave me to turn myself in once I got back to New York. I had to tackle this before my crash. I was not sure how this worked. I didn't know if I would have to spend the night in jail or if I could just pay a fine. I needed a wingman. I phoned my friend Brad Clayford for this. Brad had been a lifesaver on many occasions a number of times. He lived upstairs in the house back in North Carolina.

We devised a strategic move to extricate myself from this predicament. The game plan was that we both would go to the police station at the crack of dawn on Tuesday, turn myself in, and get the details on what the procedure was going to be. It was like Brad was the bounty hunter.

This was a bench warrant. A *bench warrant* is issued by the Court for failure to appear on your scheduled date. I should have had a lawyer with me. I thought I could represent myself. But I told Ted Williams and his law firm to take a hike back in December, so I was on my own.

That was the big plan. I went into a room with twenty or so guys who were doing the same thing I was doing, turning themselves in. They had different reasons for their warrants; everyone in that room was there of their own volition. We were all then bussed over to the Court. Brad followed by cab. Everyone got into the van, but nobody was cuffed. I guess it was an honor system. The cops didn't seem to care. We just sat in the back of the police van and talked about plans for the summer, women, and everyone's favorite kinds of food. It went something like this.

"You're crazy, I've had all kinds of chocolates from the ones in the wrappers; the white chocolate raspberry is the best in the damn whole box of those Go-Dived chocolates!" someone said.

"I don't know, the peanut butter ones are awfully tasty. It's like a real smooth peanut, it's more like butter than the peanut."

"Guys, you're talking smack. Their chocolate strawberries are the best, bar-none."

"Any fool can dip fruit into chocolate. You can do that at home. I can't make white chocolate at home. I didn't even know there was such a thing as white chocolate. It's like a flying fish. It should not even exist. It's the best of all the chocolates. You have to get that stuff overseas!" one of the guys shouted.

"Bar-none."

I spoke with utter authority. "Bar-none."

I explained the situation to the cops, and they said it's a simple, painless procedure. That no one gets jail time for this. It's mostly paperwork; you'll be out before noon. Once we got to the court and sat down, all the cops assured me and said, *"No problem, it will only take twenty minutes."*

I gave my bank card to the bounty hunter before I went to the police station. That way, when the judge sentenced my fine, Brad could go and get the cash and pay the fine to the clerk.

One hour turned into two and so forth; we sat in the court-room all day, about eight hours. Everyone I met in the morning stood in front of the judge and got their sentence. Some got community service, some got fines, and some got jail time.

And just before the court was about to close for the evening, the judge said, *"Alright, we are adjourned for the day."*

I stood up and said, "Your honor, I believe we have one more case for today."

He then waved me forward, and two young women who were appointed to the state had my paperwork. A gentleman who was appointed to me and everyone who didn't have counsel leaned over and said, *"Why didn't you show up for your court date?"*

"It's a long story," I said.

"They are going to give you community service," he replied.

"No, I want to pay a fine and get this behind me."

He shrugged, stood up, and asked the judge for a fine rather than community service. The young lady representing the Great State of New York asked for the fee to be $300. Then the judge looked at her as if she lost her marbles and said, *"One hundred."* It was a fine negotiation for skipping out on a subway fare and having two cops come to my apartment in Brooklyn.

I wanted to tell her the other $200 was paid in fear and paranoia over the winter. Brad then got up and exited the courtroom. The judge said, *"This needs to be paid today."*

"It's already done. Thank you, Your Honor," I said.

Brad returned in less than a flash with a little more than $200. The fine was paid along with the clerk's fee. A receipt was printed out and placed in my wallet, where it lived for the next five years. Brad saved my skin once again. I thought for sure this would get jail time, but the judge didn't even see my warrant or acknowledge my existence in the courtroom.

It was time for a thank you for Brad. I took him to the first bar we could find and bought him a beer. Once I got back to Brooklyn, it was as if a bag of bricks was taken off my back, and I could now fully breathe. At the end of that day, feeling that it was finally finished, this madhouse adventure. I sat in the rocking chair by the window as the sun was setting and thought to myself, *I just spent the winter in a Glass Apartment on Wheels.* And then I slept for three days.

CHAPTER 29

Returning Home After Year Two,
and The Mannequin at The Door

Getting back to Brooklyn after *Year Two*, I staggered up those stairs to my apartment. It was easy to remember every creak, snap, and pop in that brown-carpeted, old wooden staircase. It was a familiar sensation, and it felt good to be home. Nothing had changed, except the trees were starting to show their spring leaves. The entrance now had a mannequin from one of my roommate's performance projects guarding the door. *Finally, we got one*, I thought. It was standing fully posed at the top of the stairs to the right of the door to my third-floor apartment. He was dapperly dressed in a blue and white pinstripe suit and was wearing a black fedora.

When I got to the landing and turned towards the next flight of stairs for the first time, I saw him. Every time I saw him after that day, knowing full well he was at the top of the stairs, he took a year off my life. He scared the bejesus outta me. Hogarth had found him. I don't know how, I don't know where, but he found him, dressed him up, and placed him beside the door. It scared every single person that turned that set of stairs and looked up – delivery guys, people we invited over for coffee, census workers, religious fanatics, even our 82-year-old, asthmatic, seven-toed Irish landlord. He had a heart attack the first time he saw it. I heard him scream. I believe seeing the mannequin killed him, and his scream brought him back from death.

The apartment had turned into a museum. Each room had an entirely different color painted on the walls. The living room was yellow, the study was green, the kitchen was orange, and the sunroom was white. Hogarth had taken the side bedroom as his residence. It had one of the walls sky blue with white clouds. Books of poetry, playbills, dictionaries, and Shakespeare's complete works were stacked on top of each other in the study under the faux crystal chandelier. I also found out that we now had a study.

Calendars of events at local theaters and galleries were now pinned up on cork boards. Postcards from Chicago, New Mexico, and California were now hanging from bookshelves. Newspapers were neatly tied up with twine and stacked on top of the black and white checker floor in the kitchen. A new coffee mug with a festival or fair name on it would find its way into the cabinet, while cheap souvenir magnets from various states found themselves on the fridge. And another beautiful set of white hotel towels would bring new life and spruce up the bathroom. It was as if every inch had something happening all at the same time. The dark, rich colors and wonderfully complex things that popped out at you here in Brooklyn were different from the bright colors and winsome romantic places I just came from. Those places were personal and true to their owners. This was true to me.

Besides the mannequin at the door, we had a third human living with us. The railroad apartment was the entire third floor of a brownstone in Brooklyn. It was long but only had one bedroom. This was how we made three bedrooms out of one. The stairs led up to a landing with three doors: the front door (main door), the only one with a lock, then to the bedroom, and the third to a side room connected to the bedroom. The side room was just big enough for a futon and a small table, where Hogarth lived. The table, positioned in front of the window, overlooked a beautiful tree and the quiet street below. The corners of the table had to be cut just right to fit in the room, which also featured a wall painted with a blue sky and white clouds.

The main bedroom had a door to the hallway and another to the side room. The side room door was padded with a sleeping mattress, screwed to create a soundproof system that worked only in theory. This setup resulted in two bedrooms. The third bedroom was essentially the main bedroom split in half with a breakaway wall, featuring a closet and a doorway to the main hallway, but it lacked windows. This one-bedroom apartment was transformed into three. All three bedrooms had doors connecting to each other, allowing you to walk straight through every bedroom, exit to the landing, and walk down the stairs to the street. This was a railroad apartment with a sunroom, a study, a living room, two chandeliers, nine windows, a skylight window in the bathroom, three bedrooms, three ceiling fans, and three doors to enter, with only one having a lock. Each room was filled with the personality traits, tchotchkes, and keepsakes of three individuals. All this was located right off Prospect Park in Brooklyn, New York.

Enter Roger Shillingsworth: tall, powerfully rugged with olive skin and hair as black as the forbidden night. Undoubtedly a ladykiller, every day and every moment with him was an adventure. Even a simple errand, like going out for a carton of milk, could turn into the most exciting moment of your life. Every experience and encounter with another person became an emotional rollercoaster of self-discovery and pure joy. You had never met anyone so at peace with themselves, regardless of what was happening in their personal life. He was tickled pink to have his demons along for the ride as he moved about, turning everything into just another adventure. Behind his thick brown marble-framed glasses, he often looked at you in delirium. Roger worked as a bellhop at The Coconut Cardinal Hotel (CCH) in midtown Manhattan, handling the graveyard shift. He ran the show there at night, making the most of his position.

In this high-brow hotel, ordering champagne through room service meant Roger would buy a $40 bottle of bubbly from the liquor store across the street, charge the room $100, and pocket the difference. He always had that look that shined, *Everything is under control.* Sometimes, he would assist single women who had traveled long distances, checking them into their rooms and providing full-service attention. At one point, I thought he might be planning a heist at the hotel, overhearing him on the phone one day talking about getting a van, and some bolt cutters, and the name of the operation was to be called *The Overnight.*

Hogarth, a writer and reviewer specializing in the city's theater scene, had access to dress rehearsals, and press nights for recent openings. If you were lucky, he might take you on one of his reviews, whether it be a new musical on 42nd Street or an intimate drama off Broadway. After our escapades, the three of us would gather, playing the bright neon 46 O'dinetin Video Game System and exchanging our tales until the first bird sang as the sun rose on the next day. It was akin to hanging out on that concrete slab but with a larger canvas of experience and a thousand more stories to tell each other. We were in the world now and fully committed to the experience. Still unsure of the future, the apartment was transforming into the repository for all the props from shows, treasures, keepsakes, and adventures I was having in the *Cube*. And the medicine cabinet now held a bottle of Snap N'Awake pills.

CHAPTER

Year Three,
The East Stubben Hotel,
A Near Death Experience,
and Taking over The Education Bus

I walked into the lobby of The East Stubben Hotel (ESH) in Atlanta, Georgia just before the new year and checked in at the front desk.

"Yes, Mr. Hubard, the others are already here waiting for your arrival, enjoying a drink at the bar. May I take the liberty of ordering you a Mai-Tai?"

"No, thank you," I said.

"Excellent. Will you be needing to secure anything in our safe during your stay?"

"Nothing this trip, thank you," I replied.

"Outstanding! Shall I have Richard take your bags?"

Just then, I turned around and witnessed an older, silver-haired gentleman dressed to the nines in a custom-tailored bellhop uniform standing next to the revolving door. He was drawing the hotel's initials (ESH) in the sand on top of the entrance's pink, marble ashtray stand with his forefinger, smiling.

"That's alright; I think I can manage. Thank you."

"But of course. Sign here and here. Your room key. You are on the fifth floor. If you need anything, anything at all, please feel free to call me. My name is Vernon... On behalf of the city of Atlanta... Welcome to The East Stubben Hotel!" the hotel manager declared.

"Thank you, Vernon."

I took the room key, nodded to Richard with an understanding, passed the ten-foot Balsam Fir Christmas tree and all its wonderful, hand-blown, deeply-colored glass ornaments in the main lobby, rolled my suitcase to the glass elevator, enjoyed the ride up, entered the room on the fifth floor, unpacked my dress pants, button-down shirt, blazer, and sat in the white leather chair next to the window. The room had a beautiful framed black-and-white picture of the city of Atlanta just above the bed. The walls were covered with a light blue, imprint pattern that made the room feel more like a cabana tent you would find at the shore. And the rug was the color of viridian.

This year was different, judging by the last fifteen minutes. We started off in Atlanta a few days earlier at The East Stubben

Hotel. The last one in existence. The North and West ones had shut down a decade earlier due to neglect, demolished to make way for an office park and a fast-food restaurant. The South one maintained its structure, turned into luxury apartments for the smart and savvy who made millions from the *Dot-Com Boom*. This hotel survived. This was an Atrium hotel, the last of its kind. An entirely different experience.

The exterior was, brick with white stone highlights, featured three entrance doors: two glass swing doors with a revolving glass door between them. A large Christmas tree adorned with glass ornaments in green, pink, blue, and gold stood at the entrance. Tiny white lights glowed within, and thick hand-pulled candy canes hung from every other branch. The aroma was a struggle between sweet sugar peppermint and fresh-cut pine. Behind the oak dest at the entrance stood a brass eagle revealing large feathers in the hotel's colors—pink, green, gold, and blue. The manager, in a custom-made blue double-breasted suit with three vertical rows of silver buttons, stood behind the oak. His jacket opened slightly to expose the Windsor knot of his green and pink striped tie. The bellhops had hats with the same color pattern, but they remained tieless.

On the ground floor, three glass elevators went up to the twelfth floor—the hotel's height, beyond which was the glass ceiling. The second floor housed all the hotel's conference rooms, where The Stubben Family met every quarter to discuss their financial legacy. The third floor and up contained the hotel guest rooms.

On the first floor, dead center, a lounge featured pink and green striped sofas, matching chairs, and large orange and brown man-made paper mâché like boulders, creating the illusion of a quarry. The bar lived in the center, and had a white marble top and brown leather bar stools. The bartender, dapperly dressed in a white shirt and a green tie with a Windsor knot, added a touch of elegance.

In the lounge, a stream ran through the paper rocks, giving the impression of a real quarry. Glass elevators, moving at lightning speed, offered an overhead view of the area and the entire hotel. The low roar of water and the echoes of conversation filled the air, accompanied by the scent of chlorine upon entering through the main doors.

The hotel's center, looking similar to a doughnut, featured a large skylight at the top, giving natural light during the day. In the evening, each floor's hallway lights and the hidden spotlights on the rocks below illuminated the entire inside of the place. A group had already gathered at the bar by the time I arrived for the Mai Tai Happy Hour. Everyone was sitting on the pink round couches next to the rocks. You could just barely hear the instrumental elevator Christmas music played beneath the light rumble of flowing water.

Uncertain about a third spin at this, in the fall, I called Anthony to ask him about hitting the road again in the new year. Rumors were flying around at the possibility, but no solid word. We were both in contact with the New York office. I spoke to Helen a number of times, who confirmed the plans and mentioned the idea of using two *Cubes*—one for each coast. That meant they were cutting it down by half again! That meant I might be out.

I made a pact with Anthony. I said, *"Let's root for each other."* We both would be in talks with the New York office and would sing each other's praises. Peppering the conversation with reminders that the other would be perfect for the third tour. I spent most of *Year Two* on the West Coast, and Anthony spent most of the first two years on the East Coast. He had a great track record with his public relations, and was familiar with that part of the country. Not to mention, his television interviews were top notch.

Sure enough, when the decision was made to go out again on a third tour, Anthony got the East Coast, and I got the West Coast. The game had changed for this was the third year in a row.

YEAR THREE. LEANER, MEANER, ELEGANT.

Photo by Tim Parote

Year Three: Leaner, Meaner, Elegant.

This time around we knew the highways, we knew the streets, and most importantly of all, we knew the campaign backwards and forwards. This difference was just two *Cubes* on this tour. This meant they cut the project budget to a fourth of its original cost from *Year One*, but we still were to cover both coasts. They would dust off and tune up two of *The Boxes*. And place the six other *Cubes* in a warehouse in the desert with a bunch of ancient artifacts. Cover them in their green tarps and have them wait to be reactivated in the future, if need be. The West Coast. The third year. These were the players:

-REGIONAL TEAM LEADER / HUGH DANIELS
-TOUR MANAGER / PARIS SALLENGER
-ASSISTANT TOUR MANAGER / HARRY LOWE
-TRUCK DRIVER / KERMIT STEVENS
-MAN IN THE CUBE / SPOKESMAN / RANDOLPH HUBARD

Hugh Daniels, the Regional Team Leader...How do you explain him? He was the go-to guy in the office, stood as tall as a building with broad shoulders and jet-black hair with thick white sideburns. It was a contrast of color reflecting on his head. Sporting a classic 1950s boxy and stoic look, he could have easily been Superman's stunt double on a low budget serial series. His slow southern drawl added a distinctive charm to his speech, creating a suspenseful journey in every sentence. When he spoke, you thought he was not going to make it to the period, but he did. With those thick, bushy, lustrous, neatly trimmed white sideburns, he looked like he was old enough to own the company. He looked older than the company. For all I knew he was.

Between the first and second year, the marketing company transitioned from The Sparkling Marketing Group to Third Round Media-Marketing Group (TRMMG). Despite the change of ownership, they continued using Craftsmen for all *Cube* maintenance, and Roche was still backing it, and happily prepared for a third round in the campaign. TRMMG continued the campaign into the second and third year.

Helen Muse took the lead for TRMMG, reprising her role as the head of the project. Tall, with black hair, and a big fan of peanuts, she brought joy to the control booth. Having worked on *Year Two,* Helen was a great audience, I mean she laughed at by bad jokes. She had no problem speaking her mind in any situation. During a conference, she once stopped me mid-sentence, and said, *"Randolph, don't get your panties in a twist."*

Then there was Paris, our tour manager, a towering figure. I stand at a respectable six feet one inch, six feet two inches on a day with good hair. In the height department, she wasn't trailing far behind. Picture this: a pensive, soft-spoken, and handsome woman with brunette hair, accented by a streak of blonde down the center. She had spent a few years on the road with other mobile marketing campaigns, and she just finished working as an underwater mermaid for an amusement park. She was nervous about taking a lead role; she had just gotten her driver's license. Throughout the entire week of training, she managed to keep her head above water—unlike poor Amber from *Year One,* who vanished into thin air after just three days in a hot tub. When we split off for their driving training, we heard through the grapevine that during Paris's test, she ran through a red light and hit every orange cone in the obstacle course. I would have paid money to see that.

Harry, the assistant tour manager, sported hair akin to a horse's. Long and flowing, with a thick mustache to boot. A wiz kid, computer geek, and gadget freak, he was what the ancients called a technoid. Boisterous, energetic, and always seeking a good time, he resembled someone who could be a lifeguard at a country club.

Then there was Kermit, the *Cube's* driver – a man of few words, quiet as a mouse, and thin as a pencil. Wide-eyed and curious, leaving everyone unsure if he had experienced everything in the world, or if this was his first time out of the house. Everywhere we went, he had a female fan club following, almost stalking him. During one of our hotel check-ins, two young ladies in tight miniskirts and tank tops slithered up to him in the lobby, hung all over him, and then bombarded him with questions like, *"This one's cute, what's your name? Look at his eyes, couldn't you just get lost in them forever?"* and *"When are you going to take us out?"*

Despite having just met in a hotel lobby, they were ready to rip his clothes off. Kermit, with the dreamy blue eyes, curly hair, and a gentle nature, could turn the truck on a dime, blindfolded, while doing his taxes. Harry and Kermit were friends prior to this gig. They were fresh, happy, and new, with wild eyes, excited about traveling the coast and maybe seeing The World's Tallest Thermometer. They were already looking ahead to Pasadena; that was our first stop. They planned to take care of some things in Los Angeles a few days before our first event, so we all met up in Pasadena.

At The East Stubben Hotel (ESH), everyone was enjoying the atmosphere and the Happy Hour. They were taking the edge off, traveling from their homes with limited understanding of what they were about to do. These were the new batch of people. We were to meet in the conference room in the morning to go over the final details on locations, events, and protocol.

We were younger and fresher this time out, so by its nature they had us do more. The campaign still big and boisterous in its presentation but refined down to a small but essential company.
(Note: Half the size from *Year Two*.)

I skipped the Happy Hour, still nursing my coffee from the airport, I sat down at the wide oak desk. Emptying the contents of my shoulder bag on top, I organized my receipts by date, already starting to add up the expenses for the trip from New York for the reports. I was already doing math.

This was my fifth gig with these two companies (Sparkling Marketing Group & TRMMG), and I was determined not to repeat a rookie mistake from the last one. The previous spring, I landed a gig as the assistant tour manager and driver for The New York State Lottery Education Bus. At the time, I was unaware that the Lottery and the New York educational system were in cahoots, or even had a bus. Anna called me in early April, just as I'd returned from *Year Two's Glass Box Adventure*, asking if I'd be interested in driving a bus. Never having driven a bus before, it was a far cry from all the times I rode in them as a kid. I always thought of a school bus as more of a suburban tank—two axles, six wheels, a machine. Even the army uses buses for transporting soldiers and civilians alike. I had absolutely no idea how to drive a bus. If I had a blind spot out back, how would I handle that? You can't see out back! As a child, riding buses lacked all the basic and simple safety features like no seat belts, and I never thought they needed them. The entire concept of a school bus revolves around safety. It would never be in a situation requiring seat belts. I believed there was no need for them; every time a bus stopped to pick up or drop off children, every car on the road came to a halt. Painted yellow, a warning signal, it towered above all other vehicles. Yellow means *slow down.* You can't miss them. The entire idea of a school bus is that it's a safe means of transportation; a bus would never be in a situation where it would need seat belts. Tanks don't have seat belts; why should school buses? They would never have to brace for impact. Perhaps come to an abrupt stop, but nothing life-threatening. I was wrong.

———————————

It was an early spring morning, and we had just picked up the final set of students before heading to the school parking area. Most of us were half-asleep or trying to rest that last 15 minutes before officially starting our school day. I sat in the front left window seat directly behind the driver, Horatio. He was thin, with short black hair, and he always had action-packed stories of his adventures. I sat in the front and didn't want to miss a second of his tales—tales of crossing the border as a teenager or working at his father's restaurant as a kid. I was only 12 at the time. The youngsters primarily sat in the front of the bus, and the back was occupied by the older, more rambunctious teenagers. That was their turf; you knew where the imaginary line was between you and them, and you didn't cross it.

We had been on that road a thousand times, in every weather condition imaginable, twice a day for almost a year. It was in a residential neighborhood—calm, easy, early that morning.

Suddenly and without warning, Horatio stood up, rocketing from his seat. He instantly sat back down, applied the brake, then lifted his foot off as if uncertain. Slowly, or at least it felt that way, the entire bus started leaning to the right as we moved forward. I looked at Simon in the right window seat across from me. His eyes popped out of his head. We kept moving forward, tilting to the right. Horatio was now fully standing with his left foot on the bus floor and his right foot on the door as we skid on the road without the wheels touching the ground.

On this bus there was a black t-shaped safety bar right behind the driver. I grabbed the bar, and the bus was now on its right side sliding on the road. The kids behind me were now thrown to the right side of the bus as we traveled across the pavement to a stop. All the seat cushions had come off the seats and pelted everyone on the right side. Horatio was now standing with both feet on the door of the bus as we screeched to a stop. I was hanging from the bar then fell on top of Simon and all the bus seats. It went dead silent. I looked directly at Horatio's feet and saw the door and road underneath it and said, "How are we going to get out!"

Just then the alarm went off and the teenagers in the back were yelling, *"COME ON! Everyone let's go! COME ON!"*. They had opened the emergency door in the back and were throwing everyone outside. Everyone except Horatio. I walked around to see the road and saw a man in his early thirties in a black suit with curly, reddish-brown hair sitting on the curb with his head in his hands. Blood was dripping from his face and staining the black pavement below. Directly in front of him was a brown Cadillac or something that once resembled one, turned inside out. It was completely destroyed, laying not far from the bus.

Horatio was slowly climbing out of a window and now stood on top looking down at the man in black with eyes of despise. He was filled with so much rage, confusion, and compassion for that man's position in life I didn't know what, if anything, he was going to do. Horatio had an understanding of the situation. At this point no one had any idea what was going on. I turned around and about twenty of us were wandering in the front yard of a home. Some people were laying down. Some were kneeling and some were just standing, staring into the abyss of their own mortality.

For a moment I thought we were all dead, wandering in purgatory. Then the front door of the house swung open, and a beautiful woman in her early thirties, with smooth milky ivory skin, dressed in a pink transparent nightgown, came running out. I don't remember if she came to me first or last, but she said with a tender voice, *"Are you alright? Do you want to come inside?"* The next thing that happened was I found myself standing in her living room. The place was bare, with no furni-

291

ture anywhere. The interior of the home glowed yellow from the morning sun, and there were neatly stacked cardboard boxes everywhere. About five or six of us were now wandering around in this house.

On the dark, wooden steps to the left of the front door sat a young blonde-haired boy and girl, no older than 8, in their pajamas, holding each other's hands. They looked completely horrified. I turned around, and the man in black appeared out of nowhere, on the telephone in the kitchen. It was attached to the wall and yellow in color. He was making a call, yelling and screaming the whole time, but I couldn't tell you one single word he said. We tried to avoid eye contact with him at all costs. He hung up the receiver and stormed outside. Right afterwards someone started wiping his blood off the phone with a pineapple dish towel. The room reeked of alcohol.

My head started spinning, and all of us were still trying to grab onto something familiar to ground ourselves. The environment was foreign to me, and the man in black seemed to be everywhere or at least you could smell him everywhere. No one was speaking. Not my friends from the bus, not the woman in pink, not the kids on the steps—no one. I couldn't stand being in that room, in that house, or in that state of mind anymore. *Get out of this house!* I thought. The man in black was pacing back and forth in the front yard. He had a thick gash on the crown of his nose, and he kept wiping it with his white shirt. It wasn't so much that the blood coming out of his face that bothered me; it seemed like he was bleeding liquor. You couldn't get away from him.

I noticed a sign on the lawn. I forced myself to concentrate on the letters and slowly sounded out the words. It said, *For Sale*, and on top, it said, *Sold*. Then I looked at the colors of the sign and said them out loud. *"Blue, purple, and white."* I found two things that my mind could focus on. And that brought me back to earth. The three colors and the three words. And like that, I snapped back into reality. I could hear full sentences again. Some of the guys were talking and even laughing at this point. Then I knew we were alright. If someone was making fun of the situation already, I knew we were alright. You could hear sounds and you could start to make out the voices of everyone that was on the bus. We could hear the police sirens closing in. Then the man in black looked directly at me. And that was the first time in my life that I saw the death of a man's soul. It was in his eyes.

We spent the entire morning on that front lawn. Two ambulances took half the kids to the hospital, and four police cars took the other half to the police station. For some reason, I remained at the home. The man in black disappeared. There were about four or five cops forming a circle around him at one point, then he was gone.

Some of us witnessed a tow truck hauling away this mass of black, twisted metal and broken glass. On the front stone steps of that house, a fire truck worked to pull and tug that yellow monster until it flipped back to its driving position, all six tires back on the road. It had scratch marks from the road, a battered and shattered side-view mirror, and half the windows were gone, but besides that, it still retained its integrity.

The Cadillac, on the other hand, was completely mangled. That family had just moved in the day before, and that was why the grass was dead and the home nearly empty. The kids on the steps, just moved to a new town, just slept in their new beds, and apparently just witnessed a car crashing into a school bus on their front lawn.

I'd never driven a bus before. This would be the first time I would be able to experience how they work when on the open road. The company was in a bit of a pickle. The assistant tour manager broke his leg, and they needed someone with a driver's license to drive the bus. The tour manager didn't have one. I had one.

"What's the tour?" I asked.

"The state lottery puts aside some of its earnings and uses it for educational purposes. And they got a bus," Anna said.

Every year, a teacher in Upstate New York crafts the curriculum for 4th and 5th graders statewide. The State Lottery and The New York Education System collaborated, transforming a school bus into a mobile field trip so to speak. They were to use a Type B school bus as a learning device. A Type B bus is a bit smaller than your average everyday school bus.

The bus traveled to different schools in the state, spending the day as classes participated in a scavenger hunt for knowledge. The topic of the curriculum for that year just happened to be about the Erie Canal.

"Randolph, would you be interested in being the Assistant Tour Manager for the Lottery Education Bus? The driver broke his leg skiing. We need someone to take his place." Anna asked.

"How long is this tour?" I quizzed.

"It's just until the end of the school year, about six weeks."

"Sure," I said.

"Great, I already booked you a ticket on the train to Albany. It leaves tomorrow afternoon," Anna said.

I hung up the phone and packed my bags for a six-week tour. The entire evening, I tried to figure out how the bus driver broke his leg skiing in April.

The tour manager went by the name Arnold Stone. He was about six feet tall and very thin—gaunt. Blonde, curly hair with a big chip on his shoulder. He was upset, he was carrying something pretty big, something about his health. I understood why I was called in at the last minute after meeting him.

When deciding whether to take a gig, there are three rules known as the three M's: *Money, Mates, and Mobility.* There are different variations on this, and I've heard it said in different ways.

To accept a job, you need two out of three. For instance, if the money is good, and you enjoy the people you'll be working with, but you're going to a swamp, take the gig. If you're headed to white sandy beaches, staying in a bungalow, and the company is great, but the money is lacking, take the gig. If the individuals you'll be working with are less than desirable, but the money allows you to buy that new computer and you're going to outer space, take the gig. However, if you're going to the Lost City of Atlantis, working with tough people, and the money is lousy, don't take the gig.

The money was good, the position was interesting, and I hadn't explored New York outside of the city. Although I didn't know who Arnold was, that covered at least two out of three criteria. I decided to take the gig, aware that driving a bus was one of the perks. Believing the position would sort itself out, I put myself in the mindset of hitting the road again and headed out to Albany.

Despite this venture being in progress for a while, and my role being that of a janitor, it was clear on the very first day that it was Arnold's show.

Checking into the Stay Quite O' Bit Hotel (SQOBH) the night before, I briefly said hello in the lobby. With two schools to visit that day, I could tell Arnold wasn't comfortable leading and catching me up to speed. We were only in the hotel lobby, and he was already visibly shaken. Realizing I had forgotten my sunglasses and said to Arnold, "Arnold, I forgot something in my room. I'll be right back."

I hopped on the elevator, slipped into my room, grabbed my sunscreen and sunglasses, and jumped down the stairs. Back in the lobby, Arnold looked at me like I had just run over his cat.

"What are you doing, we're going to be late! You got to be ready to go!" he said with rigor, verve, and a thread of fear.

In the last month and a half of this endeavor, he assumed I was there to replace him when they restarted in September. A random guy showing up during the final phase of this gig must have been uncomfortable for him. I was a complete stranger on his ship, and I knew he had no idea who I was. I understood his position, but the other guy was in the hospital with a broken leg. Between the two of us standing in the lobby, only one of us had a driver's license. I said nothing and totally ignored him, but that was strike one.

THIS IS WHAT THE NEW YORK STATE LOTTERY
EDUCATION BUS LOOKED LIKE FROM THE OUTSIDE.

The Education Bus was a yellow Type B bus with green and pink square-like shapes outlined in black on the nose and front sides. The back window was also colored with these squares, allowing visibility only through the two rear-view windows. On top, it had two aluminum poles that would flip upright to hold a banner saying *New York Canals Exploring America's First Super Highways*. The banner went from the bow to the stern. On the left side, a second banner rolled from the roof to the ground, depicting a cartoonish drawing of New York State featuring answers to scavenger hunt questions.

The awning, chairs, bins of pencils, and scavenger hunt work sheets were stacked neatly inside. We had a different bin that held pamphlets of information we gave out at weekend events for booking The Education Bus. The entire right side of the bus would open up like two French doors, revealing flatscreen televisions and colorful images providing information on The Erie Canal. All the answers to the scavenger hunt could be found in different places on and around the bus.

We would drive to the school, and Arnold would meet with the principal. Then we were shown where to set up for the day. It took half an hour to put this thing together every time. Arnold would climb on top and set up both banners. You could open the doors and secure them with small poles that locked them in place. And then make sure the monitors were working. And we were ready.

We were the only ones allowed inside the bus. It only had two seats. Only two people could be transported inside. We had the names of each teacher and a number of how many students they had in each class.

We had the scavenger hunt work sheet. With each class, Arnold would do his little song and dance on how The New York Lottery sponsored the bus and that we drive around the state.

Everyone got a scavenger hunt, and then we supervised the class for the next half an hour. Then they went to it. They could ask us any question, any question at all about the Erie Canal. Most of the kids had more questions on how we drove that thing.

But most of the questions went something like this:

"Mr. (Ran)Dolph? Where can I find the answer to number 23?" One of the kids would ask.

"You might want to check on the right side. Close to the back tire," I would respond. Then they would whisper to their friends, *"I found the answer to 23."*

"Mr. Dolph. Do you drive the bus to the grocery store?" One of the kids would ask.

"Of course. I can fill this thing up with a thousand TV dinners," I would cry back.

"What's a TD dinner?"

After a good thirty minutes, we would call everyone to meet at the side of the bus, and Arnold would ask questions like, "Alright, guys. What year did the Canal open?"

All the young whippersnappers would raise their hands. He would then point to someone for the answer, and they would say, *"It was in 1825. October 26th to be precise."*

"That's correct. Give that lady a pencil!" Arnold would cry.

Then the lady got a No. 2 that said *New York Canals: New York's First Superhighways,* and she would jump out of her skin with excitement. There is always something very thrilling about earning a novelty. We didn't give pencils to everyone. Arnold would ask five or six questions, and not everyone found all the answers. Some of the kids were actively looking for the answers, while others were just lollygagging.

CHAPTER

Expense Reports,
and Inspecting Too Cubes

The Expense Reports were a collection of all the receipts from the week(s) prior. Things like bottled water, gasoline, cab rides, Xerox copies, or anything paid out of your pocket that was work-related. All the receipts were to be taped flat on white computer paper, and all expenses would be calculated at the bottom. That way, everything could be laid flat and filed neatly. It's a madhouse of insanity to hand someone a bunch of crumpled up and folded receipts without any point of reference on what they are. After it was cataloged and organized by date, it would then be mailed to the office. The financial officers would then have everything flat and neat to file, calculate, and determine whether or not it was work-related, and then they would reimburse you for all expenses. It was a great system and an almost flawless one.

The only problem would be if your reports got lost. If they didn't make it to the office or some unforeseen problem happened, and they got misplaced. If they got lost, you would have to eat the loss. Sometimes expense reports would be in the numbers of $500 plus. And that's your money. If a report got lost, the financial officers would accept a set of copies, but only under the circumstances with the understanding of them being lost in transit or lost under the watch of the financial officers.

During this gig, one of my expense reports was lost. I don't know what happened or how these papers were misplaced, either in the mail or due to some unforeseen accident. They were never found. To avoid making the same mistake twice, I started making two copies of every report. That way, one always had an extra for the office and one for me.

Working smarter. I wanted to have everything done at the end of each day and have my extra copy of the reports filed in a bin. This was a great idea in theory; the only problem with that system was the bin got heavier each week. I broke it into a monthly mailing system. At the end of each month, I would mail the copies of my copied expense reports to my apartment back in Brooklyn, and Hogarth would place them in my room. In turn, I'd send him care packages. These care packages would consist of what was discovered at the fairs, festivals, and the local street vendors. Things like a jug of maple syrup, a bathmat, a corkscrew, a box of chocolate chip cookies, a set of oven mitts, or a bottle of charred barrel bourbon. And then things like a dish organizer or something that was needed for the apartment—something fun and something practical, like a coloring book.

The expense reports would always reflect everything purchased on that particular tour. I would write down the dollar amounts for each item, and then add them up using my trusty No. 2 pencil that said *New York Canals: Exploring America's First Superhighways.*

The conference room at The East Stubben Hotel (ESH) buzzed with the presence of new teammates. We gathered there in the morning and headed to a warehouse where the *Cubes* awaited reactivation for *Year Three*. The two *Cubes* used were the same ones Anthony and I used the year before. Nothing changed. The loveseat sported the same gray fabric. Anthony could identify his because he aligned the windows with mini-Christmas tree lights, and I found mine by default, but I later added a red chili pepper light strand on the back window.

Everyone seeing the *Cubes* for the first time always had that sense of wonder, but for us they didn't have the same spark. Even in the third year, the new members were doing backflips when they saw them. Anthony and I were all business on the day we visited the warehouse, just wanting to know the practical updates. We both hopped inside, cranked them up, and went through them by the numbers.

1. AIR CONDITIONER/HEATING. CHECK.
2. ESCAPE HATCH. CHECK.
3. TELEVISION. CHECK.
4. STEREO. CHECK.
5. VELCRO. CHECK.
6. SEAT BELT. CHECK.

And the coffee maker. Checks across the board. Then the new tarps. Not entirely new, but the buttons were all replaced, and the zippers were now made from a stronger, metal material. Kermit was eager to put his back into the burrito flip of the tarp. We grabbed the two orange ladders that were still secured with the makeshift stopper that was made last year, and we set them up. Kermit was already done before we even started. When we flipped them back and secured them in record time, I said, "Kermit, that was fantastic. Where were you two years ago?" He just smiled.

The minivans received a facelift with new vehicle wrapping. The back window featured a vinyl wrap with small holes for visibility, this was something new. You weren't able to see out the rear-view window on the vans before, but now you could. One team tore off the entire strip on the back windows, so they could see behind them on the road. Everything was in ship shape, and we were ready to hit the road... again.

Kermit would be driving the *Cube*, Harry in one minivan, and Paris in the other. In *Year One*, I rode in the *Cube*, and in *Year Two*, I drove one of the minivans. Now, in *Year Three,* a choice between riding with Harry or Paris was presented in front of me. The truck's suspension was uncomfortable for long rides. It boiled down to deciding whether to travel with Harry or Paris. I considered flipping a coin or creating a questionnaire on conversation habits like, music and snack preferences, storytelling, and driving abilities. Who knew when to speak and when to savor the silence? Not being present during their road tests left me clueless about who was the better driver.

Harry picked up two car air fresheners, choosing scents like honey lemon breeze or cinnamon apple spice. They dangled from the rearview mirror in flat, clear plastic wrappers. The package advised opening the wrapper slowly to prevent overwhelming the vehicle with the order. Harry opened *both* and hung them inside. At that very moment I knew who to traveling with. I drove with Paris.

303

CHAPTER

Pasadena, California,
The Rose Parade,
and Harry Loves the Grannies

The 113th Rose Bowl, also known as The Rose Parade, serves as the opening ceremony for the Rose Bowl Game, a college football event in Pasadena, California, often referred to as *The Granddaddy of Them All*. The Parade dates back to January 1st, 1890, while the Rose Bowl Game was introduced on January 1st, 1902, to generate funding for the parade. The events fuel each other in terms of attendance.

The parade adheres to two key rules: participating floats must be entirely covered in flowers, including various vegetation, and they must fit under the I-210 freeway overpass. Following these rules ensures eligibility, and everything else becomes easy. Although *The Box* couldn't participate due to lacking flowers, our team was present. A quick journey from Atlanta, primarily on I-40 West, took around 32 hours. In January, the temperature was 60 degrees, and the air was filled with all the flowers.

Enormous crowds of people gathered many arriving at the crack of dawn for the best view. Positioned on the outskirts of the parade with the other vendors promoting similar and outlandish products, we witnessed the entire event.

The first thing that happened was a UFO flying overhead, revealed to be a B2 stealth bomber. It just looked like something from outer space. This was a well-organized event. The streets were clear from traffic, and they started it off with a bang. The first float was a colossal 50-foot-tall *technobot* by the American Honda Motor Co., and it stood upright. It was thin and had nothing to support it except its two legs. One would think it would not make it under the I-210 overpass. But it had 100 feet to spare. Daisies, carnation petals, roses, and orchids are just a few of the flowers used on this. And as a bonus, it also gave the thumbs-up sign.

Then came the dinosaurs. Dinosaur floats that is. All of these floats were covered in flowers, from soup to nuts. It started with a float, then a marching band, and so forth.

THESE WERE THE REST OF THE FLOATS:

Global Wonders of Communication, Bengal Tigers, Bunny Rabbits, The Golden Gate Bridge, A Home Under Construction, Bob's Home of the Big Boy, A Baby in a Huge Bathtub, Robot Horses, Woolly Mammoths, Cats and Dogs living in Peace, Harmony and Understanding, Alice and her Wonderland Friends, Butterflies, Vacation Dreams, Two Garden Parties working in Unison, Kites, Mother Nature's Playground, Piñatas, Turtles and Birthday Cake, Lazy Fisherman, Mother Goose and her Story-time Companions, Jitterbugs, A Pink Cadillac, A Taiwanese Celebrations, Wagon and Mules, Marine Animals, A Dance in the Park, Stuffed Animal Healthcare Workers, A Winged Dragon in a Boat, A Movie Theatre, A Lemonade Stand, A Honey Eating Bear in Pajamas, A Gazebo, Grandma's House, Picnics, Parks, Biblical Scenes, Neighborhood Springtime, Education Throughout the World, Man's Best Friend, Vietnamese House of Culture, Big Brothers & Big Sisters, Guide Dogs, St. Bernard, Uncle Sam on a motorbike, and R2-D2 and C-3PO.

All of them covered in, but not limited to, orchards, gerbera daisies, straw flowers, lentils, chrysanthemums, tree bark, cottonseed, rice, onion seed, roses, mums, carnations, poppyseeds, seaweed, Spanish moss, palm fiber strips, shaved coconut, cornmeal, cinnamon, kermit green button poms, lavender, and yarrow. You haven't seen anything until you've seen R2-D2 and C-3PO in a gigantic floral arrangement.

Ms. Saunders's would have flipped her bonnet. The whole thing felt like something from an ancient society mating ritual. This event also had a Queen, a Royal Court, and a Grand Marshal. The Grand Marshal for that year was a television host and personality, Regis Philbin. Three judges presided over this event: Tommy Farmer, Susie Gross, and Bruce Skinner CFE (Certified Fraud Examiner), each with different backgrounds in floral design, float design, and special events.

In addition to the floats, there were numerous marching bands. The Queen had her own float with the six members of her Royal Court riding in random order: Kimberlee Córdova, Lauren Tapp, Shannon Stockdale, Stephanie Valenzuela, Rachel Frandsen, and Katherine Stroud. The Royal Court Float was sandwiched between The Pasadena City College Herald Trumpets and The Union High School Renegade Regiment. The Boeing Company presented another series of floats, six in total, tucked between The Painted Magic Pro Rodeo Drill Team and Regis. These were the longest floats, covering over 130 feet in length, following the theme Through the Years from 1950 to the turn of the century, featuring icons from each decade.

We cracked the code on this tour, utilizing everything we had. It marked the start of the best way to travel. The larger the event, the more people attended, resulting in a larger volume of products provided to the masses. They wanted the freebies. In *Year Three*, we even started running out of dehydrated chicken soup before finishing events in each market. The office would have boxes of soup waiting for us at the next hotel, and all four of us had dehydrated chicken soup boxes stacked in our hotel rooms at all times.

At The Rose Bowl, the foot traffic was almost too much. I was surprised no one left bloody knuckles on the exterior of the glass windows. They were aggressively trying to get my attention. *Bam... Bam-Bam-Bam!* The whole *Cube* would start to waddle back and forth. Then another guy *Bam!* And yet another *Bam!* The human zoo factor was in full effect; women were screaming and lifting up their shirts for attention, guys punching the glass. Old people stood in confusion, trying to start conversations with me. Now I couldn't hear anyone outside, but they didn't know that. Some would start talking to me or talk at the glass windows, thinking this was an interactive experience. Then get annoyed that I wouldn't answer back and then start yelling as if I betrayed them. I'd never seen more female breasts in my life then I did in that *glass apartment* on *Year Three*.

The locations were perfect. The space was wide. The weather was in the sixties. The grounds were full of people. It was an event—a flower parade, leading into a college football game, combining athletic and artistic attractions. The best of both worlds.

The Rose Bowl was a dream scenario for us to promote. From my point of view you could see the tops of floats, feel the energy on the ground. Sitting on that loveseat, watching floats, the the swarm of people, and feeling the crowd's excitement, was a double blast of exhilaration.

Paris, Harry, Kermit, and I spent the day at The Rose Bowl Parade, fitting together like gears in a gold pocket watch. This was a good team. They were hungry and it very much showed. Kermit was the best driver on this whole thing. Paris and Harry were like a married couple, swapped responsibilities, and dealt with the models, *Grannies*, though Harry seemed confused when the young women put on wigs and glasses—we had to reassure him they weren't really grandmothers.

"They are models?" Harry questioned.

"That's right Harry, that's right. They're just young women pretending to be grandmothers."

"They're not grandmothers?" he pondered.

"Ohh, no, no, no. They're not grandmothers."

We worked out a daily system where I would go inside and turn on the generator, then Kermit and Harry would unroll the tarp. And it would appear like a blanket being taken off a birdcage. And the event would start. At the end of the day, Kermit and Harry would cover up the birdcage, then I would change my outfit and simply slip out *The Escape Hatch,* roll out from under the truck, and no one would be the wiser. I wish we did these things the last two years! You could hear people asking Harry and Kermit,

"Is he in there?"
"Is he sleeping?"
"Does he have a nightlight!?"
"Is he going to be in there all night?"

Harry and Kermit would play the ruse that I was still in there and all the while be standing right next to those people asking questions.

I had to make sure that it was locked and secured underneath. *The Escape Hatch* still had the problem of securing itself. If I was under the *Cube*, it could be secured. You would have to use some elbow grease, but you could lock it, though only underneath the truck. Then it wouldn't pop open when we drove back to the hotel. On longer rides, I had to have the coffee table on top. But on short, smooth, slow rides it held if I went under the truck and manually locked it. I was eternally grateful that Harry helped with the labor. And the best part was I could slip out of the *Cube*, and everyone around us, all about us, thought I was still inside.

Here in California is where we perfected the entrance and exit strategy. Traveling from town to town, the coffee table would be secured on top of the hatch. *The Escape Hatch* became the main entrance and exit. Most of Harry and Paris's work was finding ways to keep all three vehicles in the same place at the same time. They understood this. That was something that made it seem grand, having all three vehicles together. With large events and thousands of people, it was difficult to get enough space to have our little parade. And if we didn't get to events early, we would not be able to maneuver through the crowds.

This event just whizzed by. We were lucky enough to see most of the parade. I wanted to see Regis, the Queen, and all the floats. I wanted to see the game. We had a tight schedule and a lot more cities to go to. We had the entire West Coast to cover in less than three months. And it was going to take time to get to everywhere. I never did get to see the game or meet the Queen.

CHAPTER

San Francisco,California,

The Chinese New Year,

Tacoma,Washington,

and The Birthday Gift

Chinese New Year, The Year of the Horse, marked the seventh in the twelve-year cycle of the Chinese Zodiac. San Francisco celebrated this occasion with a Chinese New Year Parade in Chinatown, established in 1848 A.D. and home to The Dragon Gate.

The main attraction of the parade was, the Golden Dragon of Chinatown. Crafted in Foshan (Fatshan), Guangdong Province, China, the birthplace of Cantonese Opera, this puppet required one hundred people to operate. Stretching over 200 feet, it symbolizes power, strength, and good fortune. Lung Dragons, also known as Oriental Dragons or Sea Dragons, hold cultural significance and have appeared in various forms, including pop culture and Dungeons & Dragons (D&D).

This was the second stop on *Year Three*, marking the third year of this endeavor! Three years of this. It was becoming a career. Some people started talking about taking this overseas, touring London, France, and Ireland. The office was looking into ways to ship the *Cubes*. There are challenges to doing a European tour; the roads and driving norms differ, like steering wheels are on the other side of vehicles. One could detach the glass apartment, place it in a shipping container, send it overseas, reattach it to a local truck, and tour the surrounding towns.

What would you call it? *The Man in the Glass Box: European Edition* (TMITGBEE)? Adjusting the literature for the local language, hiring real, local grandmothers fluent in French, German, or English, and multilingual tour managers could make it feasible. Though navigating some backroads might get tricky, it seemed doable. You might have to rethink the chicken soup angle, but it seemed doable. And what would the commercials look like in foreign markets?

La Campagne de l'Homme dans la Boîte cherche à embaucher huit acteurs pour voyager à travers Europe et "vivre" dans un Appartement de Verre sur Roues.

• Doit être prêt à voyager pendant quatre mois.
• Promouvoir le nouveau produit.

Audition held at
Hôtel Coup de Foudre Aux Fraises - France
21 novembre, 9h00

Édition Européenne

These were just thoughts, flights of fancy; nothing was sold. I had been working on this for three years now, and you tend to approach things differently after traveling around a bit. We knew the market, we knew the roads, we knew the structure of the campaign, but most importantly, we knew that Roche was pleased with the success of this. However, I wasn't sure how long they were willing to support the project. It was fresh; it was new; it was exciting the first year. We did realize by the second year we couldn't wow them with the same things, but the awards they received were tremendous. Now on the third year, and with only two *Cubes* on the road, it did feel like we had already shown them all the razzle-dazzle of the campaign. But a European tour, that's an entirely different market. The key point to remember was that I've seen this thing 1000 times, but the people out there? They've never seen it. And I had to remind myself of that. This year we actually saw more people. I did at least. Granted I was in warmer climates, and that does tend to bring people outside more.

On the streets of San Francisco, the *Grannies* were mobbed, with people aggressively grabbing chicken soup packets. Adults even ripped the backpacks off them to get to the soup. At this point we needed a security department just for crowds. I just watched this whole thing. It's crucial to remember the soup is just a novelty, containing salt and chicken flavored powder – not medicine. In a single day, they wiped out our supply. And that supply was to last for the entire week.

Parked on an incline with limited space, a meat truck hauling pigs stood in front of us. The city hosted a major event, but surrounding businesses still needed to run their daily operations. Deliveries had to be made, goods and services supplied. However, vehicles couldn't navigate the streets freely. My blind spot was at the front of the *Cube*, and I could only see out of the back and the three sides. While I could see out of the top, I rarely looked up, as no one ever jumped out a window and landed on that. The cargo door was either intentionally or accidentally left open all day. Some hogs were hanging from hooks, and some were not. On the bottom of the truck, hog after hog after hog were stacked snout to snout neatly on top of each other. The truck remained parked for hours, and because it was on an incline, all the liquid at the bottom started to seep out, Kermit saw this firsthand. He called me on the intercom for support.

"Randolph?"

"What's up, do we have to move?" I asked.

"No."

"Are you alright? You sound like something's wrong," I quizzed.

"Ahh, it's nothing."

I knew something was bothering him, something brewing in his mind. He sat in the cab all day, and everyone that sat there before him went a little batty. One guy asked me about aliens, and the other guy was hallucinating on the very first day, and then flat out disappeared. I could only imagine what Kermit was thinking, what he was feeling, or what he was seeing.

On that beautiful day in San Francisco's Chinatown, celebrating the Year of the Horse, John Williams' heroic marching music (*Duel of the Fates*) played on the stereo. Coffee flowed freely as I sipped it on the gray loveseat bolted to the floor of a *glass apartment on wheels*, contemplating the future of this and the possibilities of a European tour. Witnessing Lung Dragons dancing, firecrackers popping on the streets, and confused ladies dressed as grandmothers getting mobbed for worthless salt packets created a surreal experience. This unfolded from every window as a river of pig's blood ran beneath my feet.

———————————————

Interstate I-84 and snow was our companion as we headed to Tacoma, accumulating quickly on the road. One day you're in sunny skies and it's 60° and next day you're on a mountain and it's snowing, and you can't see more than 3 feet in front of you. We observed a line, approximately two miles long, of dozens of 18-wheelers on the shoulder attaching snow chains to their tires. Kermit was our driver; he was new to the trade but he thought he could handle that mountain. However, seeing the die-hard, old-school professionals stopping and placing metal on their rigs, made us think we should do the same. Meanwhile, we were navigating up the mountain without snow chains.

The grooves in street tires are ineffective in these conditions. The rigid tire patterns in every street channel water, allowing the tire to ride on the road instead of sliding on water. However, in snowy weather, the grooves fill up with snow, losing their grip on the road. At that point the tires are useless, you might as well just be a sled on the road. In a car, only the tires make contact with the road through small areas called the contact patch. Riding in a vehicle means minimal contact with the road, especially in snowy conditions where the contact patch is non-existent. Driving in snow is like covering more ground than a car with your own two feet. Snow chains are essential for gripping the snowy road.

Every one of us, without speaking, knew we probably should put the chains on the tires, but no one wanted to stop, go out on the mountainside snowy road, and open up the brand-new box of snow chains that we had sitting in the back. Meaning you had to unzip the tarp in two places, open the door, flip the small black ladder down, go inside, get the 1000-pound box of chains, and put them on the tires. I mean, we haven't even opened the box yet. They still had that new snow tire chain smell. And no one wanted to do the grunt work of actually putting them on the tires. We did call each other a couple of times via walkie-talkies. We picked them up to make it easier for us to talk to each other rather than using cell phone data. So, we did the third option, ignore it.

(Note: Tire chains for commercial vehicles don't weigh 1000 pounds.)

Despite our schedule, every professional truck driver on the Interstate was on the shoulder, chaining up their tires. Seeing this, I questioned our chances without snow chains, considering the *Cube's* lack of weight compared to loaded trucks. We were carrying an empty box, unlike these trucks hauling substantial weight like cranberry juice, steel pipe, Furbies, and paint. But I kept that to myself.

On an average day, driving the *Cube* with Kermit at the helm, he was battling the wind. He was a kite with no string. Every sudden gust hit the *Cube*, almost swaying it off the highway. Kermit was on high alert, fighting a powerful invisible element—the wind. We were heading into the thick of a snowstorm without snow chains, so if the wind hit us just right, it would knock him off the highway and down the side of a mountain. We were all thinking about that, but no one was talking about it. After a while, we needed to take the next exit, find shelter in a hotel until the storm subsided. I finally advocated for waiting it out, and so did Kermit.

We pulled over in a small town looking for any hotel, motel, or manger. With snow falling and roads clogged, we sought refuge in a small place just off the highway—The Broadway Motel, equipped with enough parking space for the *Cube* to wait out the storm.

Photo by Randolph Hubard

Broadway Motel, air conditioned rooms.

This motel had two levels with open doors to the parking lots. It had a white exterior with red doors. Inside, to the left, was a small round table and window. To the right, there was a wall. Straight ahead was the double bed, and just beyond that, slightly to the right, was the bathroom. The rug was blue, and the walls were white. The curtains were yellow and orange, almost matching the bedspread, but on closer inspection, they didn't match at all. It was the yellow overhead light that made everything look the same. The bedspread was blue, or it was white; I couldn't tell what what was. We couldn't see the roads outside and couldn't distinguish between the bedspread in the walls. Everything was starting to blend together. And of course, air conditioned rooms.

The next day, there was no word on whether we were to travel. I went to the lobby to get myself a cup of coffee and see if I could get any information from the guy at the desk about the weather conditions on the road.

Once the weather was more manageable, we hit the road and arrived in Tacoma, Washington, by the skin of our teeth. We were scheduled at a gun show, and I wasn't sure if the glass was bulletproof—one way to find out! Scattered throughout were targets of all sorts: circular, bullseye paper targets stuffed with hay, others more lifelike, such as clay pigeons, deer, and even some as large as moose. They were all synthetic, but some of them looked too real. *Do you think I could fit one of those moose in here?* I thought to myself.

Inside were tables with rows of guns—handguns, rifles, pocket pistols—not to mention compound bows, wood arrows, aluminum arrows, hunting knives, orange vests, camouflage cargo pants, ghillie suits, beef jerky by the pound, maple syrup, and everything else you could possibly imagine. We were advertising *Tamiflu* at the show. Kermit apparently found something at one of the vendors and called me on the intercom, saying, "Randolph! I found your birthday present; it's perfect. Can I give it to you now?"

"Today isn't my birthday," I said.

"I know, but this is perfect. Can I give it to you now?" Kermit exclaimed.

"Kermit, we have to follow the rules. You know that."

"Can we make an exception? I can't wait!" he cried.

"If we don't follow the rules of sanity, the world will spiral into never ending chaos. And we will enter a new dawn where pain will become your master, and suffering will be your companion. And this will be felt in the hearts of all humanity. And last a thousand years! Do you want that, Kermit! Well, do you!?"

"No."

"Then we wait... until my birthday."

CHAPTER

Not Reno but Las Vegas,
The Consumer Electronics Show,
and Dinner with Paris at an Italian Bistro

Trying to make good time by eating our meals in the minivan, stopping on the side of the road to relieve ourselves, and increasing the speed for which we traveled. Taking U.S. Route 395 South, then to I-80, and finally to U.S. Route 95 straight to the Neon Capital of the World. Las, Vegas, Nevada.

We were scheduled to be at The Consumer Electronics Show (CES). The show is held every year at The Las Vegas Convention Center in Winchester, Nevada. It's a gathering in celebration of new technologies that will flood the market in the upcoming year. All the gadgets and toys are on display for all who attend to see and try out firsthand. It's a place to present these things to Hi-Tech writers so their readers can have a larger critique of what's to come.

It's an eerie place, the desert at night, especially Route 395. The road goes for stretches of miles without a single house light, streetlight, or headlight anywhere. The stars above are the only thing that reminds you that you are still on earth and not in a shoebox.

Paris was from Scottsdale, Arizona. She and her boyfriend spent a significant amount of time in Vegas, so she was familiar with the area and the drive to Las Vegas. I was not. This would be my first time entering the area. I had played the slot machines and spun the dreidel, maybe dropped a hundred dollars or so, and walked the boardwalk in Atlantic City, New Jersey, but I had never walked the grounds of Las Vegas before. Paris's boyfriend, however, would walk into a casino and throw down $50,000 on a single hand of poker.

We were the only vehicles on the road for what seemed like an eternity, with no visible light outside of the illuminating glow from the gauge cluster. Then after a couple of soft turns and a couple more miles, we saw in the distance a light. It looked like two mountains laying side by side with this light beaming in the center and shooting up to the stars. And slowly but surely more color surrounded it. It presented itself to the night. I thought we must be close. That was a good series of lights up ahead. Paris was driving, and we had been only listening to our thoughts most of the drive, and I broke the silence and asked, "Is that Vegas?"

Paris smiled and in a low, playful tone and said, "No, that's Reno."

We had to make haste, needing to reach Vegas that night. It's a good seven hours from Reno to Vegas, but we made it just under six. Paris and I split the driving, so by the time we got to Las Vegas, I was behind the wheel. And my driving nightmare continued. It was almost midnight, we were tired, and it was pitch dark for the last couple of hours.

Then, *"Wa-bam!"* Every single light in the state of Nevada was present. Every casino was flashing and gleaming with signs promising *The Best Slot Machines in Town. Giant King Crab Legs! Everyone Is A Winner Here! Get Married Tonight. Hassle-Free! and Win, Win, Win!!!* There were so many lights and so much eye-catching, razzle-dazzle everywhere that I could not distinguish the traffic lights from the casino ones. I had to have Paris tell me if we had to stop at each intersection. I couldn't tell if we had a green light or a free king crab leg dinner!

She was calm and guided me to the pyramid-shaped hotel and casino. My hands were still shaking as we exited the car. The juxtaposition between the dark of night, and all that light just threw me for a loop. I turned to Paris and said with all my depth, "Never put me in that situation again."

We checked into a retro, old school casino and they had parking for the *Cube* in the back parking area of the casino.

The heart of Las Vegas is what's known as The Strip. The town pulls a lot of water, and most of the people who live in the area work for the casinos.

All of the *Grannies* in Las Vegas worked in some way, shape, or form at the casinos. Some were blackjack dealers, slot machine candle lighters, cocktail waitresses, parrot ladies, casino massage therapists, wildlife control technicians, or dancers in their exotic shows. They all worked in the evenings, having their days free and often got bored to tears before going to work. A lot of them were just seeking out something to do during the day—things like dressing up as grandmothers in the hot desert temperatures and handing out dehydrated chicken soup.

Kermit couldn't get the *Cube* inside the convention center and that was the heart of the convention. The next best thing was in the parking area just outside of the action. *The Box* itself was in his elemental problem this time.

During this event Harry was jumping out of his skin, ready to go with his VIP lanyard hanging around his neck into the thick of it. Thrilled to the nines to walk around and see all the new gadgets and electronic eye candy. Getting all the free pens, computer screen cleaner, action figures associated with their products, and all the little plastic pieces of tech-paradise. And showing it off like trophies to us at the end of each day. He had the inside scoop, the 411, the word on the street, the goods on all of the gadgets. And he was loving every minute of it, then going to the casino at night to do some gambling with the *Grannies* and finishing off the night by going out for pancakes. I would say to Harry, "Are you taking out any of the grandmothers tonight?" And he would, just about every night.

The show that some of the models worked for was called *Mimzy Midgal and the Bathtub Chronicles.* It was a water show about a young woman who lived in a floating bathtub and her adventures at sea. They performed as dancers, portraying seaweed and conch shells. Some of them also worked in the Pirate Adventure show in front of one of the casinos, performing every two hours for people walking the strip, and the show was free! They would sink a whole ship. I saw it two times in one night.

If you're not a gambler and just want to hide at the end of the day, you could venture off the main strip. The strip is only 4.2 miles long, and you can walk it in an hour and some change. Beyond that is what you would call the suburban area, where most of the people who work in the casinos live. One of Paris's favorite restaurants was located not too far from where we were staying, not too far from the strip. It was a little Italian place run by a family that had a sister restaurant in Scottsdale. The place was called Il Quarto Piatto, known for their family-style dishes.

I said, "Why don't we go to your favorite restaurant for supper tonight?"

"Really?" She said with her eyes all aglow.

I could tell she was homesick and tired of eating on a paper plate.

"Sure, we got nothing on the agenda tonight. We'll get grannies to watch the kids. Let's have some Italian."

Harry and Kermit were already wandering the aisles of the casino with a *Granny* or two, so Paris and I dressed up like responsible adults and went to Il quarto piatto in the suburbs.

The restaurant was located inside what felt like a subway tube—a long half-circle with square tables in its center and red leather booths along the sides just before it curves. The floor was dark concrete, and large advertisement posters were plastered on top of each other, lining the curves in the ceiling. They said things like L'erba coltiva i pomodori, pasta gomito basilico e sedano, and quattro piatti olio d'oliva.

"Is this a BBQ place?" I ask.

"No, it's Italian," Paris laughed.

We were escorted to our table by the host, and Paris ordered a Margarita. Taking a look at the beverages, I was playfully surprised to find an old soda flavor I was familiar with. I smiled and ordered an orange pop, and we both eased into the night, enjoying the atmosphere. Both of us were a little homesick and just wanted to dress up like adults, eat a meal with real silverware, drink out of a glass rather than a paper cup, and talk about, well, anything but work.

The work I had been doing for the last three years was isolating. Being by myself all day, and every movement, every gesture, every day, I was viewed from a distance. Even the people working with me were separated from me by glass.

The *Cube* did have a series of knives, forks, and spoons in its drawer in the kitchenette. They weren't worth anything real. They were just a step above plastic. I had taken a set for myself and kept them in my rolling suitcase to use when I would check into hotels. The Il Quarto Piatto restaurant had real silverware with grapevines imprinted in the handles, and they had a nice weight to them. The tables were covered with blue and red mosaic tiles and had wine bottle drip candles. It was a beautiful little gem tucked away from the contrasting city of lights just beyond its doors. This was just what the doctor ordered. I had discovered a soda pop I thought was extinct, had one of the best Italian meals I've had in years, and no one was looking at me. Paris was a very tall, urbane, and attractive woman. People took notice when she walked into a room. She had an almost intimidating kind of beauty.

It was calm, and I had not had the time to get to know Paris until that evening, and the environment was perfect. She was telling me about the hot summers in Scottsdale where they would put plastic bags of ice in pitchers of beer to keep it cold. How she met her boyfriend and working as a mermaid. And I was transfixed by the amount of wax that was produced by these candles. We had just finished our plates of lettuce when I noticed out of the corner of my eye a man with a group of his friends kept looking in our direction. He was about thirty, clean-cut, business casual. Then he took out a camera and took two pictures of us. The flash caught Paris off guard, and she slowly turned to see who took it. The man looked at her and grinned ear to ear. She then turned back and placed her glass on the table. The color drained from her face. You could see her mood change. I looked at her and asked, "Did he just take our picture?"

And Paris said with all the sadness in the world, "Yes, that happens to me all the time."

CHAPTER 05

Salt Lake City, Utah,
The Winter Olympics,
KISS, and The Mormons

We pulled into Salt Lake City for the Winter Olympics. Park City also was the location for some of the events. That's where we were located. We couldn't find a hotel, motel, or a broom closet to rent for the week. The entire city was booked solid. The closest place we could find was in Pleasant Grove, and it took us about an hour to get out of Salt Lake and back to the hotel, that is if the fates would allow. Salt Lake City was booming. The entire world was there. This was the fourth attempt Salt Lake bid to win and host the games and they got it. Events were all around the area. They had dancers in brown and red miniskirts from The Brown Beverage Brewing Company (BBB) doing somersaults and backflips on the snow-covered streets promoting their super sweet bubbly treat.

Photo by Kevin Lyons

Salt Lake City, Utah. Olympic Games.

We barely squeezed into a parking area next to the Park City Mountain Resort where the snowboarding competition was held.

This was an interview we did with a Canadian Independent News reporter. It was the first in a series of interviews we did with the walkie-talkies we picked up just before we hit Baker, California, and saw The World's Tallest Thermometer.

This was a clever idea. Instead of the interviewer, camera-man, sound guy, producer, and myself inside, we used a pair of Motorola FV700 Talkabout walkie-talkies. We decided on using them instead of the intercom system. That also meant when the interviewer was talking, he wasn't drowned out by the hum of the generator. I could speak in a loud clear voice back and over-power the sound of the generator. The best part of this is it gave the illusion that no one else was ever allowed inside. That means that media was not inside the *Cube* for interviews. Kermit would either have one in the cab of the truck or Harry would have it on his person. If we had to move, a simple, no-nonsense call using the walkie-talkies sufficed. The picture above has me holding one of the walkie-talkies during an interview.

Walkie-talkies connected a direct line. Once everything was locked down, including myself, I just called from my end, and we could move out with no restrictions in any way. Cutting two minutes on a lockdown was the difference from a bad exit with everyone giving us the long face to a grand, flawless escape. And as a bonus, when the media wanted to talk, Harry just handed his walkie-talkie over to the guy for the interview.

A reporter for a paper in New York was talking with Kermit about the functionality of the *Cube* and its occupant. He was explaining in great detail that I was living in the unit 24 hours a day and was completely cut off from what was happening just outside the glass, spinning the tale. Then Harry opened the side door and handed me my lunch. The reporter saw this and was livid. He grabbed the walkie-talkie from Kermit and stood right in front of me and said, *"I thought you were in a sterile, germ-free environment!"*

I picked up my walkie-talkie and calmly said to him, "Don't worry about it."

We didn't get to Salt Lake until after the Opening Ceremo-ny and a week into the games. Salt Lake was chosen for that year's festivities due to available infrastructure and housing. Housing for envying the world, excluding us. The city showcased winter sports glory with enormous photographs on buildings and Olympic Rings in white lights above the Olympic Village, resembling donuts on top of a mountain of ice cream.

The Olympics were held four years all over the world. Starting in 1992 the games then held every two years. And the symbol associated with the games both summer and winter are The Olympic Rings. Pierre de Coubertin, also known as the Father of the Modern Olympic Games, designed the Pierre de Coubertin medal in 1913. This medal is awarded to athletes who display exceptional sportsmanship and discipline during the Olympic Games. In Atlanta, Georgia, there's a monument called the Gateway of Dreams dedicated to his legacy. The gold medal, the highest honor, is made of at least 92.5 percent silver and plated with gold, containing 6 grams of pure gold. But as a kid I always thought they were filled with chocolate.

The Olympic Rings are to represent the five continents of the earth. They are five circles that interlace. In the colors of blue, yellow, black, greens and red. The colors appear on all the national flags throughout the world. United by Olympism. The balance of enlightenment, culture and cooperation. With the world competing with each other. This is done with style, beauty, physical skill and grace. And that year they were glowing on the side of a mountain.

The games and the individuals that participate in them are an exciting electric pulse of kindness that vibrates through the streets and the hearts of millions. It's one of the most beautiful human experiences we share as a collective.

We only wished we had a hotel close to the action. Or I had trained a little harder to make the U.S. Ski Team that year. This was last minute decision to make the games. The city had been planning this event for years and we somehow got the green light to come in at the last second. We were lucky they let us in the city and even luckier to find any hotel in the state of Utah that entire month. This was a high-profile event, meaning we had to keep the the entire truck gleaming, spic and span. But the trick is to make it look easy, look like it always has that fresh out of the factory look. We were one mobile event amongst many. Every major American institution was present representing their products in a fresh new package. Living commercials scattered around the city. The area was organized according to the events, and small happenings like us were scattered throughout, similar to an amusement park.

We were tucked in our area, and we did have a great number of onlookers. Now, everyone at this event was not just locals; they were people from all over the world. Americans always have a flair for the dramatic, and this was no different. Foreigners were like patrons going to a museum. I could see them out of the corner of my eye, asking questions like,

"What do you call this?"
"Is this late 20th Century man in his natural environment?"
"This would look marvelous at our villa. Do you have it in orange?"

It felt more like we were an art installation. That was the only time where I felt like a thing. This was the only time where it seemed like I was the extremely large fish you would find in the aquarium at a diner. At the *WAIT HERE TO BE SEATED* area just next to the cashier, the small silver bowl of pastel butter mint creams, and the refrigerated revolving hexagon pie display case. Something that doesn't go with the layout, but everyone expects it to be there, knows your name is Buford the big fish, and talks to you like you remembered the last time they came and last thing they ate.

We were in a side parking lot rather than on a busy street. Unless you were in the lot, you had to seek us out, like going to a ride. When the sun started to set, the day trippers scattered, and the night owls came out. We would close up, and since we had a location given to us by the city, we left the *Cube* there overnight. Security was tight the last year or so.

I would slip out *The Escape Hatch,* and then we would make the drive back to the hotel. The next day, we did the same thing, sneaking back inside, cleaning the glass, and enjoying the sunshine. We had a nice, secure location with no large trees or buildings obstructing the view.

And at the end of the Winter Olympic Games in the heart of what was formerly known as Mormon Country, where almost half of its residents follow the religion founded by Joseph Smith, where the world headquarters of The Church of Jesus Christ of Latter-day Saints resides, during the closing ceremony, on a rotating stage, on top of a sea of ice, with lights shining and sparks flying, with choreographed dances and ice skaters skating, a small four-man glam rock band named *KISS* sang their hearts out. It was to be Paul Daniel Frehley's final performance with the group he helped create. The members of this hard rock band and this religious organization, not to mention everyone associated with the world games, all worked together and selflessly gave everything they had to the world that winter. And let me tell you, that winter, the whole world was there.

CHAPTER 36

Tyler, Texas,
Tube Tops,
Scottsdale, Arizona,
The Hot Box,
Denver, Colorado,
and Tarp Trouble

Downshifting from the electric frenzy of the Olympics, we suddenly found ourselves in a small Texas town called Tyler, about 100 miles southeast of Dallas. The venue was smaller, but the trouble with the local hotel was bigger.

We ended up at your standard off-the-road place. Nothing too memorable, except that it was plaid. Everything was plaid. The furniture in the lobby, the wallpaper, even the rugs in the hallway. Tiny place. I think only three people were on staff at any given time. They were friendly and soft-spoken, even trustworthy. I felt comfortable staying there that first night.

We didn't have to travel far from the hotel to our location, and we were thankful there was no snow on the ground. The next day, we were on-site with no problem finding parking, and everything was going swimmingly, almost perfect.

Then I got a couple of phone calls about tube tops.

Ring, ring, goes my cellphone.

"Hello," I said.

"This is Officer Billy Sutherland of the Tyler Police Department. May I speak to Randolph Hubard?"

I paused for a moment and then said,

"This is he."

"Hello, I was just calling about Cecile Bergman," he said.

Before Officer Sutherland called, I was unaware of a *Cecile Bergman.*

About an hour before, I received a call from my credit card company. They wanted to make sure that the fourteenth tube top that was ordered at 3 am was a legitimate purchase. This was not something that I ordered. I asked if they would cancel the order and my card, and send me a new one at the hotel in Tyler as soon as possible. Then Officer Sutherland called.

"Mr. Hubard, I've known Cecile for some time. I went to high school with her older brother... She has had some trouble in the past and she is trying to get her life together."

I had no idea what he was talking about. I didn't know who *Cecile* was or why an Officer of the State of Texas was talking to me about her and his days in high school.

"*This isn't the first time she has done this,*" he said.

"Alright, slow this down. I need to catch up... What are you talking about? I asked.

"*The credit card purchases,*" he muttered.

This was insane. This was the second time a cop called me on this gig.

"How in the world do you know about that?" I asked.

Only moments ago, I found out that my card was being used to order tube tops after midnight. And now I was talking to Billy about his time in school. It sounded like he was probably the father of this tube top obsessed girl. And he admitted this wasn't the first time she has done this!

"*Just to let you know, they just let her go,*" he said.

"Let who, go what!?" I asked.

She was the night manager at the hotel we were staying at. She came into work, looked up my card information that was on file, and went on a shopping spree. And it was not just my card but other guests at the hotel, including Kermit.

"*Well, she has had some trouble in the past.*"

"Are you telling me the person who stole my credit card works at the hotel, and they fired her for buying tube tops?"

"*Yes.*"

"Well, I should hope so; tube tops are so..."

"*Yes, you see, she has had some trouble in her past.*"

He kept saying that. But I was slow to realize that this wasn't an isolated incident. Just then, I noticed Kermit on his cell phone with the same wrinkle in his forehead that I had.

"Officer Sutherland, I just received this information. Are you concerned that I would press charges against Sarah?" I asked.

"*Cecile, yes. That's why I'm calling,*" he said.

"Listen, I'm not going to do anything like that. But she's not buying any tube tops now is she... IS SHE!?"

"*No, she is here with me now.*"

"Billy, may I call you Billy? I have to process this. Can I get a number where I can reach you?" I asked.

"*Of course.*"

He then gave me his extension. I thanked him for reaching out to me, assured him we would discuss this matter further, and hung up. I looked out the window and witnessed Kermit passing back and forth as I saw his silhouette against the setting sun and thought, *Tube Tops?*

The hotel hadn't contacted us, and I knew we were heading back at the end of the day. *This evening would be interesting,* I thought.

We walked into the lobby of the hotel. Paris and Harry sat in the matching white and red striped armchairs and watched Kermit and I approach the front desk.

"Hello, I was just checking if there were any messages for me today?" I asked the spry young man behind the computer.

"I would be happy to check for you. What's your name, sir?"

"It's Hubard, Randolph Hubard. H-U-B as in bird, A-R-D as in diamond," I replied in a calm, slow, and carefree tone.

He froze, looked from his computer right to me. He turned white as a sheet and said, "Mr. Mr. Hu... uëbard... Would you mind waiting here for a moment?"

"I wouldn't mind at all," I responded.

He got up from his computer and went into a back room. Kermit, Harry, Paris, and I took turns looking at each other from across the lobby and tried our hardest not to burst out into laughter.

A few moments later, four perspiring people came to the front desk. The one in the necktie took over.

"Um, no messages for you today, Mr. Hubard. Nothing today," He spoke.

"That's too bad. I was expecting a call from, Officer, oh gosh, what's his name?"

"Sutherland!" cried the desk clerk on duty, standing in the corner.

The man in the tie completely ignored him, started typing on the computer keyboard and replied, "Nothing for you now, sir. Nothing at all. Can I do anything for you tonight? If your room isn't adequate, or would you like an upgrade this evening?"

"Sutherland, right. The room is fine, just fine. Would you just let me know if anyone calls this evening, especially if it's the police; I am expecting some tube tops," I said,

"Of course, sir. I'll handle it personally,"

"Thank you. Have a good evening," I said.

All of the people behind the desk were hanging on every word I was saying and looked baffled that I didn't mention the incident. Kermit and I walked to the elevator and left them in a state of utter confusion.

Scottsdale, Arizona is about 1,000 miles (1,609 kilometers) by road from Tyler, Texas. It's a drive, and you could definitely call Arizona a warm state, even a hot one. It's the kind of place where folks put plastic bags of ice in their pitchers of beer just to keep them cold. I'd definitely call that a warm state.

We checked into an extended-stay place called The Pink Caterpillar Hotel. It was a one-level hotel with a living room area connected to a bedroom. It didn't have a kitchenette, but we were located close to the nightlife, and that included restaurants.

Before we set up for an event after spending some time on the road, I always checked the inside to make sure nothing was destroyed on the drive. Every other time I walked inside on *Year Three*, it looked like someone ransacked it.

When we arrived in Scottsdale, I noticed a river of sand that had found its way from the road through the vent system, like a pathway to the beach. There was a hole in the air system underneath, and it was catching all the sand kicked up by the tires. The floor was easy to clean. The vents however, were a problem.

I turned on the air conditioning, and the sand hidden inside the vents blew everywhere. It was a sandstorm. It was getting in my eyes and kicking up out of all the vents. It was like a thousand needles flying all over the place. I opened every vent and hand-cleaned the system, and it still blew sand. The solution was cheesecloth lined underneath the vents, acting like a spiderweb that caught the sand as it blew.

And as soon as I got the sand problem under control, the air conditioning stopped working. This was the Arizona desert; I was in a hot box, and there was no cool air. Nothing; it just blew in the hot air that was outside. I petitioned the office to have someone come out and fix it. I called their parents to put pressure on their children. I called their ex-lovers, their veterinarians—anyone and everyone. And no one came out to fix it. Every morning, I would turn it on to see if it fixed itself.

After that illusion passed, I would look for the shade inside and move the kitchen chair to that corner until the sun moved. And the sun moved every day. Then, I would drink a gallon of water and hope that we would finish early. As soon as we were done for the day, I would hop in the minivan with Paris, and she would ask if I wanted coffee. The thought of having coffee made me want to vomit. I just wanted to get back to the hotel where it was dark and cold. I would then turn on the air conditioning in the hotel to full blast, grab the ice bucket, fill up the tub with ice and water, and lay in it for an hour until my body didn't feel like it was going to burst into flames.

After that, my internal organs cooled down. I'd sip water, watch my soaps, and then I would realize I hadn't consumed anything solid the entire day. I'd stumble down the street to get a salad with some type of protein, forcing myself to eat. The next day, I would start the entire routine over again.

The worst of this was one day they drove to the desert. Literally the desert. There was a road that led to just sand. No buildings, no inhabitants, nothing. I thought they took me there to die. No trees, no businesses, no large structures to give shade, no people to give salt to. A place devoid of life and comfort. I finally realized why my shirt wasn't wet. It hadn't looked wet all week. It was hot, but my shirt was bone dry. It was so hot in that *Cube* that my sweat evaporated before it hit my shirt.

We had a few days in Denver before Hugh was to come out and do a ride-along with us. We'd never had a ride-along before. This was an indoor event at The Ball Arena (formerly known as The Pepsi Center).

Hugh showed up one sunny morning after we were on the street doing a guerrilla event in the downtown area. He was standing at the back of the *Cube*, and I could see him conversing with Paris and Harry. Then I got a call from Kermit on the walkie-talkie that we had to move.

"Alright," I said.

"Just give me five minutes to lock it down."

"No worries. By the way, Hugh wants to ride with us today."

"Alright, it's his funeral. Is he going to wear that hat?"

Hugh was an office guy. He spent his days calculating the miles we would travel in a week and talking to the cities to get permits to allow us in their streets. And he showed up in Denver wearing a ten-gallon hat. Many office people, when going to locations, want to look like locals. Hugh stuck out like a sore thumb.

I locked down the hatches, strapped myself in, and called back to Kermit that we were ready to roll. And we did. We hopped on Interstate I-25 and searched for a spot to set up for the rest of the day. As soon as I set up, we were kicked out. We locked everything down and searched for another location. And another and another.

On Interstate I-70, on the highway, the tarp flipped over the front of the cab, completely covering the front windows. We quickly pulled over to the shoulder. Kermit hopped out and, by himself, flipped the tarp back. We got back on the highway. A few miles later, we pulled over to the shoulder. I called Kermit.

"What's going on?"

"The tarp keeps coming undone and rolls over the windows,"

This kept happening over and over. At some point, the tarp laid against the exhaust pipe and shrunk, and the heat from the pipe melted it. Or shrunk so much that we could not pull it down to snap it secure on the bottom. We could secure it on one side and just a few button snaps on the other side. It looked like a half-wrapped birthday present. It was bad enough that the tarp caught wind like a sail when we were driving. Now we couldn't even secure it. It looked like a flag with the side slapping against the glass.

When we finally got to a secure place and finished the day, the decision was made to swap The *Cube* with another one that was in storage. It wasn't just the tarp problem. On the way to Pasadena, Kermit stopped in Albuquerque, New Mexico, for fuel. We stayed the night in New Mexico while on our way to California. It was late, and we were an hour away from our hotel. We just needed to get gas and then fall into the beds for the night. This was the first time Kermit was dealing with the truck. After fueling up, he did a turn around and hit a guardrail on the way out, damaging the backside of the *Cube*.

Kermit was losing his mind. He later told me he thought he was going to be canned. He drove with us the whole time after he hit the guardrail and drove on the highway on the opposite side of us, trying to conceal the damage. When he smashed the guardrail, he didn't even get out to assess the destruction. He just got back on the highway and hoped for the best.

When we got to the hotel, he drove the *Cube* to a shady street and left it there overnight, thinking that in the morning they could just tell the office it was damaged by some local kids looking for trouble overnight. By the time we got to Denver, Craftsmen had brought out another *Cube*, and we just switched them. Not because Kermit damaged it, but because I asked to switch it for the air conditioning.

Fairs and carnivals were slowly becoming some of my favorite locations, not just for this particular project, but for other things I have worked on or yet to work on. The Riverside County Fair and National Date Festival was our next stop—Indio, California, about 20 miles east of Palm Springs. This desert friendly festival was a lock and key event. It was all fenced in. We occupied the space between the floating duck game and a booth manned by religious fanatics declaring, *The End is Near!* on a large white banner in the back. I couldn't determine who stared at each other more – me or them.

Kermit dropped off my lunch and gave me one of their pamphlets. I felt obligated to read it; they were literally watching me read it. Word for word.

The left side was where all the games and food stands were, and on the right was the chain-link fence separating us from the vendors' cars and camper trucks. Not far away were the alligators and ostriches, though they didn't share the same space simultaneously. They had races for the ostriches and shows for the alligators.

The fair featured walk-around characters, including individuals dressed as a barbershop quartet in striped jackets and handlebar mustaches, and a clown on stilts with a basketball hoop hanging from his chest. He would bounce the ball to kids, who would then shoot it into the small hoop. Every day, before starting his rounds, he would knock on the *Cube's* glass to say hello. Because he was on stilts, we could see eye to eye. Each day, he'd come up, tap on the glass, gaze straight into my eyes with a face full of makeup, and give me a good scare. I couldn't decide what was creepier – the religious vibes watching me from the back of the *Cube* or the clown standing right in front of me.

My love affair with carnival life began to bloom during this time. The novelties, the plastic, the glass, and the vibrant colors of all those small and large oddities. A carnival barker just outside my window showcased a collection of clear drinking glasses embellished with tiny cherries, lemons, and pineapples. They caught my eye daily, tempting me to throw down good money on these crooked games. I could see myself spending $40 on a game only to leave without a single cherry drinking glass.

Turning to Kermit, I tasked him with the mission of trying to win those glasses. I asked Kermit to see if he could win them. Giving him a $20 and saying, "See what you can do."

An hour later, he calls me and tells me to open the cabinet. Sitting on the lip were four clear drinking glasses adorned with cherries, lemons, oranges, and pineapples. He won all of them. I have no idea if he won them with the twenty, or if he spent $60 of his own money on them.

CHAPTER

Savannah, Georgia,

The Trick of The Walkie-Talkies,

Hilton Head, South Carolina,

The Short Vacation,

Macon, Georgia,

and The Cherry Blossom Festival

It was St. Patrick Day. We turned into a Stay Quite O' Bit Hotel (SQOBH) and pulled up next to a white Ryder Tandem Straight Truck with green highlights. It had a large green tarp covering the back with the words *Tamiflu* written on it. It was Anthony's *Cube*. We were now in the same place at the same time. We had to be careful not to open a vortex.

You knew you were in Savannah, the large oak trees with Spanish moss were everywhere. They either hang in the air or sway in the wind. Each piece looks like a green ghost tangled in the trees, sometimes trying desperately to escape and other times at complete ease with the world. It was another picture-perfect view from the inside of *The Box*.

The morning after St. Patrick's, we were waiting in the parking lot waiting for our driver. Kermit's body emerged from the hotel, and there was nothing else in it. I've observed people battling hangovers and the aftermath of a night of partying. However, I had never before encountered what unfolded as that door swung open. Kermit was first beaten down by the morning light. Then, walking became a difficult task. We were all silent, for he was about to speak.

"Randolph, I think I'm still drunk," Kermit slurred.

"Did you eat anything?" I asked.

"I can't. I can't even stand up," he said.

Just then, Harry, with a look of concern, came out with a plate of watermelon and gave it to Kermit.

"Eat... Eat." Harry commanded Kermit. "Eat!"

Harry drove the truck to the site, and I drove the other minivan.

Once we got to the site, I climbed in through *The Escape Hatch*, and they opened the tarp with drunken difficulty. The temperature was almost 90 degrees, and the sun had just started rising. As they were placing the ladders inside the back, I opened the cabinet door and said to Kermit, "Here, drink this." I then gave him an entire gallon of water.

"And when you think you've had enough, drink more," I commanded. "Drink!"

It was spring, and everyone knew it. Since we switched out the *Cube*, the temperature outside was hot, but it was cool as a cucumber inside because the air conditioning worked. I slapped on some sunscreen and started the day. This was a fad at the time, but a large number of walkie-talkies were in use, and it was interfering with our communication system, for we were also using walkie-talkies. The entire day I kept hearing conversations like this,

"Jackie, I don't have the keys to the car, do you?"
"Where are you?"
"We are going home! No, I said if you misbehave... that's it!"
"Where are you."
"We're meeting for lunch. Are you drinking already, are you!?
"Down by the water. I'm waving at you now. Do you see us!?
"Where are you!?"

I couldn't resist. I started responding to them.

"I'm in the parking lot. I'm over by the yellow car," I said. "Did you pick up your adult diapers? I should've dated your sister." I cried.

"I started drinking the day I met your mother... the day I met her!"

Drinking? I thought to myself. Then I looked out onto the grassy field and saw Kermit laying on his back with his shirt over his head and an empty plastic gallon jug of water next to him.

We had a couple of days to kill before our last scheduled stop. Paris found a little hotel right on the beach, The Frontview Ocean Point Resort, Seacrest Oceanfront Resort (FOPRSOR). It had a huge lobby with bright, thick red rugs and white-painted wicker chairs. Wide photos of the beach in glorious color littered the walls. Quaint little gas lamps hung from the white wood walls. Complete with a clear view of the beach from the front door.

We considered this a vacation, mostly because we made good time before the festival. The protocol was to find a hiding place for the *Cube*, and they had a few out-of-the-way areas for us to park—perfectly hidden away from any passerbys. We just wanted to disappear amongst the town folk and enjoy a couple of days in Hilton Head.

We checked in, and I headed straight for my yellow room. The entire room was yellow. The carpet was an orange yellow. The bedding was yellow with blue and black drawings of dandelions and branches. The wallpaper was yellow with tiny blue dots. They even had a wicker chair painted yellow, with a yellow and blue striped seat cushion. The bathroom was painted yellow too. The only person I spoke to during the day was Paris. She would go to the gym every morning, and then swing by Bustersteins. By this time she knew my drink. And around 11 every morning she would knock on my door in her workout gear and hand me my drink.

"Do you want to get dinner later?" she asked.

"Yes, let's get the kids and have a nice family dinner."

And that was about as much as we all saw each other during our stay. I would periodically drop by the parking area to make sure the *Cube* was alright. It was in a small lot with thick, branch-like bushes surrounding it with a mixture of sand, rocks, and blacktop on the ground. The tarp was tightly secured, and no exterior damage could be seen. But I still went inside through *The Escape Hatch* to give a look around. That thing is hot without any moving air. But every day it was alright and without incident. I always parked the minivan right next to the *Cube* and then rolled underneath. It was parked with one side against the thick bushes, and it was well out of sight for anyone to see me.

The International Cherry Blossom Festival in Macon, Georgia, held at The Carolyn Crayton Park, provided a vibrant atmosphere on the midway. The festival showcased a Royal Court with a Legacy Queen, Queen, Princess, Little Miss, and Little Mister. Despite my request, lunch with the Queen was unavailable. The festival featured a parade, Emerald Ball, and musicians on makeshift stages. As an outside vendor, we worked on the outskirts, between a fried dough stand and a turkey leg grill truck. Vendor logistics in fairs and carnivals involve careful planning for space, power, and level ground. We ensured self-sufficiency with our own generator, elevated setup, and wheels on level ground. Adhering to unwritten boundaries with neighboring vendors was crucial. The aroma of grilled turkey legs from the nearby truck permeated the entire *Cube*, creating an inescapable scent of turkey since you're basically just continually inhaling your own air.

Not only did it smell like turkey legs, but all I saw were turkey legs. That's all you could see – this large grill with dozens of turkey legs wrapped in tin foil on it all day. And they couldn't grill them fast enough. I would sit on the loveseat and watch them grill the legs.

I started to grow a fondness for fairs and carnivals this time around. When the sun goes down and the colored lights start blinking, it's nothing less than awesome. You see foods that shouldn't exist like hamburgers with honey dipped doughnuts for buns, deep-fried bubblegum, foot-long corn dogs on a stick, snow cones the size of softballs, and thinly sliced potato skins deep-fried and piled high – the entire skin of the potato fried as a single piece.

You see giant stuffed animals with red ears and plaid paws, marbled colored oddly shaped balloons, and inflatable brown baseball bats. Airbrushed oversized t-shirts that say *Jason & Sabrina 4ever* with a unicorn and a dragon holding hands. Wooden, shellacked toy Air Force helicopters, transparent, fluorescent lemonade drinking devices with bendable straws, and frozen cheesecake on sticks covered in a pantry full of nuts and coconut shavings. And that's just the tip of the iceberg.

Seeing the carnies spinning the bells and whistles, creating the machine – the guys who grease the wheels for the Scrambler and the bumper cars. The electricians who are constantly producing the electrical voltage to the galaxy of blinking lights, and the barkers who speak so fast they can't catch their breath.

The candy apple makers, dipping thousands upon thousands of fire engine red balls into shiny lollipop liquids who are the third and fourth generation. And the game masters tricking you into thinking every game has a winner, who look like they would want to be anywhere else than where they are. These were the people that lived in tiny campers. That walked the clown alleys. They survived in the shadows. And when the sun went down, they came out, and it became another world entirely.

This was our last scheduled event.

We were also in Georgia, double-booked for two different happenings. We had to be at the Atlanta City Race Course (ACRC). Now when this transpired, I was completely out of the loop. Craftsmen made eight of these *Apartments on Wheels*. Two were on the road, and the other six were in storage – they were in Atlanta. Anthony was somewhere in Florida with his; I was in Macon with another. Somehow, Harry was talked or blackmailed into riding around the racetrack in one of the other ones. I had no idea this was going on. I was just staring at turkey legs all day.

Harry sitting in the loveseat in his boxers, eating bananas, and riding around the racetrack with Kermit driving – I thought they both ducked out to go on one of the helicopter rides on the other side of the fairgrounds. But Harry was inside, and you can probably guess which one he had. The one with no air conditioning. I asked Harry how he liked it, and he said, "I didn't, not one single bit, being in that thing."

CHAPTER 38

Surviving The Great Glass Adventure,
and Thanking the Old Man

We pulled into an airplane hangar off a long dirt road on the outskirts of Atlanta. Everyone was there. We parked each *Glass Box* behind a yellow and black safety marker on the ground. Everything that was not bolted down, was stripped down to its core. Each *Cube* was inspected, photographed, and cataloged from headlights to taillights. They did everything except drain the fuel. All ladders, snow chains, silverware, pillows, bed sheets, and knives were placed into storage bins and piled next to one another on tall industrial shelves. They sat in a dusty graveyard next to wooden crates, nailed shut with iron spikes from campaigns from yesteryear. This was a place where campaigns go to die. It was the final resting place.

Even though we knew no one would ever enter these *Boxes* again, I shined the glass and tidied up. Cleaned out every personal fingerprint and smudge inside. The plastic action figures snapped off the shelf with ease. The tarp was secured. I could hear Kermit snapping the buttons while I did my last walkthrough inside. It was quiet, warm, and uncomfortably hollow. I entered these things when they were new to the world and now, I was saying goodbye.

I did my final exit through *The Escape Hatch*. We signed them out on a plastic clipboard, and heard the large metal gate roll closed as we walked away. No one said a word.

Back at the hotel, sitting down at the bar in the center of the artificial rock quarry and drinking a beer, you could hear the sound of sterile, bleached, undrinkable water running in the background. Anthony took the seat next to me.

"Last day of school. Did you clean out your locker?" I asked.

He nodded and tried to hold back his sadness through his smile.

The wrap-up was really quick as saying goodbye to an adventure is. The next morning, walking to the front desk, I heard a friendly laugh,

"Mr. Hubard. Are you leaving us today, sir?"

"I'm afraid so, Vernon. I can't thank you enough for everything. You run a tight ship here."

"It was nothing. I hope we will be honored by your return sometime in the future," Vernon said with a smile.

"I hope so, Vernon. That would be nice. I hope so."

"Ah, cheer up, remember this is just the beginning," Vernon cried.

Stumbling up the stairs, half-dazed, to my third-floor railroad apartment in Brooklyn, I suddenly got greeted by an enormous sense of reality; it was over. Rolling my bag into the bedroom, opening the window, and letting the spring air in was a great feeling of peace.

In the kitchen, the dishes were piled ceiling-high on the dish dryer that I picked up the year before, somewhere on the outskirts of Arizona. And said, *"Hello,"* to the dry, brown Christmas tree still in the corner.

My roommates were on the phone and the world wides webs, hustling for their next gig as I wandered back to my room. Then, from my bag, I took out a small, brightly colored orange box and gently opened it. Inside was a tiny brass robot, the size of two fingers with microscopic buttons and knobs on its front. The face was a two-hand clock that's the size of your thumbnail. This was a treasure. This wasn't an enormous moose target stuffed with hay, it wasn't a pair of camouflaged cargo pants, it wasn't a pound of beef jerky. But it was a gift that Kermit so desperately wanted to give me when we were in Washington state. He found it at that gun show. It was a birthday present for me.

I unpacked everything in my bags, laid out the expense reports on my desk, and before I could catch my breath, I was face down on my bed asleep. The next morning, I went into the sunroom and started adding all the spacemen I had collected over the years to the shelves high on the northwest wall. There were now dozens of action figures of different colors, shapes, and sizes. Some were covered with fur, some were wearing masks with capes, and some had jet packs. Every one of them was found in small hideaways, family-owned shops, or large discount bargain basement bins all across the country. They proudly stood tall, showcasing their splendor, all facing forward.

I opened a bag of coffee from my adventure, brewed a pot, and settled in, facing the glorious display of color and detail. Just then Hogarth entered and spoke softly, "What a sight to behold, you got all of these when you were traveling through the country?"

"Yes, I got them everywhere," I said.

"They're fantastic," he said.

"Well, you can thank the old man for that," I cried.

"Who?"

"Never mind," I said.

It wasn't just these plastic, little space men I wanted to thank the old man in the wheelchair for. It was all the oddball hotels, the restaurants that served key lime cake, the snow-covered mountains, the dark uncertainty in the desert, the flickering lights in Vegas, the urns of coffee, the lonely people walking the roads, the tugboat, the *Glass Box*, Samuel L. Jackson, barefoot gnomes holding peppermint sticks, the three-ring binders, home made blueberry cobbler in Cool Whip containers, the Loch Ness monster, the two zombie half-wits, the terrified hotel desk staff, the thousand horrible birthday parties, the police officers, the heroic bus driver, the ladybugs, the tub tops, *The Runts*, the tumbleweeds, young pregnant women looking for companionship, styrofoam roosters, rollercoasters in amusement parks, the people who thought of *The Box*, the people who made *The Box*, the people who worked for *The Box*, the people inside *The Box*, the crazy stuntman driver and his incredibly attractive girlfriend, the people who worked in the office, the people who make the world run, Buck, my friends, and everything else I can't think of at the moment. The whole thing! I eased back in the rocking chair, took a sip of coffee from a roaster in the great state of Nebraska, and thought, *What am I going to do next?*

Ring, ring, goes my cell phone.

Photo by Kevin Lyons

Salt Lake City, Utah. Olympic Games.

The Man in the Glass Box
or One Man's Journey Across the United States in a Glass
Apartment on Wheels.

The Adventure Continues

NOMAD ON THE PLEASURE GROUNDS

PROLOGUE

Close to Midnight Floating on the Hudson

It was warm, the air was still and thick, the parlor was full of un-comfortable, colorful characters moving slowly about. Through the windows, you could make out the skyline in the near distance. Three, including myself, waited for her to speak.

"If I stand on this hand and you're bluffing, well, let's just say I would be very, very, very upset."

"Dealer will now double-down," I said again in a cool, low-toned, confident voice. She didn't acknowledge my statement, didn't move a muscle, just sat and pondered for a moment. I pulled the sleeves of my black jacket to reveal the red circular flame cufflinks against my white shirt, hoping to catch the lassies eye and shift her focus from the game.

There was a pause so silent you could drive a hearse through it without waking the corpse. We were the only table playing for keeps as we glided softly across the Hudson River. The inevitable pulse of the engine, begging for death, was the only thing grounding us to reality in that moment, besides the smell of stale, cheap cola. One hundred dollars was nothing to laugh at, especially if you didn't have it. Even more so if you were on a paddlewheel boat chugging along the Hudson so close to midnight. You had nowhere to go. *Is it alright for the dealer to emotionally blackmail the players in 21? Were we playing blackjack, or had we moved on to crazy eights? I wasn't sure what game we were involved in, and I was the dealer!*

"I'm not getting any younger. Are you in or out?" I quizzed.

"Hold on, I'm thinking."

"Well, don't hurt yourself." I couldn't believe I just said that to her. She eagerly sat down at my table with blissful laughter and was the only woman I interacted with that evening on a playful basis. But don't be fooled; she was playing for keeps. Her white and green sequined strapless dress kept my eyes glued in her direction. You could say she had class, only if you ignored her glowing red sunburned chest. Her dress might have been strapless that muggy spring night, but her tan lines suggested she wore a one-piece on the beach the day before. She was confident and confused at the same time.

The night was growing old; it was time to close up the hour. She and all the other passengers were dressed to the nines, worn to a frazzle after partying all night, eating chicken fingers, french fried potatoes, and sliders from the buffet table, breaking in new shoes and forgetting bandages for blistering heels, hammertoes, and broken hearts. Her mascara was losing its hold, *her* shoes were somewhere on this boat, and she had thrown her fluorescent yellow plastic party derby hat to the floor just before this hand. She wanted to end the night on a high. She wanted to break me down, read my face as false, walk away with the chips—she wanted to win.

"Marcy, are you in or are you out?"

Before I finished the sentence, Marcy slapped her last two chips on the green felt and said, *"I'm in it for the whole thing, Baron Von Dealer!"*

The fellow in the white tuxedo to her right did the same, minus the speaking of course. I don't believe he had two brain cells to rub together anymore. It looked like it was way past his bedtime. As for the guy in the plaid jacket and clip-on tie sitting softly to her left, he folded like a slice of pizza. *White tuxedo* showed his hand: two of spades face up, king of hearts flipped over.

"12," I said.

Marcy had an eight of diamonds beamed to the heavens, and then she flipped the ace of clubs.

"19, or 9, ladies' choice of course," I cried.

"You can't beat my hand. You have a jack of hearts showing. You need a 10. There aren't any more 10s in that deck, not that I've been counting. I don't even know what day this is."

I paused, mostly to see if she could stand it. I lifted my card and allowed my face to drop.

"Ah, you're bad, lousy poker face you've gots, Mr. Man. You already gave yourself away."

I let out a sigh as I played my final card face up. It was a spade, and it was a 10. At this point, red or black didn't matter. I won, but Marcy lost.

"Balderdash!" Marcy was surprised.

Just then, the captain of the boat rang the tiny bell, the staff in their blue work suits and white Navy-style sailor hats closed the lids on the buffet, and the engine downshifted to a low rumble. All those subtle things indicated we were about to dock. I gathered the final chips for the night and said to the table,

"On behalf of the good people at the *Riverside Roll & Win Gambler's Delight Cruise,* we thank you for choosing us to be your night of entertainment around the great city of New York, and we hope to see you again."

The lights on the boat started to slowly rise as we made our way into port. The music shifted from hip-hop to smooth instrumental jazz. The guests started gathering purses, shoes, their dignity, and their dates. The other dealers, carnival barkers, and game masters quickly shut down their shops of satisfaction. Wet feather boas, plastic derby hats, broken fluorescent sunglasses, evening event cards, and flashing colorful necklaces were scattered across the floor. I had closed the table for the night and shifted my focus to breaking everything down. It wasn't much, collecting the custom-made playing cards that said *Riverside Roll & Win* on them and the chips that screamed *Gambler's Delight Cruise* in a circular old-timey neon font around the edges. Just organizing circles and rectangles.

Someone softly touched my shoulder. I turned around.

"Would it be alright if I got a picture with you?" Marcy asked tentatively.

"You want a picture with me?"

"It's not every night I get to have my senior prom, especially on a boat," Marcy smiled ear to ear.

"Of course."

We both walked over to the large plastic backdrop that said, *"New York, New York: Senior Prom on the Water,"* and the man in the white tuxedo took our picture as we smiled standing back-to-back with our arms crossed as if we were partners in a buddy cop movie.

"Alright, Marcy, good luck with everything. It was a pleasure to beat you; I mean, meet you." She tilted her head, squinted her eyes, and pouted her lips. *White tuxedo* grabbed her purse, and they locked arms, heading towards new horizons together.

As the last of the night's guests exited the boat, I cried to her, "Oh, by the way, Marcy, it's April 19th. At least for another eight minutes!"

The crowd disappeared into the night, the boat was locked to the old wooden pier, and I had already slipped off my black bow tie and folded my cummerbund nicely into my backpack. The air was getting warmer, and somewhere in Jersey the bells started to toll. You could faintly hear them scurry across the harbor, and a new day had begun as I walked off the water onto the concrete path on the west side of the island—suddenly alone.

I had a good ten hours before the plane took off. If I believed New York was warm in April, Florida is gonna be an inferno. But I'm getting ahead of myself. Atlanta and the *Craftsman* warehouse were the first stops. Then back to New York, and then the drive to the *land of sunshine*. This is all supposed to happen in the next four days, not to mention the morning show we have to do live! I still didn't know what the vehicle looked like or how it's going to handle on the road. We had to chuck the log books out the window if we were going to make this happen. *Too wired now, I'll have a midnight coffee, pack my bags, wait till first light, and maybe I'll get forty winks before wheels up. And before you know it, I'll be on the Pleasure Grounds.*

Acknowledgment

My deepest gratitude to all those who contributed to the creation of this book. The people who have been rocks in my life, and the people who have spent only moments in it. My wife, Laura, whose unwavering support and encouragement made this project possible. I am also grateful to my family and friends for their patience and understanding throughout this journey. Special thanks to Roche Pharmaceuticals, Craftsman Industries, the Marketing Companies, and everyone who worked directly or indirectly on this project. Lastly, I want to acknowledge the readers whose interest and enthusiasm inspire me to continue sharing these stories. Thank you.

Writer bio.

This memoir documents actual adventurous travels across the United States, in a unique custom-made glass apartment on wheels. Randolph Hubard invites readers to explore this unique experience of the world and embrace the journey of life on the road.
"The Man in the Glass Box," the first in a series of compelling true tales of adventure, serves as a gateway to an enthralling undertaking where every turn of the page promises new discoveries and strange encounters.
While twelve people have walked on the moon, only ten have experienced life inside the glass box. This is the story of one of them.

Index:

E:
- The Elements of Style: A Practical Encyclopedia of Interior Architectural Details from 1485 to the Present: Stephen Calloway & Elizabeth Cromley / Simon & Schuster. 176.
- Eloise in Paris: Kay Thompson / illustration Hilary Knight / Simon & Schuster. 176.
- The Erie Canal: New York State Canal Corporation, a subsidiary of New York State Thruway Authority. 297. 298. 302
- Enya: New age, ambient, Celtic band / Eithne Pádraigín Ní Bhraonáin. 265.

F:
- FDA (Food and Drug Administration): United States Department of Health and Human Services. 33.
- Formica: Daniel J. O'Conor & Herbert A. Faber / Formica Corp. 95.
- Frankenstein: Mary Shelley / Lackington, Hughes, Harding, Mavor & Jones. 264.
- Dr. Fraser Winslow Crane: created by Glen & Les Charles / James Burrows / NBC / Paramount Network Television / played by Kelsey Grammer. 229. 230.
- Frisbee: Walter Morrison & Warren Franscioni / Wham-O, Inc. 170.
- Furbies: David Hampton & Caleb Chung / Tiger Electronics / Hasbro. 319.

G:
- Gateway of Dreams: sculptor Raymond Kaskey / City of Atlanta. 335.
- Ghost Riders in Sky: written by Stan Jones / sung by Johnny Cash / MPL Publishing, Inc. / Columbia Records. 73.
- The Girl who loved Tom Gordon: Stephen King / Scribner. 223.
- The Golden Gate Bridge: Golden Gate Bridge, Highway & Transportation District / California. 308.
- Gone with the Wind: Margaret Mitchell / Macmillan Publishes. 176.

L:
- The Las Vegas Convention Center: Las Vegas Convention & Visitors Authority (LVCVA). 325.
- Lakmé: Flower Duet: composed by Léo Delibes. 207.
- The Lost City of Atlantis: Plato / Timaeus & Critias. 295.
- Lot Lizards: mentioned in book Sarah by JT LeRoy / Bloomsbury Publishing. 106.

M:
- The Mall of America (MOA): Triple Five Group. 119. 120.
- Melmoth Wanderer: Charles Maturin / Henry Colburn / Archibald Constable & Co. / Hurst, Robinson & Co. / Cheapside, London. 176.
- MetroCard: Metropolitan Transportation Authority of New York City. 4.
- Miami Hurricanes: University of Miami. 307.
- Mini Skirt; Esquivel: Juan García Esquivel / Combustible Edison / Brother Cleve / RCA Records / Victor. 80.
- Modern Man in Search of a Soul: Carl Jung / Harcourt, Brace & Co. 176.
- Montclair State College: State of New Jersey through New Jersey Office of Secretary of Higher Education. 245.
- Mother Goose: Charles Perrault / John Newbery Publisher. 308.
- Motorcycle Chase: Ron Toomer / Arrow Dynamics / Knott's Berry Farm / Ceder Fair Entertainment Co. 233.
- Motorola Walkie Talkie's: Motorola Solutions, Inc. 334.
- Mr. Coffee: Newell Brands / previously owned by Sunbeam Corp. 62. 80. 84. 149. 303. 352.
- MTV: ViacomCBS Networks International / Paramount Media Networks. 57.
- Mudflap Girls: Bill Zinda / possibly based on Leta Laroe / Rachel Ann Allen. 106.
- The Museum of Pop Culture (MoPOP): Paul Allen / Museum of Pop Culture Foundation. 229. 230.

Glossary:

The Glass Box: Refers to the custom-made glass apartment on wheels used in the marketing campaign, providing a unique traveling experience across the United States. (The Cube, The Box, The Bubble, The Glass Apartment on Wheels).

Colonial Parkway Murders: Unsolved murders that took place in the 1980s along the Colonial Parkway in Virginia. Locations near or along the Parkway. The cases remain unsolved.

Craftsman Industries: A manufacturing company specializing in custom-built vehicles and mobile structures. In the memoir, Craftsman Industries is responsible for constructing the unique glass apartment on wheels used for the promotional campaign described in the book.

Ryder Tandem Straight Truck: A type of commercial vehicle manufactured and operated by Ryder Systems, Inc. This truck is commonly used for transporting goods and materials over long distances. In the memoir, it serves as a pivotal mode of transportation during the journey across the United States.

Kubota Corporation: A Japanese multinational company that specializes in manufacturing a wide range of machinery and equipment, including agricultural machinery, construction equipment, and engines. This memoir highlights the use of a Kubota generator during the travels across the United States in the Glass Apartment on wheels.

Roche: Short for Roche Holding AG, one of the world's largest pharmaceutical companies, which collaborated on the marketing campaign described in this memoir.

Tamiflu: A brand name for the antiviral medication oseltamivir, used to treat and prevent influenza (the flu). Tamiflu works by inhibiting the neuraminidase enzyme in the influenza virus, thereby reducing the severity and duration of flu symptoms.

FDA (Food and Drug Administration): A regulatory agency of the United States Department of Health and Human Services responsible for protecting public health by ensuring the safety, efficacy, and security of human and veterinary drugs, biological products, medical devices, food supply, cosmetics, etc. In this memoir, the FDA may be referenced in relation to regulatory processes, approvals, or other interactions with pharmaceutical products or medical devices.

World Health Organization's List of Essential Medicines: A comprehensive compilation of medications deemed essential for addressing the most critical health needs of populations worldwide. This list, curated by the World Health Organization (WHO), includes medications necessary for promoting public health and combating prevalent diseases, ensuring their availability and accessibility in healthcare systems globally. This list was mentioned in this memoir.

CDL License: An abbreviation for Commercial Driver's License, required for individuals operating large, heavy, or hazardous vehicles in the United States. The CDL license is issued by state authorities and involves specific endorsements for different vehicle types, such as Class A, B, or C, depending on the vehicle's weight and purpose. This license is essential for truck drivers, enabling them to legally operate commercial vehicles on public roads and highways.

Advertising Agencies: A company hired to help create and execute advertising campaigns for clients, such as Roche Pharmaceuticals in this memoir. The names for these companies we're purely a fictional creation.

Marketing Campaign: An organized effort to promote a product or service, typically involving advertising, public relations, and sales strategies.

Conventional Marketing: Traditional methods of marketing, contrasted with the unconventional approach taken in the Glass Box campaign, which broke new ground in advertising strategies.

Guerrilla Marketing: A marketing strategy that focuses on unconventional, creative, and low-cost techniques to promote a product or service. In the memoir, the concept of guerrilla marketing is exemplified through the innovative campaign devised by Roche Pharmaceuticals and a New York advertising agency, which involved placing a person inside a glass apartment on wheels to travel across the United States and promote a product.

Unconventional Campaign: An innovative and nontraditional approach to marketing, as exemplified by the Glass Box campaign, which challenged conventional wisdom and achieved remarkable success.

The PRO Awards: Awards organized by Chief Marketer, a leading marketing publication and resource for marketers. Chief Marketer is owned by Access Intelligence LLC, a business-to-business media and information company based in the United States. These awards were mentioned in the memoir.

The APMA (Association of Promotion Marketing Agencies) Globes Awards: Awards that recognize excellence in promotional marketing campaigns across various categories such as creativity, innovation, effectiveness, and strategic communication. These awards celebrate the most outstanding campaigns and initiatives within the marketing industry. These awards were mentioned in this memoir.

Ambassador of the Year Highlands and Islands Tourism Award: An accolade recognizing individuals who have made significant contributions to promoting tourism in the Highlands and Islands region of Scotland. This award was mentioned in the memoir.

The New York State Lottery Education Bus: A mobile educational initiative organized by the New York State Lottery to promote responsible gaming and raise awareness about the benefits of lottery funding for education. This bus travels to schools, community events, and public spaces across the state, offering interactive exhibits, educational materials, and resources to inform the public about the lottery's contributions to education. This bus was mentioned in the memoir.

Census: A systematic survey or count of a population, typically conducted by a government agency, to gather demographic and socioeconomic data. In the context of the memoir, census workers refer to individuals employed or tasked with conducting the census, often going door-to-door to collect information from residents within a specific geographic area.

Books: Certain book titles were created from the imagination for this memoir. Any resemblance to real books with similar names or themes is purely coincidental.

Mythical Creatures and Places: Beings and places of folklore and legend, including kelpies, pixies, gnomes, sirens, hippocampuses, vodyanoys, vampires, zombies, unicorns, fairies, mermaids, dragons, urchins and the Lost City of Atlantis referenced throughout the memoir for their symbolic significance and cultural resonance.

Hotels, Motels, Lodges, Inns, The Ranch, and the Tugboat: It's important to note that all names and descriptions of these establishments have been changed for the memoir to maintain privacy and confidentiality. These places provided temporary shelter, meeting rooms, and comfort, serving as important settings in the narrative. Any resemblance to real names and places is purely coincidental.

Fictional Names Glossary:

1. 46 O'dinetin Video Game System: A made-up product or brand name mentioned in the memoir. 123. 124. 144. 279.

2. The Angry Cobbler: A fictional name of a restaurant, bar, and club mentioned in the memoir. 245. 246.

3. The Brown Beverage Brewing Company: A fictional company name used in the memoir. 257. 258. 333.

4. Bucket O' Chicken: A fictional stage-play mentioned in the memoir. 195.

5. Bustersteins Coffee: A made-up coffee chain name mentioned in the memoir. 205. 208.

6. Clowns N' Syndicate: A fictitious clown company name mentioned in the memoir. 262.

7. Cooaireford & Sons.: A fictional mini-refrigerator company created from the imagination mentioned in the memoir. 63. 80. 122.

8. Davie Henshaw and the Tranquil Jitterbugs: A fictional swing band name featured in the memoir, representing a group known for their smooth melodies and energetic performances. 245. 246. 247. 251.

9. Double Four: Off-road Redeemer: The 2nd Journey: A made-up game referenced in the memoir, suggesting an adventurous off-road racing experience. 123. 141.

10. EyeVenture: Golden Wheat Fields of Russia: A fictitious game mentioned in the memoir, implying a journey through the scenic landscapes of Russia's wheat fields. 123.

11. Flu O' Meter: A made-up device or product name referenced in the memoir. 44.

12. Go-Dived Chocolate & Fruit Co.: A delicious chocolate and fruit company created from the imagination mentioned in the memoir. 272.

13. Hard & House Annex: A fictitious hardware store name mentioned in the memoir, offering a wide range of tools and home improvement supplies. 175.

14. Hudson & Williams LLP: A made-up law firm name featured in the memoir. 5.

15. Il quarto piatto: A fictional restaurant name created from the imagination was featured in the memoir. 327.

16. King Callant & Skylarks: A fictitious business name mentioned in the memoir. 49.

17. Major Fifty Sense: A fictitious store or business name mentioned in the memoir. 75.

18. Mimzy Midgal and the Bathtub Chronicles: Fictitious show made up for the memoir. 327.

19. Moonstruck Nanas: A fictional Banana Company mentioned in the memoir. 50.

20. Mulligan & Applefield's: A fictitious store or business name mentioned in the memoir. 75. 83. 120.

21. The National Ice Skaters Society of the USA: A fictional ice-skating organization. 111.

22. Robots Running Amuck: A fictitious name of a show about robots. 236.

23. Snap N'Awake Pills: A fictional product name used to describe a made-up brand of wakefulness-enhancing pills. 258. 280.

24. SoloMarÉ-Tech: A fictional company name introduced in the memoir. 263. 267. 270.

25. SoloMarÉ-Tech Advancement of Science and Future Center: A fictitious organization mentioned in the memoir. 263.

26. The Stubben Family: A fictional family created for the memoir, representing a group of hotel owners within the narrative. 284.

27. Supercomputer(s): Fictional computing systems with advanced capabilities mentioned in the memoir 5. 267. 269. 270.

28. Uncle Pete's Used Sheets: A fictitious brand specializing in bulk rags for various purposes. 75.

29. The Vestibule Runts: A fictional name of a group mentioned in this memoir. 95. 96. 361.

30. Wild Things: A fictitious company name referenced in the memoir. 16. 17. 129. 131. 133.

31. Ynoise: A fictitious electronics company created for the memoir. 67.